Created and Directed by Hans Höfer

INSIGHT GUIDES
Wales

Edited and Produced by Brian Bell
Photography by Richard T. Nowitz and others

HOUGHTON MIFFLIN COMPANY

APA PUBLICATIONS

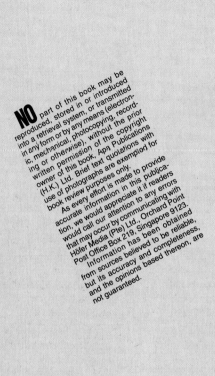
WALES

First Edition (4th Reprint)
© 1994 APA PUBLICATIONS (HK) LTD
All Rights Reserved
Printed in Singapore by Höfer Press Pte. Ltd

Distributed in the United States by:	Distributed in Canada by:	Distributed in the UK & Ireland by:	Worldwide distribution enquiries:
Houghton Mifflin Company	**Thomas Allen & Son**	**GeoCenter International UK Ltd**	**Höfer Communications Pte Ltd**
222 Berkeley Street	390 Steelcase Road East	The Viables Center, Harrow Way	38 Joo Koon Road
Boston, Massachusetts 02116-3764	Markham, Ontario L3R 1G2	Basingstoke, Hampshire RG22 4BJ	Singapore 2262
ISBN: 0-395-66281-8	ISBN: 0-395-66281-8	ISBN: 9-62421-090-X	ISBN: 9-62421-090-X

ABOUT THIS BOOK

Insight:Wales, following hard on the heels of Insight: Ireland and Insight: Scotland, is the third Apa guide to the Celtic fringes of the British Isles to be produced by project editor **Brian Bell.** Born in Northern Ireland, whose political turmoil compels all its citizens to examine their allegiances, he well understands the debates about national identity that occupy a small country like Wales.

As a London-based journalist with wide experience in newspapers and magazines, Bell was first attracted by Apa's approach to travel guides because it combined detailed reporting about what makes a place tick with a bold photojournalistic style of illustration. In a crowded publishing market, he believes, too many guidebooks content themselves with anodyne prose and picture-postcard photography; yet a country's warts can often be as interesting as its beauty spots and usually make it more enticing to the adventurous traveller.

Informed View

A journalistic perspective dominates this book, therefore. But, for an informed view of what constitutes the contentious Welsh character, Bell turned first to **Dannie Abse**, identifiable variously as a Jewish Welshman, a doctor practising in London's Soho, and one of Britain's leading poets (his collected work is published as White Coat, Purple Coat). Though born in Cardiff, he believes he was conceived at Ogmore-by-Sea in Glamorgan and retains great affection for the place. "Ogmore's my place to mope in, where I can walk under the seagulls and blown skies and think about Wales and the people of Wales and their unfathomable strangeness."

Anthony Moreton, whose contributions include chapters on Cardiff and the "Welsh religion" of rugby, returned to his native Wales after nearly 30 years in London and now covers the principality for London's Financial Times. "The combination of working for the FT and living in Wales is the best I can imagine," he says. "It's all to do with the quality of life and the easy pace of the place."

His wife and fellow-contributor **Ena Kendall**, a feature writer on the Observer Magazine, was born and brought up on a farm in Merthyr Tydfil, where the industrial valleys begin to give way to the emptiness of the Brecon Beacons. "To me, it has always been a charmed landscape," she says. "I have walked over it, bicycled along the Roman roads, driven across it many times—but it still keeps its sense of mystery. It was the one bonus nature handed to people living in the mining valleys; and in the summer, when the grass turns yellow, the hills really do look as if they could be in Israel or Jordan and you realise where those old-time preachers must have got some of their inspiration."

For an overview of Welsh history, Bell turned to Englishwoman **Sara Jackson**, an honours graduate in English and history who abandoned the security of a merchant bank for the excitements of journalism. Having immersed herself in Welsh history, she was left musing about why the Welsh consistently lost out to the English over the centuries in so many ways. It's not a question asked often enough by the English.

Frank Barrett, travel correspondent of London's Independent, grew up in the border county of Monmouthshire (now Gwent), the first in five generations not to have worked in

Bell

Abse

Moreton

Jackson

a coal mine. "I'm particularly sensitive about the present efforts to package the country's industrial heritage for tourists," he says. "Too much time and effort has been wasted on preserving the Welsh language and fighting for independence. The real problem is how to preserve Wales's prosperity without turning it into a giant theme park."

Like Anthony Moreton, **Tony Heath** returned to his native Wales after 20 years of London journalism. He now writes for T*he Guardian* and *The Observer* about Wales, which is, he says, "a blindingly emotional place—it's easy to cry, and laugh, here, and we're not ashamed to show our feelings." His wife **Dorothea** is a photographer, some of whose pictures are used in this book.

James Lewis, for 14 years a senior reporter with *The Guardian*, is a native of Wales, and retained "a fair grasp" of the language, even throughout stints as a journalism lecturer in India and the Sudan.

Paul Gogarty has been variously a teacher, a playwright, a poet and a travel photojournalist; like Dannie Abse (his father-in-law), he tries to spend a few weeks a year in Ogmore-by-Sea.

Roger Thomas, the author of five books (mainly on Wales), despairs of ever defining satisfactorily what constitutes the Welsh spirit. "Perhaps we fret too much about such matters," he admits. "We suffer from a debilitating introspection that sometimes shuts us off from the world outside. But such thoughts don't often detract from the day-to-day pleasures and advantages of living in Wales. You still find a genuine sense of community and comradeship there. It's a stunningly beautiful country. The countryside really is countryside in Wales—not the clogged, pale-green, pseudo-rural imitation served up in the southeast of England."

Emyr Griffith, who compiled the "Travel Tips" section, was marketing director of the Wales Tourist Board and now, as a travel consultant, maps out itineraries for groups as varied as Dutch naturalists and Korean handbell ringers. What irritates him most is the tendency of the Welsh to leave inn-keeping and the running of pubs to outsiders. "It goes back to a religious upbringing which poohpoohed such things. But the Welsh ought to emulate their Irish cousins and get in on the act."

Familiar Faces

The cast-list is completed by several frequent contributors to Apa guides. **Stuart Ridsdale**, a former Apa staff editor in Singapore, now works for a major public relations company in London. **Marcus Brooke**, a Scot based in Singapore, has travelled the world for 25 years, armed with typewriter and cameras, pursuing his interest in archaeology and anthropology and contributing to a wide range of newspapers and magazines. **Diane Fisher** divides her time between writing in an English country cottage and running a family farm in Connecticut. **Mike Mockler** has written on ornithology for Apa guides to *Brittany* and *The Balearics*. **Richard Nowitz** fitted in his photographic assignment in Wales between shifting house from Jerusalem to Washington D.C. **Kaj Berndtson Associates** drew the maps.

The book's progress into print depended on the skills of typists **Janet Langley** and **Valerie Holder**, proof-reader and indexer **Rosemary Jackson Hunter**, and computer tamers **Audrey Simon** and **Karen Goh**.

Heath

Barrett

Nowitz

Ridsdale

CONTENTS

History

Places

Features

Maps

TRAVEL TIPS

Compiled by Emyr Griffith
Updated by Caroline Bailey

For detailed information
see page 273

THE WELSH CHARACTER

Most tourists returning home from Wales report that the Welsh are a friendly people. Not only is there—as the song goes—"a welcome in the hillsides" but the locals appear to be particularly anxious to please: so much so that sometimes they may tell the enquiring visitor what he or she wishes most to hear rather than the truth, the whole truth and nothing but the truth.

Supposing you halt your car at some country cross-roads hoping that you are well on your way, say, to Llanberis. (*Llan* is the Welsh, by the way, for "church" or "parish".) You wind down the window in order to ask that short-statured Welshman who happens to be standing conveniently nearby if you are near your destination. "Only 10 miles to go," he will say smiling pleasantly. "You'll be by there in 20 minutes easy, mun." You thank him and you drive on. An hour later you realise that there are such things as Welsh miles and that that smiling rustic denizen was only trying to please by giving you good news.

Ebullient and emotional: This trait of friendliness and the wish to please the Welsh would recognise in themselves. Recently in the Welsh national newspaper, the *Western Mail*, one correspondent, Hilda Evans, wrote: "We are warmhearted, ebullient, inquisitive, emotional, extrovert. Our blood is mixed. There is hardly a coloured face amongst us but Irish, Welsh, Spanish and English—also I believe Italian—have interbred. We are the people of the Welsh valleys. We shock the staid English: we overwhelm them with our kindness and generosity and they frequently consider us inferior."

Inferior? It is doubtful whether these days the English do look down on the South Walians. Perhaps they used to. Nowadays, it is the North Welsh who look down on the mixed-blood South Welsh. "They're Arabs down there," they say without intending racial hostility but mindful of the fact that those in industrial South Wales often do not speak the old language. And both the South and the North look askance at the West Walians, especially those from Cardiganshire where it is said Welsh generosity has gone into reverse.

"He's a Cardi," the rest of the Welsh nation remark, meaning that, while this person from Cardigan may be friendly, he's also sly and clever and oleaginous and

stingy. "He's a Cardi. He's got short arms and deep pockets. After you've talked to 'im you 'ave to count your teeth." This, of course, is pure slander. The reputation of Cardis is as inaccurate as the Irish being thought stupid or the Scots being considered mean.

The Welsh, like many minority nations, do have a need to define their national character, to emphasise their differences—not so much from each other as from the tall, confident English. Over the past 30 years there has been, in Wales, a marked acceleration of cultural changes. Old traditions have faded or are fading, religion is holed and the

Preceding pages: detail at Portmeirion; bed-and-breakfast farmhouse, Rhyader; Conwy Castle; shepherd; Gwynant Valley; John Hughes's Grog Shop, Pontypridd. Left, guard at Welshpool and Llanfair Railway. Above, slate quarry worker.

once crowded chapels emptier, the coal mines closed down, the population forced to be mobile.

The new motorway alters the landscape and challenges the sense of where and who a person is so that the Welsh need more than ever to ask themselves existential questions. The response is often one tinged with nationalistic passion. "I am Welsh," they reply fiercely, as if they doubt it. It is no accident that large posters near Welsh towns, advertising a brand of beer, carry the slogan "Never Forget Your Welsh". This slogan, of course, is in English since 80 percent of the nation cannot read Welsh!

The Welsh-speaking Welsh have other

reasons to be concerned about the problem of identity, for the Welsh language, despite those bi-lingual signs, is in retreat. It is sad to see a language die, a culture die with it. It is natural that Welsh nationalists argue and rage. But the language is far from dead yet and great efforts are being made for it to survive.

The Welsh in their new self-consciousness—not only the Welsh-speaking community—have tended to re-invent their history. In school youngsters are told about Welsh legendary heroes—of Cunedda the Burner, of Hywel Dda and his four bitter sons, of Llywelyn the Great and Llywelyn

the Last and, most of all, of Owain Glyndwr, Prince of Wales and national hero who, in 1401, called upon his men to "free the Welsh people from the slavery of their English enemies."

Sacred dream: Here is a short extract from a school textbook: "Owain Glyndwr's grave is known, well-known. It is beside no church, neither under the shadow of any ancient yew. It is in a spot safer than and more sacred still. Time shall not touch it; decay shall not dishonour it; for that grave is in the heart of every true Cymro. There, forever, from generation unto generation, grey Owain's heart lies dreaming on; dreaming on, safe for ever and for ever."

The Welsh once were a people "taut for war" against the English but they were defeated. And according to the contemporary nationalist poet, R.S. Thomas:

> There is no present in Wales,
> And no future;
> There is only the past,
> Brittle with relics,
> Wind bitten towers and castles
> With sham ghosts;
> Mouldering quarries and mines;
> And an impotent people,
> Sick with inbreeding,
> Worrying the carcase of an old song.

Those like R.S. Thomas lament the passing of the old ways, the old religion, the old language, the righteous orators that spoke the word, scriptural or political, intensely and thrillingly. They have gone, they say, for the most part, those gesturing figures in pulpit or wild-eyed on soapbox, gone into the photographic plates of a Welsh social history book or into the remembering imagination of poets.

This is half true; but the discerning visitor will still meet their sons and grandsons, their daughters and granddaughters and recognize through them that Welsh national traits are not completely soluble. Like others, the Welsh are a perdurable people.

If the Welsh themselves are aware that they are a nation with a deep sense of their past, English visitors, too, have commented on how they have apprehended the ubiquitous spirit of history while in Wales. For instance, earlier this century, indeed before World War I, Edward Thomas, who took a walking tour through Wales, spoke of "phantoms following phantoms in a phantom land—a gleam of spears, a murmur of arrows, a shout of victory, a fair face, a scream of torture, a song, the form of some conqueror and pursuer of English kings."

Earlier still, in the 19th century Matthew Arnold, finding himself in Llandudno, remarked that Wales is "where the past still lives, where every place has its tradition, every name its poetry, and where the people, the genuine people, still know this past, this tradition." So, as that Welsh school textbook suggests, "The torch of history in Wales is handed on from age to age."

The English are aware also of other Welsh characteristics, not least Welsh talkativeness. It is not so long age that the trains

Only when the train had passed through the Severn Tunnel, only when the passengers felt themselves to be safely in Wales, only then would the carriage suddenly hum with conversation. As Rudyard Kipling wrote: "The Celt goes talking from Llanberis to Kirkwall, but the English, ah the English, don't say a word at all!" The Welsh love talking and they love those who talk well.

Why are the Welsh such eloquent talkers? They have always bred colourful trade union leaders like Arthur Horner, who could electrify a crowd of strike-bound miners. Up and down the land there have been unforgettable soapbox preachers. "I have heard most

leaving from Paddington to South Wales consisted of separate carriages—that is, they were not open-planned. Then, half a dozen strangers would look out of the window, or suck their mints, or read their newspapers, but they would not speak to each other. It was not the "done" English thing. The English are happy with few words and even fewer gestures and like to keep strangers at a comfortable distance from themselves. And in a train leaving England for Wales, who knows who is not English?

Left, chambermaid at Llandudno. Above, sheep farmers exchange gossip at Builth Wells market.

London preachers," wrote Caradoc Evans, "but I have heard few who can outdo the preachers of my boyhood."

Caradoc Evans, a Cardi and once the most reviled man in Wales because of his criticism of the Welsh nation, softened when he spoke of certain Welsh preachers. "Before theatres and picture palaces, churches and chapels were places of entertainment—entertainment that refreshed the soul and fortified man in his pilgrimage. There might have been in the pulpit more loose-livers than saints, but the biggest sinner could preach and the newest priest could recite the collect and prayers of the Common Prayer Book in a good, wholesome voice."

Then there have been fine political orators like Lloyd George, Aneurin Bevan and Neil Kinnock, all famous for the lovely gift of the gab, for true Welsh *hwyl*. The Welsh gift for articulate cadence is rooted in the fact that Welshmen and women are, for the most part, a non-conformist Old Testament people and in their childhood they early caught the accents and dignity of biblical English. Whatever the reason for their articulateness, on Sundays the shops and most other things may be closed but not Welsh mouths.

Carried away: Sometimes the natural verbal exuberance of the Welsh develops into a comic exaggeration—comic, that is, to Englishmen and other foreigners. Of Iolo Morganwg, renowned 18th-century Welsh hero, rogue, forger, poet, antiquary, it was said that he could see seven sails where there was but one. And many a Welsh hero, before and after him, has had a similar multiplying imagination.

When Shakespeare portrayed Owain Glyndwr he made that Prince tell such innocent lies that those who overheard him could only laugh. Glyndwr boasted: "At my birth, the front of heaven was full of fiery shapes. The goats ran from the mountains, and the herds were strangely clamorous to the frighted fields. These signs have mark'd me extraordinary; and all the courses of my life do show I am not in the roll of common men!" When Glyndwr swanked to Hotspur, the Earl of Northumberland's son, "I can call spirits from the vasty deep," Hotspur replied tartly, "So can any man; but will they come?" Shakespeare invites us gently, even affectionately, to laugh at Welsh hyperbole.

In our time, English poets such as Robert Graves and Michael Burn have comically continued this tradition. In *Welsh Incident*, Robert Graves makes a solemn Welshman tell of wondrous things that came out from the sea at Criccieth with accurate humour, and Michael Burn, writing his *Welsh Love Letter*, sighs:

Were all the streams of Gwynedd
In one great river joined
Dwyfer, Dwyryd,
Glaslyn, Ogwen,
And Mawddach in flood
And all in between us
I'd swim them
All!

To reach you,
O, how I love you

Were all the forts of Gwynedd
In one great fortress linked
Caer and castle
Criccieth, Harlech,
Conwy, Caernarfon,
And all in flames
I'd jump them jump them
All!
To reach you,
O, how I love you!

See you Saturday
If it's not raining

Have the Welsh themselves a sense of humour? Visitors may be misled by the ponderous and solemn manner of Welshmen when they are trying to be formal or when articulating small complaints: "Sir, members of our choir feel very strongly about the nature of the posters advertising our concert on behalf of the Powys Wildlife Trust. Why should David Evans and others be allowed an Esquire after their names when William Price has no such appellation?"

But the Welsh do have a sense of comedy and can laugh at themselves. They may be noted for their quasi-religious devotion to the game of Rugby football and for the brilliance of their male voice choirs rather than for their comedians; yet Welsh comedians do thrive and those like Stan Stennett and Sir Harry Secombe can hold their own with the best of them.

It is true that Welsh comedy often relies on the joke or the narrative going "over the top" into farce. The stories of Rhys Davies press into pure farce and novelist Gwyn Thomas (known in Wales as Gwyn the Mouth) regularly delivered wonderfully farcical epigrams.

So if those who live in Wales are carried away by the power and excitement of words and by old-time rhetoric, there are home-bred comedians and critics ready and willing to record and mock it all. Thus Dylan Thomas describes how, as a boy, he heard his older cousin, Gwilym, praying: "O God, Thou art everywhere all the time, in the dew of the morning, in the frost of the evening, in the field and the town, in the preacher and the sinner, in the sparrow and big buzzard. Thou canst see everything, right down deep in our hearts; thou canst see us when the sun has gone; thou canst see us when there aren't any stars, in the gravy blackness, in the deep, deep, deep pit; thou canst see and spy and watch us all the time, in the little black corners, in the big cowboys' prairies, under the blankets when we're snoring fast, in the terrible shadows, pitch black, pitch black; thou canst see everything we do, in the night and the day and the night, everything, everything; thou canst see all the time. O God, mun, you're like a bloody cat."

Wales, then, is the Land of Speech as much as it is the Land of Song. Not that the latter is merely a commercial tourist invention, as one can soon learn by visiting Cardiff

more stimulating than waiting for a bus. It doesn't happen frequently, but it happens.

Imagine, for example, a hot June weekday at Glamorgan's Ogmore-by-sea. The beach is almost deserted, some fifty people at most scattered here and there on different rocks, on brightly-coloured towels spread on the pebbles or sand. All is quiet except for the gentle splash of the waves. The sun throws its silver arrows into the armoured, chain-mail, glittering sea.

Suddenly, for no evident reason, a woman on the far right, sitting on a rock, begins to sing in Welsh. A companion takes up the song and then another. Soon those on the far left begin to sing and in no time at all fifty

Arms Park at an International Rugby match. The standing crowds sing the National Anthem, *Land of my Fathers*, in Welsh as if they have been rehearsing it for years. And in one sense they have. They sing it with such a martial melancholy that the auditor is reminded how "in every dirge there sleeps a battle-march".

Occasionally, the Welsh, as a crowd, will suddenly and quite spontaneously burst into song, and not just at football matches. In a queue, for instance, while doing nothing

Above, modern Welsh magic at the Folk Museum, St Fagans, Cardiff.

people on the beach, most of them strangers to one another, are singing harmoniously and with resonant yearning, *Ar hyd y nos (All through the night)*. It could be a phoney scene from a second-rate film about Wales. It is not.

Equally memorable and surprising encounters are not hard to come by, anywhere in the country. Sooner or later, if you are willing—for you cannot be alone in Wales for long except on top of a mountain—something thrilling is bound to happen: a song or a seagull flying through a rainbow, or just a signpost (bilingual) pointing backward towards a dark legend.

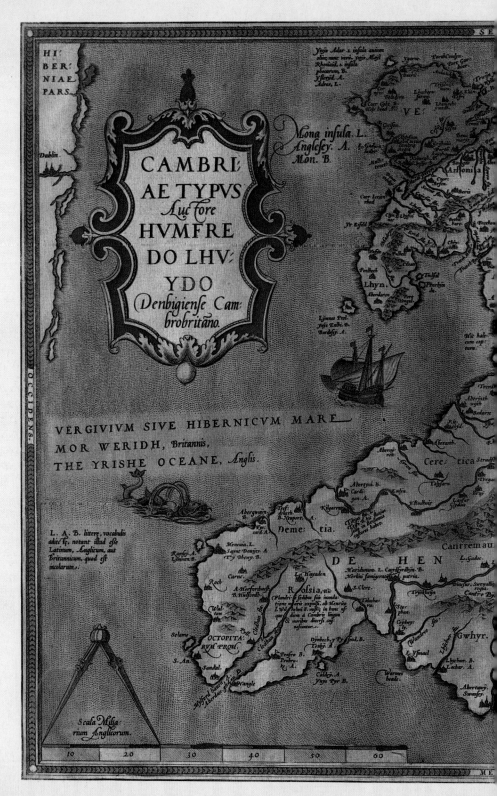

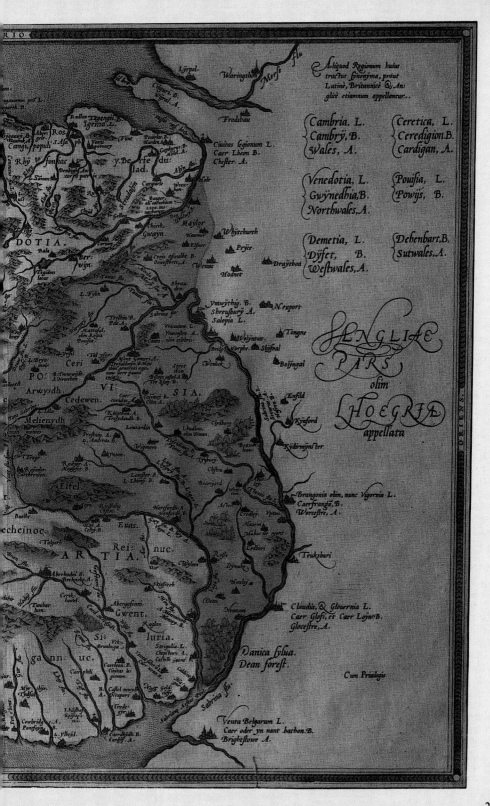

DECISIVE DATES

500-100 B.C.: The Celts settle in Wales.

43 A.D.: The Romans, under the Emperor Claudius, invade Britain. By the year 78, Wales has been conquered.

340: Defences are built against Irish raiders who eventually succeed in making permanent settlements in Wales.

410: After nearly four centuries of occupation, the Romans withdraw from Britain and the Dark Ages begin. Britain is subject to snowballing Saxon invasion.

500: The Saxons are defeated at Mount Badon, the battle possibly won by the legendary Arthur. This victory is shortlived and the Saxons continue to settle in Britain.

500-550: The Age of Saints. Celtic saints wander through Wales preaching Christianity and converting others to the faith. To the east, the Anglo-Saxons remain pagan.

784: Offa of Mercia, the powerful Saxon king, constructs Offa's Dyke, and Wales acquires an eastern boundary.

878: Rhodri Mawr, the most notable figure in Welsh history before the arrival of the Normans, is slain. The first Welsh ruler to succeed in uniting most of Wales under his overlordship, his reign also coincides with increasing Viking attacks on Wales.

927: Under the pressure of Viking attack, the Welsh kings formally submit to the English as over-king.

1039: Gruffydd ap Llywelyn, the last of the Welsh high-kings, takes to the throne, achieving a short but successful rule over Wales as a whole.

1063: Earl Harold, the future king of England, drives an army into Wales, Llywelyn is killed by his own men and England's ascendancy reaffirmed.

1066: The Norman Conquest of England. Harold is killed at Hastings and the Norman Marcher Lords are established along the Welsh borderlands.

1141: With the death of Henry I of England, Wales experiences a resurgence, strongest under the two Llywelyns of Gwynedd. Welsh culture flourishes, territory is reclaimed and Wales moves towards unity.

1267: Llywelyn II extracts from England the Treaty of Montgomery and is recognised as Prince of Wales, with overlordship of all other Welsh princes and barons.

1282: The Welsh resurgence comes to a close as Llywelyn II is killed and Wales falls before Edward I's advance. By the Statute of Rhuddlan, Wales becomes an English principality; in future the eldest son of the English king is designated Prince of Wales. Edward begins his castle building campaign in Wales.

1301: Edward's son is duly invested as the Prince of Wales.

1349: The Black Death sweeps Wales, leaving casualties of up to 40 percent.

1400: Owain Glyndwr leads revolt against England, the whole of Wales behind him.

1410: Glyndwr disappears and the rebellion is suppressed by Henry IV and his son. Defeat brings humiliation and the Welsh are made second-class citizens.

1455: The Wars of the Roses breaks out in England, the Yorks and the Lancastrians struggling for the throne.

1485: Henry Tudor, of Welsh descent and with Wales behind him, wins the Battle of Bosworth and is crowned King of England. This establishes Welsh lineage on the English throne and marks the end of the Wars of the Roses.

1536: First Act of Union. Henry VIII enacts the complete political and legal union of Wales with England. The English shire system is extended to all of Wales and the dissolution of the monasteries begins.

1588: The first publication of the Bible in Welsh appears.

1642: Civil War breaks out in England. The restoration in 1660 of Charles II is welcomed by the Welsh.

1660: The Bardic Order is in decay, suffering from loss of patronage and the influence of the new Humanism.

1718: Printing presses are introduced to Wales and the number of books printed in the Welsh language rises sharply.

1735: The Methodist Revival begins.

1795: The Iron Industry becomes well established in south Wales.

1811: The Methodists break with the Church of England and Wales becomes a "non-conformist nation".

1815: Peace in Europe after the Napoleonic Wars brings Welsh farming to crisis point. Discontent is aggravated by problems brought about by a soaring population.

1831: The Merthyr uprising: debt-stricken workers riot, ransacking the local debtors' court and raiding the town for sequestered goods. Troops are called in, leaving behind them two dozen townspeople dead. Throughout the decade, "Scotch Cattle" raids abound as miners take action against blacklegs and get their revenge on unpopular managers.

1839: The first of the Rebecca Riots. Turnpike gates are smashed in rural areas, the locals objecting to the high tolls exacted from them.

1843: Hugh Owen, in his *Letter to the Welsh People*, calls on them to take all action to further the cause of education seeing it as an essential pre-requisite to Welsh prosperity.

1850s: Coalmining in the Rhondda rapidly develops, the South Wales coalfield becoming one of the most important in the world.

1868: Liberal political supremacy is established in Wales, the Liberals holding 21 Welsh seats.

1872: The University College at Aberystwyth is founded, followed by colleges at Bangor, Cardiff, and later, Swansea.

1881: Pubs stay shut as Wales adopts the "dry" Sunday. The Welsh Sunday Closing Act is passed, proof of the influence of Welsh nonconformity on Welsh politics.

1891: The "Tithe War" leads to the Tithe Act, by which payment of tithes to the Anglican Church is transferred from resentful non-conformist tenants to the landlords.

1906: The General Election brings sweeping Liberal victories in Wales.

1908: Lloyd George is made Chancellor of the Exchequer.

1914: The Anglican Church is disestablished in Wales. Dylan Thomas, poet and author of the radio play *Under Milk Wood,* is born in Swansea.

1921: For the first time, a decline in the number of Welsh speakers is recorded.

1922: Lloyd George, having held office since 1916, steps down as Prime Minister, and with him Liberal's fortunes fail. Henceforth Labour wins increasing popularity.

1925: Plaid Cymru, the Welsh nationalist party, is founded.

1930: Depression deepens over the South Wales coalfield, unemployment in many areas exceeding 30 percent.

1936: Saunders Lewis and other members of Plaid Cymru burn a building at the RAF bombing station at Penrhos in Lleyn in protest against the construction of a bombing range.

1939: The outbreak of World War II serves to pull Wales out of economic depression.

1950: With the assistance of government schemes, limited prosperity returns to Wales.

1955: Cardiff is declared the official capital of Wales.

1962: The Welsh Language Society is founded, its members determined to arrest the decline of the Welsh language. Campaigning for a Welsh language TV channel begins.

1964: The first Secretary of State for Wales is appointed to the British Cabinet.

1966: In a local by-election, the first Plaid Cymru candidate is elected into Parliament. Plaid Cymru emerges as a threat to Labour, but Labour re-establishes its ascendancy in the 1970 General Election.

1973: Nationalist activity proves effective and the Welsh Language Act is passed, giving the Welsh language equality with the English for all purposes.

1979: In a general referendum, the Welsh vote to reject devolution. Only 13 percent vote in favour. The 1979 General Election brings a swing towards the Conservatives greater than any other region except London.

1981: Census reveals that only 19 percent of the Welsh population speak Welsh.

1982: A new TV channel, S4C (taking the place of Channel 4 in the rest of Britain), goes into action, transmitting programmes in Welsh at peak viewing times.

1987: Wales becomes the most popular location in Britain for overseas investors.

1988: The ambitious development of Cardiff's docks, a 10 to 15-year project, gets under way.

BEGINNINGS

"The enemy lined the shore with a dense, armed mass. Among them were black-robed women with dishevelled hair, like Furies brandishing torches. Close by stood Druids, raising their hands to heaven and screaming dreadful curses." So Tacitus describes the spectacle beheld by the Roman legionaries as they prepared to cross the Menai Strait and invade Anglesey. This depiction of the Celtic people is one that has always appealed to the popular imagination, fascinated by the Druid as the possible possessor of some secret, esoteric knowledge.

We know little of the Celts and what knowledge we have is derived largely from the Roman invaders who provided highly subjective and often appalled accounts of an energetic and war-like people whose religion involved human sacrifice.

It was with the arrival of the Celts (500-100 B.C.) from their homeland along the Rhine that Wales began to evolve a distinct culture of its own. Before this—and right up to the end of the Bronze Age—it had been the recipient of waves of different cultural influence. Even today's Welshman believes it is his Celtic ancestry that sets him apart from the more sedate, matter-of-fact Englishman, providing him with a whole range of romantic characteristics: eloquence, a fiery personality, a richly fertile imagination.

Roman Invasion: In A.D. 43 the Emperor Claudius launched a full-scale invasion of Britain, bringing Wales under the influence of yet another people. Despite fierce opposition from the Welsh tribes who, under Caractacus, helped maintain British resistance along the border for eight years, the conquest of Wales was achieved by A.D. 78. Although some tribes such as the Silures in southeast Wales were moved out of their hillforts into towns, many of the smaller groups continued their traditional way of life. But four centuries of Roman occupation was bound to leave its mark.

A network of forts and roads held down

the Welsh tribes, Chester and Caerlon serving as the major Welsh garrison towns. Roman civilisation, although it took deeper root in the southern and eastern lowlands where towns with columned temples, baths and piped water were built, also left its mark in the mountainous regions. Copper was mined on Parys Mountain, Anglesey, and gold in Dyfed. However rugged the landscape, the Romans imposed straight roads.

Despite Roman countermeasures, the fourth century brought increasing pressure

from new invaders as barbarian tribes descended on Britain. The Saxons raided England's east coast, and the Irish—who had not been conquered by the Romans—raided Wales. As official defences weakened, the Irish made permanent settlement in Wales, colonising both the Lleyn peninsula and Anglesey. In southwest Wales the displaced Irish tribe of the Deisi settled in Dyfed. Even today, the name "Irishmen's huts" is given to any group of round and ruined huts that nestle on a headland or hillside.

Into the darkness: After the Romans withdrew in A.D. 410, Britain slipped into the Dark Ages. During this unchronicled period, the Welsh language emerged and the boundary separating Wales from England was formed. The Saxon invasions continued, their advance checked momentarily by the British victory in A.D. 500 at Mount Badon. Speculation runs whether Badon was won by the legendary Welsh hero, Arthur himself. Nonetheless the Saxons continued pushing westwards and northwards, isolating the Celts of Wales and allowing Wales to emerge as a territorial unit.

The indigenous people took a conscious pride in the one thing they felt marked them off from their Saxon enemies: their Christianity. Although the pagan Anglo-Saxons were largely converted in the seventh and

eighth centuries by missionaries from Rome, Christianity had survived in some Welsh regions from the Roman period, while in others it was re-introduced from Gaul. In the "Age of the Saints", a period stretching from the end of the fifth century to the early sixth, Celtic saints, either alone or with a band of followers, travelled through Wales preaching and converting others to the faith, establishing churches and monasteries as they did so. The Anglo-Saxons to the east they left well alone.

A new frontier: As the sixth century dissolved into the seventh, the Anglo-Saxons resumed their gnawing expansion, driving the Welsh towards the foothills of the central mountains. By the eighth century, Mercia was one of the most powerful kingdoms in southern Britain. It was at this time that Offa, the greatest of all Mercian kings constructed "Offa's Dyke", a boundary marking the frontier between the Celtic Welsh and the Germanic Mercians. Wales had for the first time acquired an eastern frontier, and one not greatly differing from the present national boundary.

The Wales of this period was splintered and disunited, a country of squabbling princes constantly at war with one another. Out of this confusion rose Rhodri Mawr, king of Gwynedd. In the face of an increasingly serious Viking menace, he used opportunistic marriages as a tool for forging the Bardic dream of a united Wales able to safeguard Welsh social and cultural traditions. But he was killed in A.D. 878, with Welsh unity still unattained.

The English kingdoms, in contrast, were becoming united. After Alfred's death in 901, Wessex became increasingly stronger, Wales increasingly fragmented. After a brief period of stability under Hywell ap Cadell, Rhodri's grandson, Wales again sank into a century of political instability.

The High Kings: Their kingdoms ruled by fratricidal brothers, wracked by recurring and destructive invasions of Northmen who raided monasteries and farmland alike, the Welsh kings in 927 made a formal submission to the English. The two people were to fight together against a common enemy, with Athelstan as over-king and the Welsh kings as sub-kings. Here, Wales entered the political arena as a junior partner to England.

The last of these Welsh High Kings was Gruffydd ap Llywelyn, who in 1039 took the throne of Gwynedd. Engaging himself in constant warfare, not only along the border but in Wales too, he extended for the first time the rule of a High King into every corner of Wales. His success was short-lived. Earl Harold, England's future king, drove an army into Wales, and in 1063—in what was becoming a Welsh royal tradition—Llywelyn was killed by his own men.

Just three years later, Harold himself lay dead on the battlefield at Hastings, as the English fell in turn before the invading Normans. This victory provided no relief for the Welsh, for the triumph of William the

Conqueror over the English was to change Wales as violently as it changed England.

The Normans: Because Llywelyn's defeat had returned the country to the local rule of warring princes, Wales was in no position to face the Norman threat. Although William the Conqueror had no plans for the outright conquest of Wales, he set up powerful Norman barons along the Welsh borderlands in order to secure the flanks of his new kingdom. These were the Lords Marcher, who immediately began the attack of Welsh lands around them, dispossessing their rulers and seizing for themselves the legal rights and powers of the displaced.

The rights of the Lords Marcher, far ex-

Teifi, south of Pynlimon, and even as far westwards as Pembroke. But, although the Normans held and colonised the lowlands of south and mid-Wales, the north and the uplands remained largely Welsh.

As the Normans advanced, they built castles and fortifications. The original motte and bailey castles made of earth and wood were later replaced by those whose ruins still litter the Welsh landscape. The Norman dominated areas became strongly feudal (a system alien to the existing Welsh system of landholding) with the castle as the centre of administration, and the Lord surrounded by holdings of his vassals who were bound to him by duties of military service in exchange

ceeding those of their fellows in England, were often almost regal in their extent. As William was obliged for the present to turn a blind eye to such accumulating power, these barons, commanding bands of trained knights on horseback, advanced on Wales.

When William died in 1085 and was succeeded by his son, the power of the Lords Marcher increased even faster. The little kingdom of south Wales suffered the greatest. The Normans swept into the valley of

Left, Kingship preserved at Conwy Castle. Above, Caerphilly Castle at dawn conjures up ancient mysteries.

for land. Under the castles' protection and encouraged by the Lord's granting of both charter and guaranteed trading rights, towns such as Cardiff and Swansea sprang up.

Under the spreading influence of the Normans the church was also transformed, its structure reorganised first into diocese and down into deaneries and parishes. The changes introduced were welcome, renewing the Welsh church's vigour and bringing it into closer contact with a reformed papacy.

However, the death of Henry I in 1142 led to new disruption as disputes broke out over the succession. Wales, as it was so often to do, took advantage of England's weakness.

BEATI PACIFICI

JAMES I.
KING of GREAT BRITAIN
FRANCE and IRELAND
Defender of the Faith &c.

Paulus Vansomer p.　　An Original Painting in the Palace of Hampton Court.　　G. Vertue Sculp.

The period following Henry I's death became known as the Welsh resurgence. Lands were recovered, the arts and scholarship flourished, monasteries became centres of learning, and princes encouraged the bards, giving them an established position and duties at court.

So rose the Welsh tradition of the great bards, with this "second generation" ranking with those of the sixth and seventh centuries. Precious folk legends were collected and preserved, including *The Mabinogion*, the great medieval collection of Welsh prose. In 1136 the Welsh historian Geoffrey of Monmouth had written his *History of the Kings of Britain*, a vital source to later historians.

The resurgence went much deeper than political and military success alone. In the mid-14th century, as Wales was grappling with the social problems that followed yet another military defeat, lyrical, naturalist and love poetry flourished as never before and Wales produced its finest early poet, Dafydd ap Gwilym.

The resurgence was strongest under the greatest and last princes of Gwynedd, the two Llywelyns. Llywelyn the Great (1194-1240) and Llywelyn the Last (1246-82) were accomplished military commanders who learnt much from their Anglo-Norman foes. They absorbed Welsh territories to unite large parts of the country and formed a feudal state guarded by stone castles. Laws were codified and taxation systemised. As a matter of policy, the Llywelyns arranged marriages with both the English royal family and the powerful Marcher Lords.

Peace at any price: It soon became evident to the English crown, however, that the threat posed by this new and strengthening neighbour could no longer be tolerated. Llywelyn I had contended with a relatively weak English king, Henry III, and Llywelyn II achieved his greatest success when England was divided by the barons. England had needed peace at all costs and so, by the treaty of Montgomery (1267) Llywelyn had gained control of nearly all of Wales and was recog-

nised by Henry as Prince of Wales with overlordship of all other Welsh barons and princes. But, with the accession of Edward I, Llywelyn was confronted with the most powerful of English medieval monarchs— and one determined to subdue Wales.

When Llywelyn II was killed in 1282 in the middle of the second of Edward I's Welsh Wars, the Welsh defence was quickly overcome. To secure his conquest, Edward built a chain of castles at Rhuddlan, Conwy, Beaumaris, Caernarvon and Harlech, all on

defensible water sites, so that they could if necessary be supplied by sea.

The statute of Rhuddlan (1282) reinforced the Treaty of Aberconwy, imposed on Wales on its defeat. Wales was henceforth to be an English principality, and in future it would be the eldest son of the English king who would carry the title Prince of Wales. In 1301 Edward's son became the first such prince to be invested with the honour. The statute established five new shires, on the English model and strengthened the grip of Canterbury over the Church of Wales.

Some Welshmen and princely families, seeing the Llywelyns' policy not as an asser-

Left, Stuart King James I. Above, detail from Conwy Castle.

tion of Welsh independence but as a threat to freedom and a heavy financial burden, had almost welcomed Edward I's settlement. So did others who benefitted by the conquest from increased contact with the outside world brought about by entering service with the royal armies in France or the administration of the Crown. But the peace imposed was shortlived; resentments ran too high, dissatisfactions too deep.

The last revolt: The Wales of 1282 was not united with England and there had been no intention of its being an equal partner. Indeed, much of the administration lay in English hands and England seized control of trade. Discontent centred on the subordi-

private territorial dispute between Glyndwr and a Marcher Lord.

Glyndwr's campaign began in 1400 in northeast Wales. He then consolidated his hold on the southwest to establish in 1404 a base in the northwest in the mountain core of Gwynedd. From this base, Glyndwr attempted to institute reforms and national institutions, including two universities, to give him the trained administrators his new state would need. Glyndwr attempted to give to Wales the attributes of 15th-century nationhood.

England retaliated and with devastating success. The crisis of his reign over, Henry IV and his son Prince Henry (whose military

nated Welsh position, on galloping social changes and on memories of what might have been. In 1349 this discontent was exacerbated by plague when the Black Death swept Wales as it had swept the rest of Europe. Four people in 10 were said to have died.

The stage was set for uprising and rebellion, and with the accession to the English throne of Henry IV, a Lancastrian and a usurper, revolt could be justified. All that was required was a leader. He appeared in the form of Owain Glyndwr, born in 1354 of noble Welsh lineage. The rather ignominious trigger for a widespread rebellion was a

talents were to ensure him victory at Agincourt) could turn their attention to Wales. By 1410 Glyndwr had disappeared, the last rebellion had died.

Defeat this time involved humiliation. The lands of the rebels were seized by the king, who imposed severe fines. Most importantly, the Welsh became second-class citizens: they were not allowed to bear arms or to be appointed to public office; no Englishman could be tried by a Welshman or have evidence given against him by a Welshman. Intermarriage was forbidden. In the border towns, the Welsh were denied citizenship.

Just 50 years later, however, England

became embroiled in the internecine bloodbath of the Wars of the Roses as the House of York and the House of Lancaster tussled for power. After the prolonged turmoil was over, the only surviving claimant to the throne was Henry Tudor, whose grandfather had been of pure Welsh stock. To the delight of the Welsh, a Welsh dynasty sat on the throne of England in fulfillment of centuries of bardic prophecy. When Henry landed in Wales in 1485, the bards hailed him as the new Arthur. Henry met the English forces led by Richard III at Bosworth, where Richard was betrayed and killed in battle. Henry was crowned King of England, inaugurating the Tudor dynasty. Shakespeare,

tion to the Welsh problem: the complete union, political and legal, of Wales with England.

London supreme: The Acts of Union of 1536 and 1543 are frequently seen as the beginning of the end of Wales. They undermined the dominance of the Welsh language by proscribing it for many official and almost all legal purposes. They introduced English law and led to a widening social division between the anglicised Welsh gentry and the ordinary people. The former, who had been the mainstay of Welsh higher culture, increasingly entered English educational institutions and Inns of Court in English towns and cities.

chronicling the Tudor line, was to portray Richard as an evil, scheming hunchback in his melodramatic *Richard III*.

Henry VII rewarded his followers generously: Welshmen entered local positions of power on a large scale and were made welcome at his court. Something resembling a Welsh job rush from Wales to London began. Henry introduced few reforms in Wales, however, and it was left to his successor Henry VIII to institute that drastic solu-

Left, stained-glass window in Ruthin Castle's banqueting hall; Welsh hero Owain Glyndwr. Above, Tudor times depicted in Cardiff.

The Acts of Union are also seen as initiating the decline of Welsh cultural life, replacing it with a London-based culture. Administratively, Wales was abolished as a separate entity. Crucially, the ancient system of nomenclature disappeared. English lawyers found the Welsh *ap* (son of) confusing and so the Ap Hywels became Powells and the anglicisation of surnames extended to all levels of society.

At the time, however, the Acts were welcomed. At last Welshmen had equality with Englishmen before the law. The new legal and administrative arrangements brought a stable and peaceful life, which in turn opened up opportunities for individual advancement and financial gain. At Henry VIII's accession, Wales had been in turmoil and lawlessness prevalent. The new shires, the chief units of administrative and legal control, were given boundaries that remained barely changed until the 1970s.

With Union came reformation of the church. Again there was little protest as the old religious structure was smashed and the dissolution of the monasteries began. Monasticism had long since lost its hold on people and the Welsh did not feel strongly over papal supremacy. Indeed, most of them were glad to be rid of the financial burdens this distant figure imposed.

Under the Tudors, Wales—although still not rich by comparison with England—enjoyed a degree of prosperity. The period saw an increase in the population, the development of coal and lead mining and the growth of trade. Almost every sector of the Welsh economy found an outlet in a new and much larger market.

The Welsh transferred the loyalty felt towards the Tudors to England's next dynasty, the Stuarts, who took over the throne in 1603. But when Civil War broke out in England in 1642, many of the Welsh remained Royalist. They tried to remain aloof from the tumult of the times, and the ruling

Puritans, despite their reforming zeal, had little success in imposing their values on the Welsh peasantry. Wales generally welcomed the restoration of the monarchy in 1660, when Charles II came to the throne.

Crisis in culture: By the 18th century the cultural separation of the two layers of Welsh society was complete. The upper, anglicised layer looked to England for its standards of social behaviour, literature, speech and religion; but in the years that followed the Civil War even the lower, Welsh-speaking strata was to undergo a profound change.

The Bards had been central to the Welsh social structure in a manner that had no parallel in English society. Welsh high culture, poetry and music had been oral, the Bard its guardian. They were also the historians, genealogists and musicians. However, under Elizabeth I's rule in the late 16th century, Welsh literary culture suddenly seemed narrow, reactionary, even barbaric, and the Bards were urged to modernise their art. By 1660 the Bardic order was in decay.

A few diligent scholars attempted to bridge the gap between the new and the old learning. Although Welsh was excluded from state administration, it returned as the language of Anglican liturgy in Welsh churches. The use of Welsh in the churches played a crucial role in both preserving the language and spreading religious zeal. In 1567 the Prayer Book and New Testament were translated into Welsh, with the whole Bible following in 1588.

As the vigour of the ancient traditions of music, history and literature declined, a new, serious, pious book-reading public arose, and the old oral culture was replaced by a printed culture. The culture was not of literature and learning but of piety and devotion. Between 1660 and 1750 the stream of Anglican tracts in Welsh became a flood.

Before the 18th century had run its course, three revolutions were to have struck Wales. The cultural revolution opened the doors for the Methodists and a religious revolution, while at the same time industrial revolution wrenched the Wales of history into the Wales of today.

Left, Henry VIII and Jane Seymour, one of his six wives, portrayed in Cardiff Castle. Right, Welsh mascots have to be bilingual.

HOW WELSH IS FIGHTING BACK

Driving into Wales on any major road supplies a painless and instant introduction to the Welsh language. The road signs are in Welsh as well as English and even the dimmest of linguists can scarcely fail to take on board sooner or later that *milltir* means miles, *lôn* lane and *toiledau* exactly what you would expect.

Welsh is now widely in evidence all over the country, *de rigueur* from British Rail to the Post Office, gas boards to water authorities, banks to supermarkets. Cities and towns carry their Welsh names as a matter of course: Cardiff/*Caerdydd*, Swansea/*Abertawe*, Newport/*Casnewydd*, Abergavenny/*Y Fenni*. A Welsh television channel, S4C, not only backs up the language but establishes a market for actors and actresses, writers and film producers working in Welsh.

All this is the outcome of a battle to promote the official status of a language at one point threatened by terminal decline. If nothing else, Welsh has now slipped into the psyche of the four-fifths of the population of the principality who do not speak it as part of the natural order of affairs.

Despite many Welsh people's deep pessimism about its fate, the language's most remarkable quality must surely be its powers of survival. Living in the closest possible relationship with English, one of the most powerful and all-pervading languages on earth, the miracle is that it was not swallowed without trace centuries ago. Yet, according to the 1981 census, 503,000 people (18.9 percent) speak Welsh. That's a far cry, admittedly, from the million who spoke it at the turn of the century, but it's holding its own better than Scots or even Irish Gaelic.

The most hopeful sign is that there has been a slight upturn in the number of those speaking Welsh who are under 14. In the past decade or so, there has been a notable surge of interest in the language, not least in anglicised South Wales. Many parents want their children educated entirely through the medium of Welsh and the number of schools offering this has shot up. There are 67 bilingual primary schools, with a further 16 at secondary level; 25 years ago, there was just one secondary school.

The Welsh equivalents of the Irish *Gaeltacht*, its language strongholds, are the north and west. Just as Welsh seems poised for recovery, a growing threat presents itself in these areas. Historically, in South Wales, the hold of the language was broken by the Industrial Revolution and the massive influx of immigrant workers from England and Ireland.

History seems on the point of repeating itself in the rural north and west, where a wave of immigration is changing the old pattern of life. Twenty years ago, the relatively cheap and empty acres of West Wales, along with farmsteads left vacant as properties amalgamated, became a spiritual klondike for seekers after an alternative way of life, largely people from the big English cities.

In the north, second homes are seen as a major threat in previously homogeneous Welsh villages. Many incomers make strenuous efforts to learn Welsh, but a learned language must invariably be second best to a mother tongue.

For many Welsh people, the fate of the language, compounded by immigration, adds up to a sensitive, not to say explosive, issue. But as that distinguished Welshman, Sir Ifor Williams, once put it, the people of England and Wales are formed of the same racial ingredients, although not necessarily in the same proportions: the same is true of Christmas cake and Christmas pudding, only one has been baked and the other boiled.

Welsh is not a particularly easy language to learn, but to know it is to have the key to a rich literature going back through the hymns and folk ballads of the 18th century and medieval storytelling to the age of bards in the sixth century, and the odes and elegies of Taliesin and Aneirin.

They were writing in the earliest British language—Welsh, which with Cornish belongs to the Brythonic branch of Celtic speech—and references to Catraeth (Catterick) show that their Britain went far beyond present-day Wales. There is a sense, therefore, in which Welsh belongs to the whole of Britain and that those Welsh road signs are as much a part of a Northumbrian's heritage as a North Welshman's.

HOLYHEAD MARKET

METHODISM AND MINING

The decay of the old oral culture left a void into which stepped the forces that moulded the familiar Wales of non-conformist chapels, preachers, miners' choirs and pubs closed on Sundays.

The fervent wave of Methodism that swept Wales began in earnest in 1735 with the conversion of Howell Harris, but previous movements heralded this "religious revolution". The Society for the Promotion of Christian Knowledge (SPCK) had been active during the reign of Queen Anne, but more crucial were the efforts of Griffith Jones, vicar of Llanddowror. He organised a system of preachers travelling from parish to parish, spending three months in each, where they taught the illiterate to read.

Although Jones was concerned not with education but with religion, he played a vital role in making Wales literate, and literate in Welsh. By the end of the 18th century, most people had some degree of literacy in their own language, and this aided the rapid spread of Methodism.

Comparisons with Calvinism: Welsh Methodism originated independently from English Methodism and remained closer to Calvinism than Wesleyism. The Established Church soon came to be seen as the church for the English and the gentry, while the chapel held the loyalty of the people. In 1811 the Methodists severed their connection with the Church of England to become a separate denomination—a break that was to have unexpectedly serious consequences for the latter.

And so Wales became a "non-conformist nation", Methodism and non-conformity reflected in a radical political tradition and representing the "Welsh way of life". The level to which religion influenced politics is illustrated in the 1881 Sunday Closing Act, prohibiting the Sunday opening of pubs—an Act that remained enforced in parts of Wales until the early 1980s.

Chapels sprang up everywhere, the ac-

companying choral singing turning Wales into the "Land of Song". After two decades of concern over diminished spirituality and increased materialism and one decade of zealous activity on behalf of the Methodists, Methodism in Wales peaked in the great spiritual revival of 1904-05.

Why did the Methodists achieve such overwhelming success in Wales compared to the much more modest following achieved in England? The Methodists appeared at a time of vacuum in Welsh culture

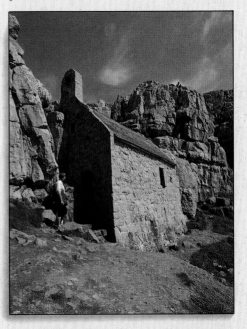

and used new methods to reach parts of the population other religions had failed to reach. They depended on the power of the spoken word, whose eloquence could induce frenzy in congregations. To further Methodism's appeal to the people, hymns were often set to versions of popular folk songs or even hits from the English theatre.

But there were also negative reasons for its startling success. In England there was deep-rooted Anglicanism to contend with, a powerful force. Wales, in contrast, lacked an established church, and had few other rivals for the people's interest—no great commercial and business activity, no sophisticated

Preceding pages: Holyhead market as it looked for centuries. Left, traditional Welsh woman. Above, the oldest chapel, at St Govan's Head.

PRINCES OF WALES

Not for nothing is Wales called a principality. It is a land once ruled by warrior princes, whose memories live on in the names of counties and towns as well as in the first names of many of its more patriotic citizens.

Charles, heir to the British throne and the present Prince of Wales, is a thoroughly modern prince who went to university at Aberystwyth, did a crash course in Welsh, and is involved in many good works in his principality, where he is a regular visitor and well liked.

Some, however, do not recognise his title. His ceremonial investiture in Caernarvon Castle in 1969 attracted people with lapel badges proclaiming "No Englishman is Prince of Wales" and much time was spent, before the great day, scrubbing off wall slogans declaring that "Llewelyn Lives".

A couple of years later an advertisement was solemnly printed in *The Times*: "In Memoriam—David—last ruling Prince of Wales, of the Royal House of Gwynedd, gallant and heroic defender of his country's honour in her most tragic hour. Barbarously tortured and executed at Shrewsbury, October 3, 1283".

There were principalities in Wales before the Norman Conquest in 1066, ruled by the families of Gwynedd, Powys, Dyfed, Ceredigion (Cardigan), Brycheiniog (Brecon) and Morgannwg (Glamorgan). They were engaged in endless quarrels for supremacy but the Welsh were united, after a fashion, by Gruffydd ap Llywelyn, just before the Conquest.

From then on, Wales was to be regarded as a danger and English earls were encouraged to extend their territories into Wales from border cities such as Chester, Shrewsbury and Hereford. They made considerable inroads, though without subjugating the people, and it fell to a new generation of princes to try to drive them back out.

The 12th-century skirmishes between the Welsh princes—Owain Gwynedd, Rhys ap Gruffydd and Owain Cyfeiliog of Powys—are best recorded by Giraldus Cambrensis (Gerald of

Barry), the son of a Norman settler who became a noted scholar and churchman and wrote of his tour through Wales in 1188 while seeking recruits for the Crusades.

In this period there arose Llywelyn ap Iorwerth, later to become Llywelyn the Great, Prince of Gwynedd, and the most powerful ruler in Wales since the Norman invasion. But it was his grandson, Llywelyn the Last, who embarked on the biggest campaign to drive back the English. He was joined by his brother, Dafydd (the David whose memoriam was recorded in *The Times*).

Edward 1 retaliated and Dafydd was executed and Llywelyn killed in the battle at Cilmeri. Thus ended a great princely dynasty. In an effort to placate the Welsh, who were still mounting minor rebellions, Edward revived the title of Prince of Wales and conferred it on his son, who was born in Caernarvon.

The next attempt to establish an independent Wales was mounted by Owain Glyndwr (Owen Glendower), a descendant of the princes of Powys and Deheubarth, who sought alliances with the Scots and Irish and negotiated with the French. Declared Prince of Wales, he held parliaments—at Machynlleth, Dolgellau and Harlech—and went on to appoint bishops, to demand the independence of the Welsh Church, and to plan the building of two Welsh universities. But his rising also failed and, though twice offered a pardon by Henry V, Glyndwr, the last Welsh Prince of Wales, was forced into outlawry and died ignominiously in some hiding place which was never discovered.

So, while a small minority of nationalists still raise their glasses to Llywelyn and Glyndwr, the rest pay their allegiance to the ceremonial princes of today.

Edward VIII, later Duke of Windsor, who was invested Prince of Wales in 1911, was held in much affection in South Wales, where he seemed genuinely shocked by the poverty he witnessed during his visit to the coal-mining areas in the depression of 1936. "Something must be done," he announced publicly. He was seen as a martyr when he abdicated shortly afterwards, which is doubtless why a surprising number of South Walians are called Windsor.

aristocratic life nor energetic political centre.

Renaissance and romanticism: The Revival gave Welshmen a new respect and strengthened the position of the Welsh language. Although it filled a gap, it couldn't appeal to the intellectuals who were also looking for a new order; instead, they attempted a national revival by restoring Wales's ancient history and literature.

The Druids were romanticised and placed at the forefront of Welsh history. In 1701 the Eistedfodd was revived. Welsh authors arranged publication of new editions of ancient texts of dictionaries and grammars. After 1718 printing presses appeared and the

inventing new ones. He forged poems by Dafydd ap Gwilym so brilliantly scholars have only recently been enlightened.

In their patriotic fervour, the Welsh also sought to resurrect past heroes. A clamour rose up around Prince Madoc, believed to have sailed to and discovered North America in 1170. In a report of the discovery of a tribe of Welsh-speaking Indians, lay the opportunity to prove the claim beyond doubt. Amid great enthusiasm and anticipation, one John Evans sailed up the Missouri to find them. The Madocs, when discovered, were undeniably Red Indian, but possessed as keen a knowledge of Welsh as an Australian Aborigine.

number of books printed in Welsh soared.

But by far the greatest number of poems written in Welsh in the 18th century were hymns—the vehicle of Methodist revival. A mini-Renaissance was under way, with London Welshmen playing a leading role as London Welsh societies flourished.

In his passion to restore the glories of the Welsh past, Iolo Morganwg, at the heart of the Welsh Renaissance, had no qualms about

Left, Prince Charles is invested as Prince of Wales by the Queen at Caernarvon Castle in 1969. Above, slate quarrying became a major industry in North Wales.

It was, however, neither the cultural revolution nor the religious revolution that was to have the most enduring effect on Welsh society, broadening horizons while ensuring the steady infiltration of the English language and the corresponding decline of the Welsh. These changes were to be wreaked by the transformation of the Welsh economy from an agrarian to an industrial base.

Revolution to riot: Industrialism in Wales developed as a result of the use in iron smelting of coal and coke in place of charcoal. The Welsh mountains were rich in both coal and iron. In the south the most rapid industrial growth occurred in the 1790s as the number of iron works along the northern outcrop of the south Wales coal-field multiplied. By 1796 the iron industry of Glamorgan and Gwent, with its growing coal dependency, had outstripped Shropshire and Staffordshire to produce 40 percent of Britian's pig iron.

Communication networks were vastly improved. In 1804 Trevithick's steam locomotive made its first run alongside the Welsh canals. Roads were improved by the establishment of road trusts, and, in one of the age's greatest engineering feats, Thomas Telford constructed a road that ran through the wilds of Snowdonia to extend across the Menai Strait by means of a suspension bridge.

But while one face of Wales underwent industrialisation, different pressures bubbled in the rural areas. The great population explosion struck Wales a blow as it struck the rest of Europe. At the first census, taken in 1801, Wales had a population of 587,000; by 1921 the figure was 2.6 million—almost five times as many over three and a half generations.

The result was an increase of poverty in the lower sections of society. The old system of parish relief broke down, its provisions quite inadequate to cope with the swelling populace and the conditions prevailing after 1815.

Wales between 1815 and 1848 was a country of social unrest and riot. The Napoleonic Wars had brought some prosperity to the richer farmers, but with peace and the reopening of trade with the continent, prices tumbled. Victory over the French also entailed the iron works losing their best customers, the army and navy, and a spate of enclosures only aggravated the seething discontent.

King Coal: Between 1846 and 1914, 43 million Europeans emigrated to the United States. Yet Wales, from the 1890s until 1914, was the only country apart from the USA to register net immigration. By the 1880s the South Wales coal empire was all-pervasive. Mining towns and villages developed a unique, intensive culture, with their choral singing, demands for education, and later, fervent loyalty to the local rugby team. From 1850 the southeast sucked in people from the rest of Wales and beyond until nearly four-fifths of the Welsh population

was lodged in this increasingly English-speaking region.

But the miners of south Wales worked in appalling conditions and before long their resistance, like that of the farmers, took on a violent aspect.

The 1830s was a decade of "Scotch Cattle" power in Monmouthshire. In a campaign against blacklegs, unpopular managers, profiteers and the like, raiders came from the next valley, unrecognisable in women's clothes, animal skins and with blackened faces, the leader wearing horns on his head. The Scotch Cattle approached at night amidst much lowing and horn blowing and embarked upon a ritualistic smashing-up of

windows and furniture and roughing up of occupants.

South Wales's most serious outbreak of violence took place in Merthyr Tydfil, in 1831. Merthyr was the biggest town in Wales, born with the recent industrialism and having no deep roots in the past. In 1831 agitation for the Reform Bill was at its height, along with renewed protests against the system whereby workers had to take wages in part in goods supplied by the coal or iron owners. The town, plunged into a debt crisis by the recession of 1829, rose up in May 1831, sacking the local debtors' court and ransacking the town for sequestered goods. Troops were called in, incensing the protesters, who attacked them. The soldiers opened fire and left two dozen dead.

It took two pitched battles before order was reimposed, but the newly militant working-class consciousness was to last for over a decade. It was only with the doomed Chartist attack made on Newport in 1839 that this working-class militancy began to give way to the working-class Liberalism that was to be, for so many decades the leading force in Welsh politics.

The Daughters of Rebecca: Rioting was by no means confined to industrialised areas. The Highways Act of 1835 placed road improvement in the hands of road trusts who

dressed as Rebecca, the justification for their actions found in Genesis: "...and they blessed Rebecca and said unto her, let thy seed possess the gates of those which hate them".

A major campaign begun in 1843 led to gates being cleared from a large expanse of southwest Wales. Before long, the Daughters of Rebecca began to extend their targets beyond the destruction of toll gates alone: in Carmarthen the hated workhouse was attacked.

Stirred in part by the sympathetic coverage given by *The Times*, government commissioners began in 1843 to investigate the all too evident grievances. The resulting re-

advanced the money and made their profit from toll gates set up along the road. In poor areas the trusts would increase their revenue by increasing the number of gates, and long journeys made by farmers became cripplingly expensive. The first attack on a turnpike gate occurred in May 1839 in Pembrokeshire. It was demolished by a party of men with blackened faces and wearing women's clothes. These attacks are known as the "Rebecca Riots", as the leaders were ad-

Left, the Menai Straits Bridge, one of Telford's lasting achievements. Above, friends bringing wedding presents to a "bidding".

port was sympathetic to many of the farmers' aims and the government acted quickly. The trusts were unified, tolls made uniform and even, in some instances, reduced. The Enclosure Act made any enclosure dependent on an initial public enquiry and the 1847 Poor Law Board began making the Poor Law more humane.

It was, however, the ever expanding coal fields that were really to relieve the pressure by absorbing the rural population explosion.

The radical tradition: Wales in the 19th century was a melting pot of a variety of movements and developments, affecting different sections of the populace. In north

Wales the people remained primarily concerned with religion, as the Methodists firmly established themselves. During this period the gulf between the nonconformist Welsh-speaking countryside and the anglicised industrial areas became entrenched, creating a division that remains today.

The latter half of the 19th century also saw Wales gain a new sense of political direction, a sense of "Welshness". By this time 80 percent of the principality belonged to a chapel and by 1891 the Liberals were in control, their power based on opposing landlords and rallying the anti-established church. It was the non-conformist and chapel aspect that was to give to Welsh Liberalism direction flourished even further after the government's publication in 1847 of the "Blue Books", a survey into the state of education in Wales, an area in desperate need of attention. The conclusions drawn— that the Welsh language was a "barrier to the moral progress" of the people, and that Welsh country women were universally unchaste—caused widespread outrage. A united non-conformist front was formed, and popular leaders achieved success as they spread political awareness amongst the common people, providing them with a single, coherent philosophy.

Hugh Owen, in his *Letter to the Welsh People* (1843), called on them to organise

its individuality, generating "Welsh Radicalism" (as opposed to English Liberalism) and giving direction to the new Welsh nationalism.

Welsh non-conformity reveals its power in many ways. Numerous government Bills were introduced to lift the disabilities of the non-conformists and to disestablish the Anglican Church (the latter became law in 1914). The 1881 Welsh Closing Act typifies the fusion of non-conformity and politics. Tenant farmers refused to pay tithes to the Church of England, so the 1891 Tithe Act transferred payment from tenant to landlord.

A sense of Welshness and of national primary schools and apply for Privy Council Grants (which had long been available to them), to take all action to further the cause of education. He dedicated 40 years to the creation of such schools and training colleges, to establishing a National Eisteddfod and to equipping a Welsh middle-class with grammar schools and universities. Owen prepared the way for a new prosperous and respectable Wales. In 1872 the University College at Aberystwyth was founded, subscriptions provided even by those from the most rural of areas with the lowest of incomes. In the 1890s colleges at Bangor and Cardiff were also established.

This sense of national mission grew to such an extent that by the 1880s and 1890s many were pressing for Home Rule. The nationalist party, Cymru Fydd (Young Wales), accordingly flourished, but nationalism was not popular in the great centres of power in southeast Wales, the anglicised towns and cities, and the movement died a decisive death.

The Great War: Welsh Liberalism began enjoying its golden years. The party scored sweeping victories in Wales in the 1906 election, passed a law disestablishing the church in 1914, and saw the rise of the Welsh radical, Lloyd George, to become first Chancellor of the Exchequer, then Prime Minis-

ter. Optimism and pride in nationhood, were felt by the most rural of communities all of which had donated their pennies to found a distinctively Welsh university.

Lloyd George remained Prime Minister from 1916 until 1922, heading a coalition government; but, by the end of his term, the political climate in Wales had changed. World War I had a dramatic impact on Welsh life and religion, and cleared the stage for the triumph of the Labour party. The Liberals

Left, Victoriana revisited in a Hay-on-Wye shop window. Above, Victorian confidence in the face of John, Marquess of Bute, Cardiff's mayor in 1890.

feared both Labour's rise and the increasing militancy and violence of the industrial areas, of which the Tonypandy Riots of 1910 are a chilling example.

Liberal optimism had belonged to a period of economic prosperity; Welsh speakers had been on the increase and chapel membership had never been so high. But after 1918 the optimism vanished. The non-conformists, under the influence of rural depopulation, industrial slump and the advance of the English language, experienced decay and loss of faith.

The chapel which had served small communities found it hard to adapt to the new society with its open communities, mobile population and scattered families. The spread of mass media entertainment only served to weaken the chapel as the centre of cultural life. (On the other hand, the Anglican Church proved much more successful in attracting the English immigrants who arrived in Wales in increasing numbers after 1945.)

In the face of the international concerns of the world after 1918, Welsh Radicalism suddenly appeared irrelevant. Britain had now to face the real cost of the war and, when Lloyd George stepped down from office in 1922, the Liberals' fortunes fell with him.In the coalfields, Labour's dominance was absolute by the 1930s. The Welsh economy depended so much on export that the collapse of the coal trade, with the turn to oil and consequent pit closures, crippled it. Strikes erupted, but in an economy of falling demand they could achieve little.

Mining's legacy: In 1913 south Wales produced almost one-third of world coal exports. More than a quarter of a million men (41,000 in the Rhondda alone) worked in 485 Welsh collieries. South Wales *was* coal. In the 1880s and 1890s no-one had been concerned that south Wales's total dependence on heavy industry and on export made it impossible for secondary or spin-off industries to develop as an economic insurance policy in the narrow valleys.

In fact, the region had never been properly industrialised at all. And so the Depression of the 1930s, whose effects were worst in the heavy industry that formed the basis of the Welsh economy, came to hang heavily and seemingly irremovably over the mining communities.

THE DEVOLUTION DRAMA

Although a few areas of Welsh industry—such as Swansea, with its oil refining interests—were less badly hit by the Depression, disaster faced the coalmining heartlands and the eastern valleys in the 1930s. The tide of immigration turned to one of emigration.

The Welsh fled to the English Midlands and the southeast, areas which still possessed an expanding light industry. And, as the industrial areas turned increasingly towards Labour, and the Liberals retreated to the Welsh-speaking areas, the gap widened between north and south, between industrial and rural Wales.

Work and war: Government commissioners were appointed to rehabilitate Britain's worst hit areas, one being South Wales. Reduced rents, rates and taxes were introduced to encourage new industries. Retraining schemes aimed to give workers the skills required in growth areas of the country, and grants and loans were offered to assist workers and their families to move elsewhere.

It was the outbreak of World War II that really pulled Wales out of depression. Once again, the metal industries had a market; munitions factories sprang up on or by coalfields. Crucially, the new industry provided employment for women, who until then had been forced to find work in England. The war created a new workforce, skilled in factory operation, and left behind old munitions factories as ready floor space for light industry. With the arrival of peace, the government started a major programme encouraging new industry into Wales, once again by means of grants and low-interest loans.

Steel expanded, the Abbey Plant at Port Talbot becoming the largest in Europe. New enterprises started up on a scale unknown in Wales and government investment in roads, motorways and new towns contributed to economic expansion.

Trade unionism provided a cohesive force, not only protecting workers' rights but also producing strong bonds of loyalty

Preceding pages: farming flourished in mid-Wales, though goats were outnumbered by sheep. Left, Aneurin Bevan, keeping oratory alive in the 1950s. Above, Japanese factories move in to the Valleys.

among workers. The movement gave birth to many leading politicians, the most celebrated being Aneurin Bevan, universally known as "Nye" Bevan. The member of parliament for Ebbw Vale from 1929 until his death in 1960, he was the life and soul of Britain's post-war Labour government and, as Minister of Health, launched the pioneering National Health Service.

By the mid-1950s Wales had achieved nearly full employment, but the 1960s brought more pit closures. Between 1947

and 1974, 150 collieries closed; in 1960, 106,000 men worked in the South Wales coalfields, compared with 10,000 today. The steel industry met with the same fate, a decade or so later. The decline in the British car industry, coupled with rising supplies from the USA, Germany and Japan, led to more redundancies.

By 1966 most of Wales was classified a "Development Area", receiving direct government assistance. Although diversification had cushioned the fall, the recession of the 1970s proved Wales to be still far more vulnerable to economic slump than many parts of England.

THE ENGLISH INVADERS

Rural depopulation, a hurt as debilitating as inner city decay, is not unique to Wales. Neither is the cheque-book stampede to snap up houses and farms which otherwise would end up derelict reminders of a past age. But in Wales there is a difference: the language spoken by a fifth of the principality's 2.5 million people.

Inevitably, an influx of monoglot English speakers dilutes local communities whose mother tongue is still Welsh. Second-home owners who seek to impose the standards of metropolitan England on essentially uncomplicated villages get short shrift—not to mention short change. Fortunately most newcomers are sensitive to cultural differences. Lions and lambs lie happily side by side, though it is not always clear exactly who is cast in which role.

Nevertheless there is resentment. Since 1979 arsonists have attacked more than 130 second-homes in Wales. The shadowy perpetrators have hijacked a famous name behind which they hide; the Sons of Glyndwr have nothing in common with the 14th-century Welsh prince. It is a conjunction most Welsh people condemn.

The arguments rage. After all, the injection of outside cash is not to be sneezed at. Without subventions from England—and elsewhere—many communities would be reduced to isolated enclaves of the elderly, unable to maintain acceptable standards of housing and social care. Fresh faces mean that local skills and local services are retained. The builder, the carpenter and the plumber are in demand again and the village shop is better able, with swollen summer takings, to weather the long winter.

On the down side is the inevitable anglicisation of community life. To a city dweller from across Offa's Dyke, that may seem unimportant, a small penalty to pay for economic gain; to a Welsh speaker proud of his heritage it represents a wound to Welsh nationhood.

About 20,000 dwellings in Wales are officially listed by local authorities as second homes. Perhaps another 10,000 come into that category—

those "winter lets", houses rented out by absent home owners from October to Easter. In some districts, notably the areas covered by Dwyfor and Merioneth councils in the northwest, as many as 20 percent of all dwellings are second homes.

Part-time residents form one strand in the tangled skein of the English invasion. Permanent settlement is another, less discussed until roaring property prices in the more prosperous parts of Britain sent many eager buyers hurrying to Wales. The rush got under way in 1988 after the government dramatically cut taxes paid by high earners. Soon it was not uncommon to chance on new arrivals who, having sold their home in Surrey or Sussex for a figure that looked like a New York telephone number, were settling down to live on the interest payments made possible by the change of location.

The equivalent of a £150,000 house in southeast England costs about £50,000 in Wales, and the £100,000 balance provides a steady income without the traumas of city life. So paddocks where rogue sheep once grazed are being turned into manicured gardens. There are rows about long-established rights-of-way. White plastic garden furniture is beginning to sprout in Snowdonia. Plastic gnome alerts are frequent.

The invasion has its positive side. New skills are brought in. The Welsh, notoriously laid back when it comes to business, are finding that it is possible to be an entrepreneur without behaving like some rapacious robber baron. Capital is being invested in craft industries which otherwise would have simply muddled along. And returnees—Welsh people who spent years in the fleshpots of London or Manchester—are finding a welcome when, to quote a song of great sentiment, they "come home again to Wales".

The north coast resorts have special significance in the Anglo-Welsh mix. Llandudno, Rhyl, Colwyn Bay, Prestatyn and lesser-known locales are increasingly populated by the retired. The density of blue rinses and walking sticks is such that a 20-mile stretch of that bracing seaboard is known in Wales as the Costa Geriatrica. Older armies, arriving without the fuss surrounding the cash-rich younger cadres, may yet command the greatest attention.

The rising yen: The quest to strengthen and stabilise the Welsh economy goes on. In 1980, the steel plant at Port Talbot was losing millions of pounds a week; today, it works at 100 percent of its manned capacity. The flow of new companies, inward investment and government incentives made Wales the most favoured location in Britain for overseas investors, attracting the largest number of Japanese investors.

There are plans to develop Cardiff into a leading financial centre, with merchant banks such as N.M Rothschild leading the way. At the same time, 2,700 acres of Cardiff's docklands are being redeveloped as part of a 10 to 15-year project to create in the

jobs and brings to Wales £1,000 million a year. However, only 4 percent of foreigners visiting Britain come to Wales for an overnight stay; to increase this figure and particularly to encourage the much courted "big-spending Americans", hotel facilities were improved and the inevitable Holiday Inns arrived in Cardiff and Swansea.

But the face of Welsh tourism is changing. As more and more English holidaymakers take package tours to the Spanish *costas*, Wales has tried to compete by offering short breaks and activity holidays. Today the Rhondda has a Wild West Park, Merthyr a Mountain Railway. South Wales has heritage parks, North Wales has Llechwedd

Welsh capital "a city for the future".

The "Valleys Initiative", a three-year project, set out to rejuvenate former mining areas suffering from old housing, high unemployment, poor roads and industrial dereliction, for if Wales had an "inner city problem", it was located not in Cardiff but in the industrial valleys.

Tourism, displaying the highest profile of the new Welsh industries, provides the most

Left, old Welsh cottage, a lure for English settlers. Above, yesterday's Welsh miner commemorated at Blaenavon Big Pit; and his successor today.

Slate Caverns. The Big Pit mining museum (in Blaenavon, north of Newport) allows the visitor to go underground to experience something of what working in a pit must have been like.

But economic change and development have put predictable pressures on the fabric of Welsh society. In particular, the language question threatened to become a crisis.

The mobility offered by railways in the 19th century and the increased exposure to English in the 20th century through the mass media made Welsh more vulnerable than ever. The depression of the 1930s had driven Welsh speakers out to anglicised coastal areas and even to England, and the prosperity of the 1950s brought in non-Welsh-speaking immigrants.

A pattern developed: as the standard of living rose, so the number of Welsh speakers fell. By 1961 only a quarter of the population spoke Welsh.

Even great literary figures no longer used it as a medium. Dylan Thomas, the Welsh poet, was a master of language—the *English* language. A product of an Anglo-Welsh background, growing up in Swansea, he could speak no Welsh. Although his love of Wales permeated some of his finest poems, his sentiments were expressed in English.

Those who saw the language and Welshness threatened in the post-war world could only resent Thomas's growing reputation. Perhaps the best known Welshman internationally since Lloyd George, he was not Welsh-speaking, and to some he therefore represented not Welsh achievement in literature but the relentless anglicisation of Welsh literary culture. The threat to the Welsh language and the resulting tension fuelled every movement in Welsh politics.

Welsh nationalism: In 1925 Plaid Cymru, the Welsh nationalist party, had been founded by the merger of two groups of intellectuals headed by the poet Saunders Lewis. Their main objective was to ward off threats to Welsh language and culture; almost as a by-product of this, they advocated self-government for Wales. Although abounding in intellectual talent, the party had little political know-how. It attracted distinguished figures concerned at the erosion of the native culture, but found little support outside the limited circle of writers and university teachers.

Its pacifist members were outraged when, disregarding general protest, the government constructed a bombing range in Lleyn, in the heart of a deeply Welsh farming community. In September 1936 Saunders Lewis and two other leaders of Plaid Cymru set fire to the construction hut at the new aerodrome at Penrho. They gave themselves up and Plaid Cymru gained its first martyrs. Such a gesture and any public interest in Welsh nationalist activity were, however, soon eclipsed by the more urgent concern of World War II itself.

Then, in 1962 Saunders Lewis came out of retirement to broadcast on BBC Wales his views on "The Fall of the Language". He called for the use of "revolutionary methods" to preserve the language, proclaiming its preservation as being central to the survival of Wales itself. Out of this broadcast grew the Welsh Language Society.

Immediately a campaign began to blot out English words on road signs, and slogans were emblazoned demanding a separate TV channel for Wales. Sit-ins in the studios of the BBC and HTV were staged. A few members even perpetrated bomb explosions in public buildings, and attacked aqueducts bringing water to England from Wales.

The activities of the Society were effective. In 1973 the Welsh Language Act was

passed giving the Welsh language equality with English for all purposes. In 1982 a new TV channel began transmitting programmes in Welsh at peak hours.

Britain's Labour party, whose position in Wales, strengthened by the Depression of the 1930s, had appeared so stable, suddenly found itself in the 1960s under threat from the nationalists. The climax of Labour's ascendancy came in the 1966 general election, when it won 32 out of 36 Welsh constituencies. It had expanded its appeal from the hardcore working-class vote across the whole spectrum of Welsh society, replacing the Liberals as the "national" party of Wales.

Then, in the 1966 Carmarthen by-election, the president of Plaid Cymru, Gwynfor Evans, was elected into parliament with a sensational 17 percent voting swing against Labour. Plaid Cymru, which had never been taken seriously and had remained a small and struggling group emerged instantly as a real threat, able to command votes the Liberals and Conservatives would never get. Labour's majority vote collapsed in by-election after by-election.

As a gesture of good intent, Britain's new Labour administration had, in 1964, appointed the first government minister with special responsibility for the principality: the Secretary of State for Wales. But great

Devolution debate: With the approaching depression of the mid-1970s, Labour looked for all the support it could muster, and was prepared to make concessions to both Scottish and Welsh nationalist feeling. Both were offered their own assemblies. On 1 March 1979, St David's Day, the Welsh voted by referendum whether they wanted such a measure of self-government.

The result was a decisive No. Only 13 percent of votes were cast in favour of this very modest degree of devolution. Welsh-speaking Wales feared perpetual domination by the anglicised South. Plaid Cymru worried that such an assembly would create a permanent Labour majority. Others antici-

gaps remained between his powers and those of his ministerial equivalent in the Scottish Office: the former could supervise the application of government policies but could seldom initiate. Although the 1970 elections re-established Labour's safe dominance, and relegated Plaid Cymru once again—after its brief period of glory—to the ranks of a small fringe party, the Welsh Language Society still carried out high-profile Welsh nationalist activity.

Left, the poet Dylan Thomas, who didn't speak Welsh. Above, the politician Gwynfor Evans, who did.

pated increased bureaucracy.

But the real fear was simple enough. It was that political devolution would be economically destructive, that the Welsh would lose their new prosperity. Wales therefore opted for security—with the rest of Britain.

In the 1979 general election Wales also swung harder towards the Conservatives than any region in Britain apart from London, a trend that has been repeated in subsequent elections. To some, this breaking with decades of political tradition of Welsh radicalism is yet further proof of the relentless anglicisation of Wales.

This anglicisation has been furthered as

English buyers acquire "second homes" in Wales—cottages ripe for renovation, available as a result of rural depopulation. This trend has also served to push up property prices in Wales, so fuelling local resentment. Retired couples come from England to settle in the north and west of Wales. About 70 percent of second home ownership is in coastal Wales, especially around Lleyn Peninsula, one of the densest Welsh-speaking areas.

The concern is that this can only serve to further dilute the language. In the Welsh heartland, 80 to 90 percent of the population speak Welsh, but such areas are fragmented by towns, holiday areas and a wedge of

has been energetic enough to arouse the resentment of monoglot English speakers, who consider themselves just as Welsh as anyone else. After all, four-fifths of the Welsh people can speak *only* English, and there is bitterness that Welsh language speakers are allocated too many of the limited resources available, that there is too much TV in Welsh at peak viewing periods, that attention is being diverted from more pressing social and economic issues.

Despite economic advances, it is the language question that will provide the fulcrum of debate in the near future. In this, as in the issue of devolution and the nationalist cause, the Welsh appear to be as far from presenting

English speakers across mid-Wales. In the anglo areas the number of Welsh speakers falls to 20 percent and, in some cases, to below 10 percent.

The response of a Welsh nationalist minority was to start burning unoccupied English-owned second homes. The campaign spread to London, with extremists planting firebombs in the premises of estate agents who sold such properties.

Government policy has been to discriminate positively in favour of the language. Welsh-language schools exist in most areas, and the language is used widely on TV and radio. Indeed, the official backing for Welsh

a united front as they have ever been.

Strangely enough, increasing tourism may prove an ally rather than an enemy. Many of the new tourist attractions strongly emphasise the language and its place in Wales's cultural identity. A wider understanding has been forged outside Wales of the principality's "otherness" and certainly there is little danger of encountering a repetition of the infamous index entry in the *Encyclopaedia Britannica*: "For Wales, see England".

Above, modern tourism takes hold at Betws-y-Coed. Right, modern industrial needs have meant Japanese children in Welsh schools.

WHY THE JAPANESE LOVE WALES

Once a year, on a summer Sunday, coachloads of Japanese families descend on the Edwardian spa town of Llandrindod Wells. They come from Wrexham and Llay in the north and Bridgend, Cardiff and the Gwent valleys in the south. As the women and children meander around the shops, the men head for the hills, eagerly pulling their trolleys *en masse* towards the golf course.

The occasion is the annual match between Japanese executives in Wales and a business team of Welshmen. A good time is about to be had by all, especially by the golf-mad Japanese.

A few weeks earlier those same families will have enjoyed a rather more relaxed afternoon at a garden party in Duffryn, a large country house in the pastoral Vale of Glamorgan just outside Cardiff. For a couple of hours the adults of both cultures mingle among the lawns and rose beds drinking tea, or stronger Japanese spirits, and eating the thin cucumber sandwiches redolent of blue skies and all that is best about British summer afternoons in the garden.

That these two social events should not only take place but also attract hundreds of participants reflects the strength of the Japanese "invasion". The Japanese have taken to Wales in a surprisingly big way; to the rugger and the weather, the singing and the working. Especially the working.

Britain, as an international trading country, has always had more than its fair share of overseas companies and Wales has shared in this invasion. Americans have been long-established: Ford, General Motors, Kelloggs, Chemical Bank, 3M, Alcoa and the rest. European companies have been here for ages, too. But the first Japanese company, Takiron, only arrived in 1972. The next year the giant Sony set up shop in Bridgend to produce television sets and since then there has been a continuous flow of big—and small—names from the Orient into Wales.

Sony has now made over two million television sets in its plant at Bridgend and hundreds of thousands of tubes and other parts for export. Another big TV producer, National Panasonic,

part of the Matsushita group, has plants in Cardiff and Newport. Orion has made over one million video recorders.

Up in North Wales Sharp makes microwave ovens, electronic typewriters and paper copiers in Wrexham and Brother makes electronic typewriters, printers and microwave ovens on the other side of the town. Hoya Lens makes ophthalmic glass and plastic lenses in a very modern factory on the Wrexham industrial estate.

Many of the Japanese concerns have brought high-technology skills to a country that until the early 1960s relied heavily on traditional industries such as coal, steel and textiles. But not everyone has welcomed the Japanese with open arms. Some critics allege that their factories are merely engaged in screwdriver operations, assembling parts bought in from elsewhere.

The Japanese have also helped to change work practices. They have not sought to ram down Welsh throats the physical jerks that are obligatory for every operative back home. No Welsh man or woman is expected to stand by his or her bench and do a couple of dozen knee-bends every morning before starting work. But they do all wear the same uniform, right up to managing directors, and they do all have the same canteens and car parks. They also work for the same trade union—which in Wales, with its strong attachment to the Labour movement, took some getting used to.

In return, the Japanese have had to come to terms with Welsh culture. They have taken happily to singing and rugger and quite enjoy a pint in the local. But the wives have often had a more difficult time as they are less likely to be fluent in English. Japanese executives, like top businessmen the world over, work long hours and the wives and children have to exist to a considerable extent on their own resources, especially when the men are away—there are no women executives in Wales—or out playing golf.

Some help is now being provided for the children with a Japanese school in Cardiff which takes in as many as 100 of them every Saturday morning. Japanese restaurants are also beginning to appear. It may not be Tokyo, but for these families it is a step in the right direction.

A land beneath which men burrow tirelessly for coal and on which others perform fearless feats with the oval ball—rugby football, not soccer, is the Welsh national game—is guaranteed to supply an abundance of heroes. Some observers will not be shifted from the view that the gladiatorial figures in red jerseys (hopefully running rings round an English XV at the National Stadium) are the greatest and bravest in Wales. The reverential glee which greets these men (capped, not medalled, for their country) when they take the field at Cardiff is peculiarly Welsh.

The hero count in Wales is high and hundreds with legitimate claims queue to join the roll of honour. Some heroes are self-selecting: the Welsh soldiers who in 1879 defended Rorke's Drift against the Zulu Impi, winning 11 Victoria Crosses (Britain's highest gallantry award) in the process, for example; or the mines rescue teams who went into the inferno after Gresford Colliery blew apart in 1936 to try to find survivors.

But, after much deliberation and not a little argument, Wales plumps for the political and cultural giants as the best, the bravest and boldest—men and women whose lives deeply affect the nation's psyche to this day.

Orator extraordinary: Before politics was taken over by image makers and presentational gurus, **Nye Bevan** (Aneurin Bevan, purists insist) towered over British parliamentary proceedings. He died in 1960, a gifted life cut short at 63. A monument to Nye, who began as a miner, stands at Waun-y-Pound, an unexceptional hill-top near his home town Tredegar, a Gwent mining community now sadly reduced by contractions in the coal industry. No huge likeness carved by some great sculptor stands on the windswept hill. Instead there are four large monoliths. Three represent Ebbw Vale, Rhumney and Tredegar, the towns comprising the Ebbw Vale constituency he represented for 31 years; the fourth is bigger, representing Bevan himself, planted for all time on the

spot where he spoke to the people of Wales and to the world beyond the Valleys which nurtured him.

Radical, rebel, *bon viveur*, scourge of conservatism, champion of the underdog: Bevan was all these. But he is best remembered for the creation of Britain's National Health Service, the forerunner of which was the ponderously named Tredegar Workmen's Medical Aid Society. The negotiations leading to the establishment of a nationwide service showed the depth of Bevan's intellectual ability. He could charm even the most reluctant to his way. The British Medical Association, the doctors' trade union, took its medicine manfully after first opposing "socialised medicine"; today the BMA is among the stoutest defenders of a health service which puts care above cash.

Was it realism or resignation which caused Bevan to declare towards the end of his life that no British foreign secretary should be allowed to enter the conference chamber of nations naked—that is, without a British nuclear weapon to back up his arguments? The conundrum is still unresolved. In Tredegar, Nye is still a name that comes to the lips as readily and frequently as ever.

David Lloyd George would be rated by some a greater Welsh figure than Nye Bevan. True, he achieved the ultimate in British politics, becoming Prime Minister in 1916 and holding power through the flush of victory in 1918 after which the Liberal world began to come apart. His guile amply demonstrated Welsh cunning. His notorious womanising won envy, admiration and loathing . Quite a catalogue for a man born, strangely enough, in Manchester at the height of Lancashire's textile boom. He was brought up in the tiny village of Llanystumdwy in North Wales under the tutelage of his uncle Richard Lloyd, a cobbler and chapel elder.

When he died he was buried there in a simple grave—at least, simple for a world-renowned statesman—by the River Dwyfor. A museum of Lloyd George memorabilia nearby is much visited.

His flamboyance was legendary. Flowing hair, voluminous cape, generous moustache

Preceding pages: slate workers at Llechwedd. Left, David Lloyd George and his wife go camping in 1913.

and overwhelming charm captivated every-one. Women adored him and his sexual exploits were the subject of much gossip and secret envy. He neglected his Welsh wife and favoured English company between the sheets. Political honours were auctioned to swell party funds, company shareholdings were acquired in dubious circumstances. It hardly seemed to alter Lloyd George's popu-larity one bit. A hero he remained, perhaps because he rode the storms with such ease. An enigma to foreigners, accused by Welsh-men of swapping his country for worldly satisfactions, he was Wales's most exotic son for decades. Towards the end of his life he was made an Earl—a long journey which is unlikely to be matched by anyone cur-rently on the Welsh political stage.

Pyrotechnic poet: One of Wales's more re-cent heroes, the poet **Dylan Thomas**, evokes similar feelings of ambivalence. He also provokes equally fierce defences of a life and talent which rose like a rocket and ended with the big bang of an alcoholic in a hotel room in America.

Thomas started life as a journalist on the local paper in Swansea. Tradesmen rather than professionals, journalists have been known to develop strong tastes. Thomas's was for words, beer and whisky. His words remain as stimulating as the spirits which consumed him. Remembered for impromptu recitations in London's Soho pubs as well as for the exquisitely honed lines of *Under Milk Wood*, he was as flamboyant as Bevan and as captivating as Lloyd George.

He worked mostly at Laugharne on the Carmarthenshire coast (now Dyfed). From the wooden shed near his home, known as the Boathouse, he looked out over the Taf Estuary, a swelling river at high water and a vast expanse of mud flats when the tide drained away. He was a regular at Brown's Hotel in the sleepy little town's main street. The Boathouse is now a major tourist attrac-tion full of Dylan Thomas memorabilia. Photographs of the poet, a cigarette charac-teristically stuck in the corner of his mouth, are on display. A video recounts his life. Dylan Thomas postcards sell by the hundred.

Thomas had enemies among the Welsh-speaking literati who were envious of his magic and scornful of his inability to con-verse in their tongue. But the fact remains that he is counted one of the 20th century's literary giants, a wizard with words whose place in the Welsh hall of fame is secure.

Richard Burton was another of Wales's most revered figures. Arguably he can be rated one of the world's greatest classical actors, although most critics believe he rarely achieved his potential. The son of a miner, he was born Richard Jenkins at Pon-trhydyfen, a village which in a sense he never left, even though he travelled far and wide and was feted like a king. Love of his home patch marked him out as a true Welshman.

A sensitive and perceptive school teacher, Philip Burton, took the young Jenkins under his wing and "Richard Burton" emerged.

The name change was more than symbolic. His mentor fostered the young Richard, whose father became increasingly addicted to that great Welsh drug, alcohol. Just how much Richard Burton owed to Philip Burton will be mulled over and disputed for a long time. The importance of personal relations never dimmed throughout the actor's glitter-ing career, even if his companions and lovers were less than permanent.

He was a man of great appetite and insa-tiable passion, and his marriage to Elizabeth Taylor was an epic which generated im-mense public interest. As his life drew to-wards a close, the need to operate at full throttle receded. In the end he came home again to South Wales for that final embrace of his native soil. The funeral attracted the world's press but the importance of its actual location was not universally understood.

Burton never lost his Welshness despite all the worldly seduction which attended his brilliant career on stage, on film and off the set. He never let go of the simple Welsh beliefs in the virtues of work and commitment—and drinking, an activity at which he rivalled Dylan Thomas. That addiction, however, and his unrelenting love of women, took second place to a love of words.

Wales has always embraced people of

other lands other cultures. New arrivals with panache and individuality are especially welcomed in South Wales, itself a hotchpotch of nations. Until the discovery of coal and iron, the Valleys were silent places, peopled only by farmers. Internationalism in the shape of workers from many lands changed that.

One person from far away who vividly stamped her imprint on Wales was **Adelina Patti**, a great and glamorous opera singer.

Left, opera singer Adelina Patti. Above, actor Richard Burton, whose voice was no less distinctive.

She was born in Madrid in 1843 of Italian parents. A year earlier the impressive Craig-y-Nos (Rock of the Night) Castle was built on the steeply sloping side of the upper Swansea Valley. Adelina Patti—Madame Patti as she was known—bought the castle in 1886 and lived there until her death in 1919.

The composer Verdi thought her the finest soprano of her time. She was fabulously successful, touring the world in grand style and captivating audiences everywhere. A single tour of South America earned her £100,000—a bonanza in the 19th century.

Energetically, Madame Patti made extensive additions to Craig-y-Nos. A clock tower rose above the castle and formal gardens were massaged into shape. The greatest triumph was the construction of a theatre inside the castle. There she gave concerts for her friends and admirers; the auditorium seated more than 100. Lavish balls were held in the theatre, the floor of which was raked but which could be levelled for dancing by a series of concealed jacks.

Madame Patti married three times, outliving a French marquis, a French tenor and a Swedish-born baron. There were other men in her life—one who was turned away because he arrived late for an appointment was King Edward VII. When she died, her body was laid out in the private chapel at Craig-y-Nos before the burial. The castle later became a hospital. A few years ago the patients were moved to new premises down the road and Craig-y-Nos was sold for use as a residential centre for musicians and others where, the artistry of Madame Patti will be remembered.

Wherever you travel in Wales, you will hear of other heroes. The novelist **Kate Roberts** and the trenchant dramatist **Saunders Lewis** both wrote in the Welsh language and are widely revered among the 500,000 who speak "the language of heaven".

In the industrial valleys, **Will Paynter**, a charismatic orator and miners' leader, and the socialist **Keir Hardie**, a Scot who was MP for Merthyr Tydfil from 1900 to 1915 and is remembered for his championing of the unemployed, are names to conjure with. No list can be complete. A nation which is renowned for argument—invariably constructive, always closely reasoned—would not want it any other way.

THE CHAPELS

From Llangollen to Llanelli, from Colwyn Bay to Cardiff, the chapels punctuate the landscape. Few villages are too small to have their four-square Bethel or Bethania, their Siloh, Soar or Saron. Whatever the elusive "Welsh way of life" may be, the chapels play a crucial part in it.

Architectural gems are rare. The founders of Welsh Nonconformity despised outward show—that was for the Anglicans and Roman Catholics. All that was needed was four walls and a roof, hard wooden pews, a pulpit and, perhaps most important of all, an organ or harmonium.

Most date from the mid-1800s, by which time the Church of England had come to be seen—and rejected—by the Welsh as representative of the landowners, Toryism and Englishness. The next 70 years—the golden age of Nonconformism—was the great age of chapel-building, by the Calvinistic Methodists, and Wesleyans particularly, but also by the Baptists, Congregationalists, Presbyterians and other, smaller sects.

A religious census in 1951, a pretty slapdash affair, showed that, if seating capacity was any guide, Wales was far and away the most religious part of the British Isles. Its churches and chapels had seating for three-quarters of the population. In some areas, indeed, notably the old counties of Breconshire and Merioneth, there were actually more seats than people.

Mass appeal: The golden age of Nonconformity was carried forward by the great pulpit orators and itinerant preachers, often of humble origin and little formal education, who preached to vast congregations out of doors. They had the kind of mass appeal that evangelists such as Billy Graham have exercised in more recent years. And they created the climate for three great religious revivals which swept the principality in 1840, 1859 and 1904. The last of these was the most emotional and saw large-scale conversions reckoned to swell chapel membership by 90,000 people.

Preceding pages: the village church and graveyard at Bosherston, Pembrokeshire. Left, and above, an outdoor hymn service and a church at Criccieth.

By World War I, the total number of chapel-goers was estimated to be more than 500,000. Nothing like that number now attends regular worship, but the chapels cling on tenaciously with impoverished congregations. And still there is no better singing in Wales.

It was the chapels that gave the principality its *hwyl* (pronounced *who-ill*), a word which has no precise English equivalent but expresses a mixture of extrovert fervour and emotion. This found its outlet in the singing

of hymns, some with dozens of verses, which went on for a whole day—or sometimes, even, two or three.

Though it was fire and brimstone from the pulpit, the congregations could, did, and still do, let rip with the stirring hymns. Day-long prayer meetings, too, were outlets for bursts of impassioned oratory which many of today's theatrical giants would find hard to equal. As Trevor Fishlock observed wrily in his perceptive book, *Wales and the Welsh*: "In terms of sheer prayer hours, Wales must have a handsome credit balance in heaven!"

The chapels were the birthplace of the great male voice and mixed choirs which, before the end of the 19th century, had made Wales, in the popular parlance, the "Land of Song". Those same chapels, ironically, nearly put paid to the harp which, for no reason that would bear intelligent scrutiny, was labelled "the devil's instrument". The playing of it declined dramatically, though perhaps only in public.

Drummed out: Condemnation came easily to the hell-fire preachers. There are still Welsh people alive today who can recall, now with shame, the ritual drumming out of chapel of some hapless servant girl who had got herself in the family way; and the man responsible, too, if he could be found.

Cruel sanctions could also be imposed on

The influence of the Nonconformist chapels on the Wales of today is something for future historians to quarrel about. Certainly there are many who argue that their puritanism and fundamentalism stifled debate on progressive ideas such as Darwinian biology; that they generated tensions and subconscious feelings of guilt and sinfulness, particularly in sexual matters.

Equally clearly, the chapels offered hope and a sense of community for poor, isolated and ill-educated communities. Also, without doubt, the fervour of Nonconformity in Wales saved the threatened Welsh language, and the chapels are still an important ally in its critical fight for survival today.

illegitimate children if they were found out. And there are still elderly chapel folk who will say, as in the tones of the fundamental revivalist preachers, that "We're not here to enjoy ourselves."

So the chapels were, and often still are, at war with the brewers, though there are probably now few "Bands of Hope" where youngsters of tender years were warned through song against the "demon drink". There are no records to show how many young people acquired an interest in alcoholic drink through the Band of Hope and thus grew up to break the "pledge" they readily signed at such a tender age.

The imminent doom of the Welsh language had been prophesied from the time of the Act of Union in 1536, which made English the language of administration and of the courts. Though the fears were exaggerated, the bias in favour of English language and culture grew inexorably. This was partly because of English immigration and Welsh emigration, and partly because the Welsh were persuaded that the surest route to material advancement and the good things in life lay through learning the language and ways of England.

But there were the beautiful words of Bishop Morgan's 1588 translation of the

Bible, read in the home and in the pulpit every Sunday. God himself, it appeared, was indeed Welsh. And Bishop Morgan's Bible was, more importantly perhaps, read in the Sunday School, where many of today's older Welsh speakers learned the language at a time when it was not widely taught in the schools.

The Sunday Schools, which had been going since the late 1700s, did not even have to be held in chapels: they could be convened in barns or farmhouses. One of the founders of the Sunday School movement, Thomas Charles, even set up a society in London to raise money to print New Testaments in Welsh. The teachers were unpaid and the

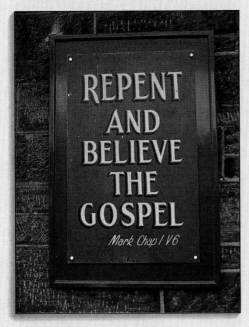

only qualification that was demanded of them was the ability to read.

The pupils, adults as well as children, recited and sang what they had learned at Sunday School and thus acquired a limited sort of education when no other was available. Urdd Gobaith Cymru, the still-vigorous Welsh national youth organisation, also had its origin in the chapels and, through its annual eisteddfod, camps and other activities, still gives young people a chance to

Left, the chapels nurtured the great Welsh choirs. Above, a message at Ffestiniog Railway Station.

preserve and rejoice in their Welshness.

The Welsh preacher-poet continues to thrive and is often to be found chaired or crowned at the National Eisteddfod of Wales and at the scores of smaller, one-day chapel *eisteddfodau* which often carry on far into the night, particularly in North Wales.

It was the chapels, too, which were responsible for the creation in 1872 of the University College at Aberystwyth, known as the "college by the sea" and the first higher education institution to be established in Wales apart from the Anglican college at Lampeter, in West Wales.

Aberystwyth's first Professor of Music was Joseph Parry, vividly described in Jack Jones's novel, *Off to Philadelphia in the Morning*. And since there were, at that time, no Welsh orchestras or concert halls, or even any great tradition of orchestral music, most other composers found their main outlet in the composition of hymns.

The hymns are still sung, as lustily as ever, though the number of singers has steadily dwindled. Even in the 1920s chapel membership remained at about 400,000. Figures are hard to come by, but the total now is likely to be nearer 200,000.

Broken down: The dramatic decline in the number of Welsh speakers since 1920 has played its part. The emigration associated with the Depression of the 1920s and 1930s dealt a further blow. Cultural influences from the other side of Offa's Dyke provided alternatives to chapel-going. The geographical and cultural isolation of so many Welsh communities was further broken down by newspapers, books, cinema, radio and, more recently, television.

In the more industrialised and Anglicised areas especially, the kind of sabbatarianism which was the hallmark of the chapel now counts for little or nothing. Licensing laws have been liberalised, making the "dry" Sunday in Wales almost a thing of the past.

Old animosities between the Church in Wales—created by the Disestablishment of the Church of England—have mostly given way to a new spirit of ecumenism. Chapels have combined, and theological colleges have closed.

But the chapel buildings remain. They played a crucial part in creating the principality of today, and Wales would not be Wales without them.

"We'll keep a welcome in the hillsides," runs the opening line of that maudlin Welsh song beloved by male voice choirs. But its sentiments of a warm, open-hearted welcome offered by the close-knit mining communities of the valleys are now something of an anachronism. There are large, cheerful miners waiting to greet you when you "come on home to Wales", but these days they are likely to be people on Government job creation schemes dressed up as miners, acting out a role assigned to them in the latest "industrial heritage park".

Is Wales becoming nothing more than "a nation of museum attendants?" asked Swansea academic Hywel Francis in 1981 in an article in the Welsh magazine *Arcade*. "My Orwellian nightmare," he wrote, "is a big black sign at the Severn Bridge: *You are now entering a protected industrial relic. Pay £5 to view this disappearing society.*"

At the time he was writing, before the wholesale closure of the coal and steel industry, the idea of Wales as an extended industrial museum could still seem far-fetched: Francis's nightmare had a touch of macabre humour about it. Today his vision seems to be rapidly coming true.

New initiative: In 1988 Peter Walker, Secretary of State for Wales in Margaret Thatcher's government, outlined a £500 million package of measures to revitalise the depressed mining areas of South Wales. At the heart of his "Valleys Initiative" lay fresh plans for attracting tourists. For example, £36 million was set aside for creating the site at Ebbw Vale for the National Garden Festival in 1992.

There was much local amusement in the area at the coming of the Garden Festival, which seemed absurdly at odds with the area's desperate social and economic difficulties. The Government's hope was that the Festival would serve as an elaborate public relations exercise for the Valleys as a whole, proving to the outside world that

Preceding pages: the traditional tourist image of the wool spinner. Left, military might recreated at St Fagans Folk Museum. Above, a slate industry rockman.

there can be life after the death of industry. It's a sort of empty "get well soon" gesture— like an expensive toy given to a boy who has just had his appendix out—a reward for having suffered the agonies of more than 30 percent adult male unemployment, but holding little long-term significance and promising no serious improvement.

The Great White Hope for boosting tourism in Wales has been the industrial heritage park: the "living history" museum. The concept originated in Wales with the

opening of the Llechwedd Slate Caverns at Blaenau Ffestiniog and the slate museum at Llyn Padarn near Llanberis. Here they discovered a new meaning to the old adage: "Where there's muck, there's money." The idea has rapidly spread.

A new scheme, the development of the Rhondda Heritage Park on the site of the old Lewis Merthyr Colliery near Pontypridd, raised the possibility that soon there would be more mining museums than mines in South Wales. And the Rhondda Heritage Park plan contained a particular irony: it was at this colliery in 1983 that the miners held a stay-down strike which presaged the subsequent national strike held to save jobs. (A further irony is that the man who led that first strike became an advisor on the plans to turn the colliery into a museum.)

There are moral arguments against industrial museums in South Wales. Dr Kim Howells, research officer for the National Union of Mineworkers in Pontypridd, describes them as "working-class vampirism". While he admits that the museums create some jobs—"It's better someone working than no-one at all"—he sees the museums as "insulting". "The valleys were once the world's greatest nodes of economic power, now it seems their only hope for the future lies in attracting visitors

government expense from job creation schemes: the unemployed of the 1980s paid to pretend to be the employed of the 1920s.

For these "museums" the temptation is to "sanitise" the past: trim out the nasty bits, omit the poverty, the hunger and the strikes—to see life as a cinema newsreel film of the 1930s and 1940s, where the working classes are always irrepressibly cheerful, despite all the dreadful odds.

What particularly worries critics like Hywel Francis and Dr Kim Howells is that the "museum-ising" of the Rhondda and other areas of South Wales implies that normal life has reached a full stop.

The Welsh Folk Museum in St Fagans,

from areas where industry is still burgeoning."

Bogus history: There are other objections. In his book *The Heritage Industry*, Robert Hewison highlighted the dangers of industrial museums which recreate the past in a way which we would like it to have been, rather than the way it really was. The Rhondda Heritage Park is the latest in a series of large-scale British heritage parks such as Ironbridge in Shropshire, the Black Country museum in the West Midlands and Beamish in northeast England which include a "cast" of characters in period costume. For the most part these are people recruited at

near Cardiff, is an agreeably arranged repository of buildings and artefacts of pre-industrial Wales—what Francis describes as the "Cymric Merrie England": "Welsh dance, costume, barns, crafts, coracles, carts and idyllic sterilised white-washed cottages". Now the museum is preparing to absorb the era of industry, placing the life of the collier beside that of the coracle maker. As far as Wales is concerned, both are now part of history.

The St Fagans museum is on the look-out for a good example of a Miner's Institute which it can dismantle and remove piece by piece to the museum grounds. At the

Rhondda Heritage Park, stark terraces of miners' "two-up, two-down" houses are being preserved as part of the "mining experience". In a search for novelty, the Rhondda experience—unlike those offered by Beamish and Ironbridge which look back 60 years or more—will be more contemporary: the Welsh Valleys 1947-50. The period when coal mines were nationalised and workers had reason to suppose they would have jobs for life.

But what of the financial argument: the claim that the packaging of industrial heritage in this way generates prosperity?

For the last few years, each July the Gwent town of Blaenavon has put on a celebration

dilapidated: Broad Street, the main thoroughfare, is scarred with closed-down stores—each empty shop window as bleak as a gravestone. The Workmen's Institute, one of the finest of its sort—built entirely from workers' subscriptions as a place to hold choir concerts and improve education with its lending library—now stands deserted and boarded up. Perhaps this could be the one that will be shipped to the Folk Museum in Cardiff.

Throughout the 1980s, the town has been counting on tourism to safeguard its fragile existence. In 1982, the main colliery near the town, Big Pit, reopened as a mining museum—for the first time allowing tourists

of "Welsh/American heritage". The highlight is "Olde Worlde Day", when local residents dress as American Southern Belles and Red Indians and others wear Welsh period costume.

The celebration and the dressing up is part of an effort to promote tourism in the town. On the face of things, this seems a forlorn hope. In the 19th century, Blaenavon was one of the more prosperous towns in South Wales. Today, the place is sad and

Left and above, locals who would once have worked in factories now conduct tours or practise crafts.

kitted out in hard hats and miner's lamps to travel down a mineshaft to see what life was really like for workers underground.

In financial terms, Big Pit has been moderately successful. With job creation labour, a further project is under way to turn Blaenavon's old ironworks into another "industrial heritage" attraction. It will show that the town played a pivotal role in the Industrial Revolution both in pioneering manufacturing techniques and, later, in trade unionism. The Chartists' movement for workers' rights grew up around Blaenavon: from here in 1839 they marched on Newport with hopes of insurrection.

But for the residents of Blaenavon, tourism is seen to have been a false dawn: the promises of prosperity are unfulfilled. Lynn Howells, who is on the town's tourism committee, says that the mining museum has brought no benefit to Blaenavon itself. She explains that people call at the museum and then travel on to somewhere else—often to nearby Abergavenny which in style is more a typical English market town than anything you are likely to find in Wales.

"This is why we launched the Blaenavon American week to bring visitors into the town," says Ms Howells, who runs a baby wear shop in Blaenavon. The tourism committee hoped originally that American

visitors might be attracted. There are connections: Gilchrist Thomas of Blaenavon sold his steelmaking patent to American industrialist Carnegie. Hundreds of Blaenavon workers left for Pennsylvania to establish the US steel industry. Now with steel factory closures in the States, Pennsylvania is as depressed as the Welsh valleys: there are few American tourists to Blaenavon.

The Big Pit museum itself succeeds largely on attracting school parties, many of whom are working on school history projects about the Industrial Revolution. The men who kit you out in hard hats and lamps,

and who lead the tours underground, are ex-miners. The museum—and the guides—don't "sanitise" history: these, after all, are real miners, not people on a job creation scheme pretending to be miners. They talk of how women and children worked below ground, the hard physical back-breaking labour of hewing coal, the pit ponies that stayed in the dark for 50 weeks of the year.

It's shocking, and very moving: but is it good box office? How long before the marketing men step in and, in order to "maximise revenue", demand more of a showbusiness style? There have been serious suggestions of presenting a Hollywood *How Green Was My Valley* tableau: miners singing "Myfanwy" as they clock on for the morning shift, their lamps flickering in the dawn, life-like canaries tweeting on their shoulders.

One of the ex-miners at the museum admitted that his new work as a guide wasn't much of a job. "I'm glad I've got a job but it isn't real work. Coal mining was hard but there was a sense of doing something: and there were good times with your pals." He looked up towards the pit-head baths, which now house a cafeteria: "This isn't right."

Dancing in the streets: Lynn Howells, of Blaenavon's tourism committee, agrees: "What Blaenavon really wants is not tourists but proper jobs. If someone announced that they were opening a new colliery which would offer 300 to 400 jobs for at least the next 20 years, you could send one of your photographers up here and take a picture of people rejoicing and dancing in the streets."

Does it therefore make sense to pay people to pretend to be miners: wouldn't it be better to pay them to be real miners, since that's what they want anyway? Tourism officials see projects like the National Garden Festival at Ebbw Vale and the Rhondda Heritage Park not only as tourist attractions in themselves, but as ways of attracting other employers to the area—"beacons" waving a message of hope from the community.

Unhappily, the people of Blaenavon and Rhondda fear that they may not be waving, but drowning.

Above, tomorrow's generation turn their backs on industrial decay. Right, the Rhondda still struggles for prosperity.

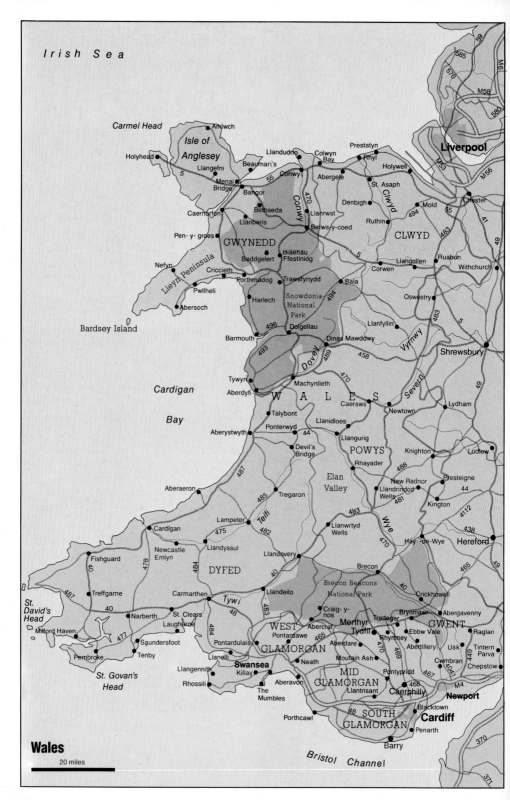

Wales

20 miles

PLACES

Like Richard Burton, one of its most celebrated sons, Wales can assume many different guises yet remain recognisably itself. There is the Welsh-speaking Wales in the north and the west, a community whose distinctive culture has been shielded by its ancient language from a world hell-bent on homogeneity. There is the close community of the Valleys, gradually shaking the coal dust from its boots and redefining its future. There is the "English" Wales in the east and southwest, where the two ancient enemies have reached an understanding of sorts.

The visual contrasts within this small community are as striking as the differences in character. The Wye Valley, the first stop for many visitors who cross the Severn Bridge, offers gentle scenery, sleepy villages, ruined abbeys and castles. The Brecon Beacons National Park combines mountain and moorland to convey a feeling of space rare in an overcrowded island. In the Valleys, the dramatic geological rifts that form the heart of South Wales, the coal mines have been eclipsed but some rivers still run black.

Cardiff, like many capital cities, does not claim to be a microcosm of the country. It is noticeably anglicised, and has cosmopolitan convictions—though it assumed the role of Wales's capital as recently as 1955. Swansea, Wales's second (and indeed *only* other) city, is a personable and personal place—"an ugly, lovely town," as the poet Dylan Thomas called it.

Glamorgan's Heritage Coast remains one of Britain's best-kept secrets: the seaside pleasures of past times have remained uncorrupted by the juggernaut of tourism.

The coastline continues to the southwest into the Pembrokeshire Coast National Park, an area where seafaring traditions combine with Celtic myth and tales of Merlin. Mid-Wales, unsullied by motorways, has retained its unspoiled rural charm. To the north lies Snowdonia National Park, a dramatic mountain landscape and a magnet for climbers and outdoor enthusiasts. Those looking for fun will head instead for the string of north coast resorts, doggedly maintaining the candy-floss tradition of the British seaside.

As the signs say, *Croeso i Cymru*—Welcome to Wales.

THE SEVERN BRIDGE

Just across the **Severn Bridge**, on the Welsh side of the M4 motorway, there is a road sign that makes it unmistakably clear to all drivers and their passengers that they are entering another country. *Croeso i Cymru*, it says. And underneath, it adds in English: Welcome to Wales.

The bridge is now the main way into South Wales and so busy that there are plans to build another one, a few miles downstream, to handle the rising number of cars and lorries squeezing through the nine toll booths. Friday teatime and Saturday morning are the peak periods: Friday is commercial-traveller time, with all the businessmen returning home to Wales for the weekend; on Saturday the traffic is the other way, day-trippers going over to sample the English air or heading for London and a day out.

Tailback time: On a busy day 50,000 cars and lorries make the crossing. But on a really busy Saturday in August, with all the holidaymakers on the move, the figure goes well over 66,000.

This is all a very long way from the little ferry that used to ply across the Severn before the bridge was opened in 1966. Then, the usual way into South Wales was along the A40, past Oxford's dreaming spires, Cheltenham and Gloucester, down the A48 through the little Severnside towns of Newent and Lydney, crossing the border out of England, just before the bridge across the river Wye and Chepstow's steep winding streets.

The scenery on the Welsh side is very different to that on the English, as every driver going west along the M4 can see. Through Wiltshire and Avon, the countryside is rolling but relatively flat; houses are built in the soft yellowing Cotswold stone; rich pasture land borders the road. Across the water it is very different. The **Wye**, one of Britain's great salmon rivers, at whose mouth Chepstow lies, is steep-sided, with tra-ditional oak, beech, birch, ash and chestnut covering the slopes. It is an area which may have provided inspiration for the poet William Wordsworth, who spent some time there (perhaps looking for another host of golden daffodils).

Beyond Chepstow, in the far distance, are the **Black Mountains**, and, even further, the **Brecon Beacons**, where the peak of **Pen-y-fan**, snow-capped through much of the winter, reaches 2,907 ft (886 metres), making it the highest mountain top in southern Britain.

The bridge is now the gateway into this very different country. It is, technically, not one bridge but two, though it takes an engineer to spot the join. A thin isthmus of land divides the Wye from the Severn and the piling for the bridge comes down on this strip of land, still part of England, before carrying the bridge on over the Wye into Wales. It's not one of Europe's dramatic borders: indeed, drivers will not notice this point at all and the first indication they are in Wales will be the *Croeso i Cymru* sign welcoming them half a mile further on.

When the Severn Bridge was first opened it was one of the longest single-span arches in the world. It could live in the same league as the bridges across the Hudson and the East rivers in New York. But since the mid-1960s a lot of bridge building has taken place and now the Severn just about gets in the top 10.

Pay as you go: As drivers quickly discover, it is a toll bridge—though the cost is much less than the cost of petrol for the alternative route, a circuit of 60 or more miles, through Gloucester. However, the tolls are a matter of considerable debate because there appears to be neither rhyme nor reason to the charges levied for crossing water in the United Kingdom.

Anyone crossing the Severn Bridge, though, is going over one of the seven engineering wonders of modern Britain. And anyone fortunate enough to approach the bridge from the English side just as the sun is setting at the end of a fine day is seeing one of the seven finest views in the country.

Preceding pages: Porthmadog railway station; a train heads for the summit of Snowdon; New Quay in Cardiganshire. Left, the Severn Bridge.

THE WYE VALLEY

As an introduction to the Wye Valley, **Chepstow** offers few hints of the magnificent pleasures to come. This small town near the mouth of the Wye was once one of the most handsome and prosperous places in South Wales. The years, however, have not been kind: industrial decline and a series of curious town planning decisions—the worst has involved driving a by-pass through the most attractive quarter—have almost entirely robbed the place of its charm and character.

The Norman Castle, its greatest treasure, remains impressively intact, dominating the river with tremendous presence. Although playing a key role in the Norman control of the turbulent Welsh, it came into its own in the English Civil War, achieving particular significance during the ebb and flow of the battle between the Roundheads and the Royalists.

The castle is particularly associated with Henry Marten, a leading Parliamentarian who signed King Charles I's death warrant and suffered for this "treacherous" act when King Charles II was restored to the throne. He was kept prisoner in the castle for 20 years; the tower where he was held is still known as Marten's Tower. (In fairness to the Restorationists, Marten's imprisonment seems not to have been especially arduous: he lived with his family in some comfort and was given permission to come and go from the castle.)

Near the river, in the old streets at the bottom of the town, one can imagine how Chepstow must have been 200 years ago: busy with ships and boats travelling further up the Wye and out to the Bristol Channel, its dozens of ale houses crammed with sailors and prostitutes. Like most ports, it was often mad, bad and dangerous to know.

Two miles (three km) from the centre of Chepstow, heading north towards Monmouth on the A466, you pass **Chepstow Racecourse**, a popular venue for enthusiasts of steeple-chasing. On Sundays the car park here is given over to a busy market.

Shortly after St Arvans, a mile further on, the Wye Valley opens up to reveal its full grandeur. It is worth making a small detour up to the **Wyndcliff** which offers a breathtaking view of the valley, the horseshoe bend of the river and beyond to the Severn Bridge. This view was one of the highspots of the "Wye Tour" enjoyed by pioneer tourists of the late 18th and early 19th centuries who travelled in search of such powerfully romantic settings.

For most visitors, however, then and now, the true highspot is probably **Tintern Abbey,** five miles (eight km) north of Chepstow. It would be difficult to imagine a more handsome setting for an abbey, set as it is beside the river, framed by steeply wooded slopes. The abbey inspired William Wordsworth to write one of his finest poems, *Lines composed a few miles above Tintern Abbey*. The poem, which Wordsworth actually wrote in Bristol, isn't really about Tintern Abbey at all but rather a

Left, the River Wye. Below, Chepstow Castle.

statement of his pantheistic belief that God is to be found in nature:

And I have felt
A presence that disturbs me with the joy
Of elevated thoughts; a sense sublime
Of something far more deeply interfused,
Whose dwelling is the light of setting suns,
And the round ocean and the living air,
And the blue sky, and in the mind of man.

The area around Tintern is superb walking country. There are footpaths in all directions, many of them well marked trails on signposted circuits. A few miles above Tintern, and perhaps the very spot where Wordsworth had his first inspiring glimpse of the ruined abbey, is **Devil's Pulpit**. There's a well-marked footpath from the village, crossing the river Wye over the footbridge: the early part of the climb is steep.

A more interesting route to Devil's Pulpit—and a more level one—is along the **Offa's Dyke footpath**, which begins near Tidenham; for a couple of miles you can follow the surprisingly well preserved line of the 170-mile (270-km) Dyke built in the eighth century by Mercian King Offa. It was erected to mark the western boundary of his kingdom and to provide a defence against Welsh raiders. Perhaps it looked more of a barrier 1,000 years ago; today, a small dog could leap over it.

At Devil's Pulpit, a rocky knob which does look rather pulpit-like, legend has it that the devil stood and raged against the monks in their handsome abbey below, pelting them with rocks. Not much sign of the devil now, but there are still piles of small rocks lying around (discarded brimstones perhaps?) From the Pulpit, the view of the Abbey, the Wye and the wooded valley is one of the best views in the world: enough to move anyone to verse.

Don't leave Tintern without visiting the Abbey, a splendid Cistercian build-

Below, Tintern Abbey. Right, Offa's Dyke path near Chepstow.

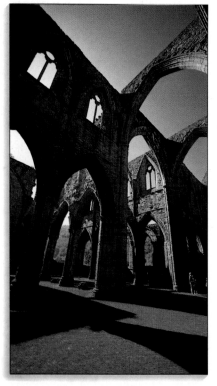

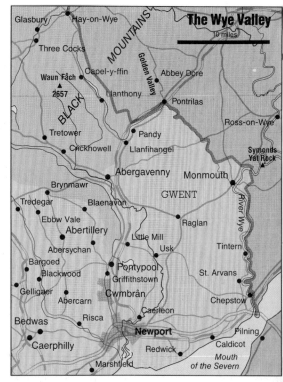

The Wye Valley

10 miles

Glasbury — Hay-on-Wye — MOUNTAINS
Three Cocks
Waun Fâch — Capel-y-ffin — Abbey Dore
2657 — Golden Valley — Llanthony — Pontrilas
BLACK
Tretower — Pandy — Ross-on-Wye
Crickhowell — Llanfihangel — Symonds Yat Rock
Abergavenny — Monmouth
Brynmawr
Tredegar — Blaenavon — GWENT
Ebbw Vale — Raglan
Abertillery — Little Mill
Abersychan — Usk — Tintern
Bargoed — Pontypool
Blackwood — Griffithstown — St. Arvans
Gelligaer — Cwmbrân
Abercarn — Chepstow
Bedwas — Risca — Caerleon
Newport — Pilning
Caerphilly — Redwick — Caldicot
Marshfield — Mouth of the Severn

OFFA'S DYKE

Crossing the border from England into Wales is an anticlimactic event. You'll sometimes see a sign telling you that "You are now leaving England", though you'll more often find a roadside notice-board depicting a red dragon accompanied by the greeting *Croeso i Cymru*, Welcome to Wales. And that's about all.

Things were different in the dim and distant past. The understanding of territorial boundaries then was often a matter of life and death, and always a cause of potential conflict. Tenth-century travellers, for example, knew precisely where they stood, for Saxon law stated that "Neither shall a Welshman cross into English land nor an Englishman cross into Welsh land without the appointed man from that other land who should meet him at the bank and bring him back again without any offence being committed."

The "bank" in question was a reference to the earthen dyke which served as the first official boundary between England and Wales. Speculation surrounds the purpose behind the construction of this great earthwork known as Offa's Dyke, or *Clawdd Offa* in Welsh. It was built at the command of King Offa (A.D. 757-796), ruler of the Midland Kingdom of Mercia.

That much can be stated with certainty. But was it a military defence put up to keep the unruly Welsh out? Or did it serve as an administrative boundary—a demarcation line, if you like—to clear up, once and for all, any territorial ambiguities that existed between the Welsh to the west and the Anglo-Saxons to the east? Was it intended as a lookout to give the Mercians a sense of security and control in dangerous hill country? Or was it simply meant to discourage cattle thieves?

Compared to Hadrian's Wall, built to keep the Scots at bay, Offa's Dyke can hardly be regarded as a serious line of defence. Unlike the heavily fortified Wall, it was not intended to be permanently manned. Neither was it a continuous structure. The dyke ran from Prestatyn on the North Wales coast to Sedbury near Chepstow on the Severn Estuary, a distance of 142 miles (227 km). But there were many breaks along the way: in thickly wooded river valleys, for instance, where construction would have been very difficult—and pointless, the forests acting as a barrier in themselves.

The building of the dyke must, nevertheless, have represented a monumental effort. A deep ditch was dug on the Welsh side. Above this, an earthwork barrier rose up to 20 ft (six metres) high. The overall structure, ditch and earthwork, was in places over 70 ft (22 metres) wide.

This 1,200-year-old barrier has vanished along much of its route. Where it does survive—usually in high, lonely, obscure places—it conveys a profound sense of the past. The untravelled uplands around Knighton, Powys, are such an area. These undulating hills are one of the best places in which to see the dyke in its full glory. Here, the earthwork still stands more or less to its full height, miraculously well preserved as it snakes across remote, grassy hill country like a miniature railway cutting.

Knighton's Welsh name of *Tref-y-Clawdd* means "the town on the dyke". It is a real meeting of the ways. Not only does it stand on both the ancient dyke and today's official border between England and Wales (the route of which only bears a rough approximation to the eighth-century prototype); it is also on the long-distance Offa's Dyke path, which follows the line of the earthwork wherever possible. Moreover, Knighton is the home of the Offa's Dyke Information Centre, so is the perfect place at which to begin an exploration of the dyke. The long-distance footpath runs for 170 miles (272 km), sometimes through demanding, tough moorland but also along gentle lowlands of outstanding beauty. Walkers will regularly come across evidence of the earthwork, sometimes faint, at other times conclusive.

Did Offa's Dyke lay the foundation stones for Wales's sense of separateness? Without it, would the Wales of today still harbour that unsatisfied longing for autonomy? Perhaps Offa's Dyke represents one of those ironies often thrown up by the fickle hand of history: a boundary, created by an Anglo-Saxon king, which contributed to the survival of Wales's national identity.

ing suprisingly well preserved. The Cistercians are a strict order who eschew most comforts, including warmth. But they certainly treated themselves with the site of the Abbey and its handsome construction. Even without heat, you can almost have envied them.

Old railway: Below the Offa's Dyke path, running parallel to the river, is the route of the old Chepstow to Monmouth railway. The Wye Valley railway line was closed 25 years ago, and the tracks ripped up with indecent haste. It must have been a magnificent ride; memories of the line are preserved at the Old Station in Tintern, now a picnic site with an exhibition of memorabilia from the line's heyday.

In the **Old Signal Box**, from May to October, is an exhibition of the life and works of Flora Klickmann, one of the foremost women journalists and writers of the first half of the 20th century. As well as being editor of the *Girls' Own Paper*, the leading women's magazine of its day, she also wrote and edited more than 50 books, including the well-known *Flower Patch* series which lovingly chronicled life in her small Flower Patch cottage near Brockweir (one mile north of Tintern). Flora Klickmann is buried in the delightful Moravian church in Brockweir and her grave is still visited by "Flower Patch" pilgrims who come from all over the world.

In autumn, the hues and tints of the Wye Valley rival the New England fall. The wooded stretch of valley from Brockweir to Llandogo is particularly magnificent.

Llandogo (two miles north of Brockweir) was once a busy river port where the flat-bottomed boats known as "trows" called en route to and from Chepstow and Bristol. In Bristol today there is still the "Llandoger Trow", a famous old pub on Welsh Back named after the boats which plied to and from Llandogo; this pub is said to be the model for the "Admiral Benbow" in Robert Louis Stevenson's classic story of adventure, *Treasure Island*.

The Wye Valley.

After Llandogo, the road crosses over Bigsweir Bridge and continues to Monmouth on the English side of the river. During the highest spring tides, usually in April, both banks are crowded at night with men fishing for baby eels (or elvers, as they are known). These tiny, almost transparent creatures make their long arduous journey across the Atlantic Ocean from the Sargasso Sea only to be scooped out of the river in special nets. The elvers are boiled and then pressed into an elver "cheese" which can be fried with bacon. A popular pastime practised in a number of pubs are elver eating contests.

Redbrook, five miles (eight km) north of Llandogo, has a dour, industrial air about it. Indeed, like other places in the Wye Valley, it used to have a busy ironworks industry, linked to the streams that rushed down the valley sides. When large supplies of coal were discovered further east in South Wales, the iron industry moved away.

In the two-mile drive from Redbrook to Monmouth, the valley begins to flat-ten out. The scenery is less dramatic but no less beautiful.

Monmouth can claim several places in history. Geoffrey of Monmouth, who might have been a monk of the Benedictine Priory in the town, produced a history of England, the *History of the Kings of Britain*, which was more fantasy than fact but which, like Shakespeare's history plays, became accepted by many as the unvarnished truth. A more recent celebrity was Charles Rolls, co-founder of Rolls-Royce, who until his death in 1910 in a flying accident lived in The Hendre, a handsome manor house near the town. (Near the former Rolls home are the Rockfield recording studios, frequented by more contemporary celebrities such as Huey Lewis, Queen and Black Sabbath.)

Monmouth's most famous son, however, is without doubt Henry V (Good King Hal), who won the Battle of Agincourt—Monmouth's main square is called **Agincourt Square**. He was born in 1387 in Monmouth castle, which was

Twin heroes in Monmouth: Henry V and early aero-engine maker Henry Rolls.

largely destroyed in the Civil War: a few walls are all that remain. The town museum has plenty of information on Henry, Rolls and Geoffrey—but its star exhibits concern quite a different character, Admiral Lord Nelson.

Nelson came to Monmouth only twice, but such was his status—equivalent to that of some sort of TV superstar today—that these visits had a profound effect on local sensibilities. A Naval temple was erected on the **Kymin Hill**, which has a stunning view over Monmouth, to commemorate Britain's success at the Battle of the Nile and other naval victories.

Lady Llangattock, Rolls's mother, built up a collection of Nelson memorabilia which was bequeathed to the town after her death in 1923. This collection, which includes Nelson's sword and models of his ships, forms the basis of the Nelson museum.

The town's most outstanding sight is the 13th-century **Monnow Bridge**, Britain's only surviving fortified bridge and still in regular use today (its low headroom constitutes a continuing menace to double-decker buses). But of the once famous Monmouth caps (mentioned by Shakespeare in *Henry V*) there is alas today no sign.

Echo of Camelot: After leaving Monmouth, the valley once more takes on a more precipitous shape. **Symonds Yat Rock**, three miles (five km) northwest of Monmouth, is the valley's most famous viewpoint, offering dramatic views up river and beyond to the Malvern Hills. Here the river flows through some of the finest scenery in the country. Landmarks include the **Seven Sisters Rocks** and **King Arthur's Caves** which, like most things that are attributed to the great king, probably had nothing whatever to do with him.

A short way upstream at Whitchurch is the **Jubilee maze**, planted in 1977 to honour the Queen's Silver Jubilee and first opened to the public in 1981 on the day of the wedding of Prince Charles and Lady Diana Spencer.

Seven miles up the A40, past Goodrich Castle and Flanesford Priory,

Monmouth's fortified bridge.

you cross the border from Wales to England to reach the elegant town of **Ross-on-Wye**, with its famous market house at the centre. Ross is a place to be enjoyed not so much for any particular sights or great public monuments, but for its easy-going charm.

From Ross, the Wye meanders up to Hereford through small delightful villages, with names that summon up the essence of rural England: Brampton Abbots, Kings Caple, Hoarwithy, Holme Lacy, Hampton Bishop.

After the succession of sleepy villages, **Hereford**, 15 miles (24 km) from Ross, comes as a surprise. Technically a city, with a handsome cathedral, Hereford has more in common with a quiet rural market town: there are no bright lights. The place is at its busiest on market day, a Wednesday, when farmers come into town to trade their world-famous Hereford cattle.

On market day, too, there is certainly heavy consumption of Hereford's other great product, cider, made by locally-based Bulmers. In some countries of the world, cider is an innocuous alcohol-free concoction enjoyed by maiden aunts. In this part of the world, cider can be a ferocious brew to be taken only in modest quantities.

There has been new development here, but the character of the old city— once the capital of Saxon Mercia—has been well preserved, particularly in the cathedral precincts. The **cathedral** should be visited to see its 13th-century *Mappa Mundi* which shows a flat world with its centre in Jerusalem and at the top, of course, is Paradise. To raise funds, the priceless map was on the verge of being auctioned off in 1989, but was saved. The cathedral's other great treasure is its monastic library, claimed to be the largest of its sort in the world, with 1,500 chained books. One of the best known books here is the famous ancient version of the bible known as the "Cider" bible: its translator, conscious no doubt of local tastes, has substituted the word "cider" for any mention of "strong drink".

For such an untheatrical sort of place,

Left, Agincourt Square outdoor market in Monmouth. Right, Ross-on-Wye.

Hereford has strong connections with drama and music. The city was the birthplace of famous Shakespearean actor David Garrick and home of actress Sarah Siddons. Its best known theatrical daughter, however, is Nell Gwynne, who is believed to have been born in a house in what was formerly Pipe Lane (since renamed **Nell Gwynne Street**). She became famous as mistress to King Charles II.

Civic variations: Hereford was also home for a short period to one of England's greatest composers, Sir Edward Elgar, who moved to the town in 1904. Elgar was closely associated with the Three Choirs Festival held in Hereford, Gloucester and Worcester (Elgar's home town). Elgar, it seems, was better thought of in Hereford than his home of Worcester—it was even suggested that he should become Hereford's mayor.

Eleven miles (18 km) west of Hereford is the small, charming village of **Bredwardine**, which has recently achieved literary celebrity. From 1877 until his death in 1879, it was the parish of the Reverend Francis Kilvert, a mid-Victorian minister who kept a diary of his daily life in the area. Long after his death, the diary was "discovered" and published, becoming widely successful. Kilvert is buried in the graveyard of the village's lovely Norman church.

Across the river from Bredwardine is the small village of **Willersley**, which has further literary connections. This was once the home of the de Baskervilles, a long-established Norman family connected with the legendary hound. Sir Arthur Conan Doyle borrowed the legend for one of his most famous Sherlock Holmes stories.

If all these literary allusions have whetted your appetite for books, then **Hay-on-Wye** is the right place to visit. This sleepy border town has become the "Biggest Second-hand Bookshop in the World" (*see panel*), but has still managed to retain its rural character. The dry business of browsing through old books can be remedied at one of more than half a dozen excellent old pubs in the town. It's worth remembering that little more than 20 years ago, when the whole of

Wales was "dry", Sunday drinkers there would have had to cross the border into England for a glass of beer or cider.

From Hay, the road following the Wye moves on towards Builth Wells and begins to climb into the **Black Mountains**. The scenery subtly shifts from lush green, open, rolling hills to a starker, harsher landscape. There is a sense of dark Celtic mystery in the air: there are certainly no shortage of myths and legends connected with the area. Near Erwood, 10 miles (16 km) from Hay, for example, is **Craig Pwll-du** where it is said a castle once stood with a chatelain who had a fondness for ravishing local womenfolk; after enjoying his pleasure he would hurl them into the dark pool down below in the river.

Nearby is **Llangoed Castle**, a house handsomely remodelled by Portmeirion architect Sir Clough Williams-Ellis. After falling into neglect, the house was acquired by Sir Bernard Ashley, husband of the late Laura Ashley (founder of the worldwide chain of shops bearing her name), and is now a luxury hotel.

Books in bulk at Hay-on-Wye. Right, Richard Booth, who began the book boom.

A Town That Turned Into A Bookshop

For bibliophiles, the tiny market town of Hay-on-Wye, straddling the border between England and Wales, is either paradise or a vision of hell. In more than a dozen bookshops, ranging from the cosy to the gargantuan, glossy art books rub spines with the battered works of long-forgotten novelists, battered Barbara Cartlands consort with frayed Ian Flemings, and antiquarian treasures share shelf space with volumes of *Pennsylvania Constitutional Development*.

It all began in the early 1960s when Richard Booth, who had local family connections, set up a books and antiques store in the town with the aid of a legacy. The antiques didn't do so well, but the old books moved. Booth was on his way. Every time a commercial property came on the market, he snapped it up. Soon the old Plaza cinema was packed with books; so was the former fire station, the workhouse, a chapel, even the castle. Booth, an engaging, unkempt man with a penchant for self-promotion, proclaimed himself "the world's biggest secondhand bookseller".

His philosophy was simple. Hay was facing economic extinction as local shoppers were lured away to the supermarkets of larger towns nearby, and its only salvation was to specialise.

"Books are essentially an international and not a purely metropolitan market," he argued. "Hay is a suburb of nowhere, but there's a bigger market here than in London because people who live within 100 miles can easily take a trip here—and that includes Bristol, Manchester and Birmingham. Books are a part of tourism and I want to give bookselling a carnival image. I think a town where the bookshops are bigger than the supermarkets can be a major attraction because it is offering a retailing service that no other town in the world offers."

Booth installed himself in Hay Castle, a decrepit building he bought for £6,500, and filled it with books. Outside stood wooden stocks "erected in 1690", complete with bookrest and a sign proclaiming that, even in the 17th century, Hay was a Book Town and that malefactors locked in the stocks were permitted to read. Tourists queued to photograph this antiquity, which in reality had been cobbled together by a local carpenter for £55 plus value-added tax.

But the hype began to work. Bus tours included Hay on their itinerary, and soon other booksellers were seeking premises in the town. Rents, they found, were amazingly low by city standards and so were warehouse costs. Even Oxfam opened a secondhand bookshop.

Booth himself, ever quotable, became a celebrity. One day he would attack the "bureaucrassities" of the Wales Tourist Board; the next he would rage against the parish-pump politics of the "Hay Clown Council". It was time, he insisted, to ban the destructive motor car and reinstate the horse economy, thereby creating jobs for blacksmiths, grooms and stable boys. Declaring the town an independent state, he printed Hay passports (for carefree travel, 50p post-free) and national currency (denominations of £1,000, £5, £1).

Not everyone shared in the joke. Many of the 1,200 townspeople resented the razzmatazz and didn't take to the "trendy types" who were moving in. Hay divided into the supporters of "King Richard" and his detractors.

Inevitably, Booth's book-keeping abilities couldn't keep pace with his bookselling skills and the most frequent topic of conversation in the gossipy town became the likelihood of Richard Booth's bankruptcy. Certainly the 1980s brought a host of problems: a fire destroyed much of the castle and Booth was forced to consolidate by selling off many of his properties. But other booksellers such as the burgeoning Leon Morelli Group were all too ready to snap them up.

In 1989 the first Hay-on-Wye Festival of Literature was held. Hay had become firmly established as a book town and the tourists continued to pour in, even though their chances of finding a rare book for 10p on the dusty shelves had markedly diminished. The new intake of booksellers had imported professionalism, and were not so given to buying books unseen by the container load. They did, however, happily embrace Richard Booth's stirring slogan: "Every publisher in the world is working for Hay-on-Wye."

BRECON BEACONS NATIONAL PARK

People in South Wales used to regard the **Brecon Beacons National Park** almost as a private fief. Just as the world at large thought of Cardiff as a grimy and industrial coal city, so it vaguely imagined that the South Wales coalfield reached to the fringes of Snowdonia. A glorious landscape hid its secret behind the myth of black industry until the M4 motorway reached out, demolished the myth and abolished the fief.

As incomers began to move in, part of the national park even became tagged, in that ironic South Wales manner, the Hampstead Highlands. But despite being the nearest serious hill country to London, Parc Cenedlaethol Bannau Brycheiniog, in the old tongue, still retains its remoteness and a certain sense of mystery.

Its most valuable asset in an overcrowded island is the feeling of space presented by mile after mile of empty mountain and moorland, dappled by cloud shadows, ever-changing but planting an enduring mental snapshot. **Highest peak:** The park is almost defined by its hills: the five ridges of the **Black Mountains** on the eastern border; the more isolated **Black Mountain** in the west, with its legend-haunted twin lakes, **Llyn y Fan Fach** and **Llyn y Fan Fawr**; and, dominating the centre, the Beacons themselves, crowned by South Wales's highest peak, **Pen-y-Fan** (2,907 ft/886 metres).

These are soft-focus grassy heights with few rocky outcrops or glowering cliff faces, superb hillscapes of wide horizons, turning the colour of a lion's mane even in an averagely decent summer. But mountains—and wild ones—they certainly are: hard on the legs, sharp on the senses, demanding on the body. They would scarcely be the chief training ground for the soldiers of the SAS if they were otherwise.

The Army, the Beacons and the Mynydd Eppynt ranges above Sennybridge have been partners for generations. In some places, we're told, they beat swords into ploughshares. Here, farmers' wives have been known to make stools and foot-rests out of spent artillery shells, stitching together covers to disguise their original purpose.

Half the park's 519 sq miles (1,344 sq km) is enclosed farmland with a patchwork of small fields whose soil turns red under the plough because of the predominant old red sandstone of much of the geology. The pinky-red stone is used in many of the older buildings on the eastern side of the park: travelling west, the harder outlines of the villages are sometimes softened with painted plaster and the farms lime-washed white or pink.

Hedges have survived to a far greater extent than in many other parts of Britain because this is cattle and sheep country and they are needed as shelters and wind-breaks. The hills are the breeding grounds for Welsh ponies whose concave profiles and delicate muzzles are said to be a legacy of Arab blood brought in by Roman packhorses. The park's four million sheep easily

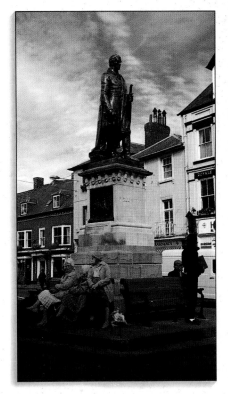

outnumber the human population of Wales.

A recent law has enabled some upland commons to be fenced along the roadsides to save the sheep from cars but there are still too many "mutton miles" for comfort as they break through to get at the sweeter grass of the verges. There are at least two major roads crossing the park, the A40 London to Fishguard trunk road running east-west along the northern edge and the A470, north-south; sometimes the conflict between road engineering and National Park aims is blatantly obvious, and not just in the numbers of dead sheep. Who wants the standards of urban streets applied to country lanes—unnecessarily straightened, widened and concrete-kerbed? Or the intrusion of bollards with red reflectors at **Storey Arms**, the landmark at the high point of the Brecon Beacons.

The human hand has been scarcely less heavy in other directions. There are 18 reservoirs supplying Cardiff, Newport and the industrial valleys—one of the earliest was built to supply clean water to Merthyr after a raging mid-19th century cholera outbreak—and thousands of acres of conifer plantations. Even together, they account for less than 10 percent of the park.

Historically, the Welsh have never been great ramblers and even now many of the groups on the hills are visitors. Too often, these may be seen making the trek up the much eroded path from Storey Arms to the top of Pen-y-Fan, when there are at least 45 to 50 known hill and ridge routes, mainly circular, to choose from in the Beacons and Black Mountains. Such walks do not include the uncharted ones here and further west for exploration by those who scorn nannying and who see that one of the greatest threats in any national park is the erosion not of footpaths but of the scope for finding your own way.

This is a difficult balancing act. By a happy geological accident, the park's most popular tourist attraction, the **Dan-yr-Ogof Showcaves**, said to be

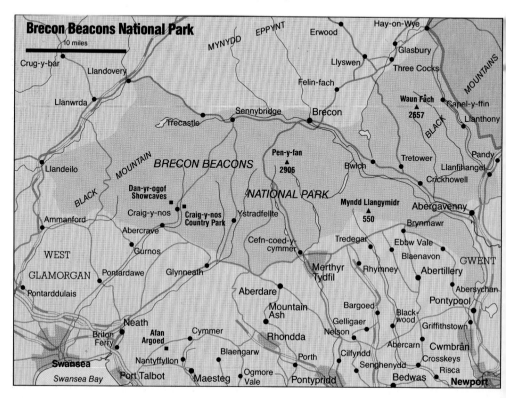

the largest showcave system in Western Europe, is on the southwestern edge and heavy internal traffic is avoided. Near the caves, with their vast chambers and limestone formations, is a **Dinosaur Park** with life-size replicas of these prehistoric animals.

The nearby **Craig-y-Nos Country Park**, 40 acres (16 hectares) of woods, a lake and gardens in the grounds of Craig-y-Nos Castle, once the home of Madame Adelina Patti, the Victorian opera singer, is a classic example of the honey-pot—an attraction catering for family outings and casual day-out visitors and easing pressures elsewhere.

Just off the Heads of the Valley road, travelling along the park's southern boundary near Merthyr, the narrow-gauge **Brecon Mountain Railway** runs for two scenic miles into the Beacons. Attached to the main station with its high-quality shop and restaurant is a fascinating workshop where small engines from as far afield as South Africa are being restored for work on the line.

Brecon, population 7,200, a small town of great charm, is the park's "capital", internationally noted for its jazz festival held every August and also home for that impudently successful brew, Welsh *chwisgi*. Both the Romans and the Normans have left their mark on Brecon—in Welsh, *Aberhonddu*—from its site at the meeting place of the Rivers Usk and Honddu. Six Roman roads converged at Bannium, the Roman fortress built near Brecon after the conquest of Wales, and much of the extensive Roman road network is easily traceable today.

One of the most remarkable features of the Beacons landscape are the memorial stones such as the nine-ft high (2.7 metres) high **Maen Madog**, the stone of Madog, alongside Sarn Helen (Helen's Causeway), the Roman road from Brecon to Neath. This is one of 12 such stones found in Breconshire, now Powys, and its Latin inscription tells us it is a memorial to Dervacus, son of Justus. A half-Welsh, half-Irish chieftain called Brychan was victor in the

Plastic dinosaurs at the Dan-Yr-Ogof Showcaves.

WHEN NATURE TURNS NASTY

Easter and October are the year's crunch points for the four mountain-rescue teams that cover the Brecon Beacons National Park. October marks the year's final flush of warmth; Easter signals, however dubiously, the end of winter—and both are times when the hills are a lure for the unwary.

These southern mountains look benign and tempt walkers to over-estimate both their stamina and their capabilities. The most unpredictable factor is the weather that can be markedly localised: brilliant sunshine blotted out by heavy mists, rain-bearing clouds unloading their burdens with sudden intensity, winds springing up that are brisk and biting.

The temperature drops five or six degrees for every 1,000 ft (300 metres) of ascent and, although the sheep may appear quite unconcerned by it, humans find it a lot harder to take. The danger is less that of falling off a rock face than suffering a nasty bout of exposure.

Because of their similar rounded shapes, the mountains can be confusing for navigation and it is all too easy to lose one's bearings in unfamiliar territory, especially if map reading is not a strong point. Learning how to read a map properly is effort well spent. The mountains are often harder than expected to walk. Making your way through miles of knee-high tussocks of grass— which is what that distantly glimpsed smooth terrain is really like—can slow up progress considerably and you should allow ample time to finish a walk before dark.

In an emergency, the recognised distress signal is six long whistle blasts, shouts or flashes of the torch. These signals are repeated at intervals of one minute.

The park is not a major climbing area. The old red sandstone is too friable for climbing until a good frost in winter binds it and then the hard climbing men come in. In fact, the riskiest areas of all for the visitor are not so much the mountains as the Ystrad Fellte Falls in the west of the park; there, limestone ravines and gorges and their racing, falling waters have been the cause of several fatalities and many broken bones, largely through people venturing on to dangerous rocks in inadequate shoes.

The Morlais Mountain Rescue Team, based at Merthyr, is called out 50 to 60 times a year— nothing like as frequently as their colleagues in North Wales and the Lake District, in itself a reflection of lighter pressures of tourism. The Beacons are used for military training, in particular by SAS troops, and a military mountain rescue team is available to tackle Army emergencies.

All calls for assistance from mountain rescue teams must be made through the police, who co-ordinate all rescue work in the Beacons from Brecon itself. Morlais is just one of four civilian rescue teams on standby, the others being based in Brecon itself and Bridgend. The fourth, the Longtown Mountain Rescue Team, is a group who come together to help out when needed.

The professionals, though, are the RAF Mountain Rescue Team operating from St Athan air base just outside Cardiff. Five men under a sergeant are based full-time on the team and they are backed up by another 20 servicemen who give their time on a voluntary basis as needed.

The RAF team was formed to rescue aircrew involved in service accidents or passengers in civilian crashes. However, 99 percent of their time is spent on assisting the police in the Beacons. Their patch is not just the Beacons: they may be called out to help in a murder hunt—searching for a lost body, for instance—or to help an old lady who has fallen over and twisted her ankle. Sometimes they might even be called out to help a dog that has fallen down a pothole. The Beacons are full of crevices; potential danger lurks almost everywhere.

Walkers should dress for the mountains and not for the season. This means wind- and water-proof anoraks, one sweater on, one in reserve, strong leak-proof footwear, warm socks, gloves and head-gear. Carry a torch, a whistle, food, maps and a compass. Do not set out without having some idea of where you are making for and what alternative return routes are available. Make a preliminary check on what weather might be expected. Use common sense and the hills become your friends.

tribal battles that followed the Roman departure; Brecon is named after him.

It has always been a farmers' town—**Ship Street**, one of its main thoroughfares, refers to sheep rather than matters maritime—though with strong military and ecclesiastical overtones, and despite a reputation Brecon people have elsewhere in South Wales for a certain reserve, there is a pleasant intimacy about the town. So far, it has escaped developers' rash.

Norman relics: William the Conqueror's half-brother, Bernard Newmarch, built **Brecon Castle**; its surviving tower and battlemented section of wall are nearly all in the garden of the Castle Hotel. That same Bernard Newmarch also had a hand in the building of nearby **Brecon Cathedral**, though the only relics of the Norman period are the north and south walls of the nave and the 12th-century font.

The largely 14th-century church is, in the words of E.A. Freeman, "noblest of a class of which a good many structures occur in Wales, massive cruciform churches with central towers... invariably presenting a picturesque external outline". The cathedral was finally restored and completed by Sir Gilbert Scott no less than 650 years after work began.

Across the Usk is **Christ College**, a public school founded by Henry VIII, and a riverside walk along the Promenade allows superb views of the Beacons. From here, you can see **Newton Farm**, a Tudor house on the site of the birthplace of Davy Gam, the one-eyed Welsh squire (as his nickname, Gam, suggests) who saved the life of Henry V at Agincourt but lost his own, and is said to have been the original of Shakespeare's Fluellen. Brecon was also the birthplace of Sarah Siddons, the actress, in 1755, and of Dr Hugh Price, founder of Jesus College, Oxford's Welsh college.

When the Gurkhas were given the freedom of Brecon in 1988 they won an honour also granted the South Wales Borderers (24th Regiment) in 1948, commemorated by the numerals XXIV

Left, house-proud in Brecon. Right, Brecon Castle.

in the town's coat-of-arms. The Border-ers have 23 Victoria Crosses on their roll, nine of them awarded in the battle of Isandhlwana and the defence of Rorke's Drift in 1879 that inspired the award-winning film, *Zulu*. The splen-did museum in **Brecon Barracks** illus-trates the history of the regiment from its birth in 1689 to its amalgamation into the Royal Regiment of Wales in 1969.

The **Brecknock Museum** in the col-onnaded Shire Hall, built in 1842, en-capsulates the history and life of Bre-conshire and has one of the largest col-lections of Welsh lovespoons in Britain.

Where the ground falls to the river at this point is the **Captains' Walk**, where French officers who were prisoners on parole during the Napoleonic Wars used to exercise. Not far away on the Bulwark, the town's centre, stands a statue of their conqueror, the Duke of Wellington, put up four years after his death in 1852.

Llangorse Lake, six miles (10 km) east of Brecon, is the largest natural lake in South Wales and has long been be-devilled by the demands of recreation and conservation. The lake is privately owned and, while sailing and fishing are long-established, water ski-ing and power boating also have a slice of the action. You may need to belong to a local club or pay for use of facilities.

The decline in wildlife has long been a source of worry, though the run-off of fertilisers from surrounding fields into the water may be as much to blame as the lake's long-term use as a play-ground. This has gone on long enough for some of the birds to adapt their behaviour: sensibly, they fly off in the morning to spend the day elsewhere, returning in the evening when all is peaceful.

Crickhowell (*Crug Hywel*, Hywel's Cairn) is the only other town in the park, 14 miles (23 km) along the incomparable **Usk Valley** from Bre-con. Though scarcely more than a vil-lage, it has some excellent shops and good pubs and is popular with new settlers in search of the rural dream.

So is **Abergavenny**, six miles (10

Cottage in Abergavenny.

km) along the A40, not actually in the park, but like Merthyr Tydfil, 17 miles (27 km) to the west, a gateway. A smart new shopping centre complements the twice-weekly market (Tuesdays and Fridays) when farmers' wives still bring home-made butter, free-range eggs and fresh cut flowers as their perks to sell in the market. Abergavenny used to be noted for its Welsh white flannel and exported large amounts to India. Rudolf Hess spent the war here, imprisoned at Maindiff Court, once the home of Crawshay (Cosher) Bailey, the Victorian ironmaster.

The town is in a hollow, surrounded by hills, the **Sugar Loaf** (1,955 ft/ 596 metres) **Skirrid Fach** and **Skirrid Fawr**, and the **Blorenge**, or Blue Ridge, on the summit of which is the memorial to Foxhunter, legendary showjumper of the 1950s, whose rider, Sir Harry Llewellyn, lived in the Usk valley.

Abergavenny is a splendid jumping-off point for the 80 sq miles (207 sq km) of **Black Mountains** with their oppor-

tunities for pony trekking, caving and good old-fashioned exploring. Ruins of a high romantic order are to be seen at **Llanthony Priory** in the Vale of Ewyas, an Augustinian monastery founded in the 12th century. Llanthony Priory—the name is an abbreviation of *Llandewi nant Honddu*, the church of St David on the Honddu brook—now houses a hotel and restaurant in what used to be the Prior's Lodge and south-west tower.

The row of 14th-century pointed arches seen by moonlight is a sight not soon forgotten. Walter Savage Landor, poet and author, once lived in the Priory house but died in 1864 without realising his plans to restore the ruins.

Four miles (six km) up the valley is **Llanthony Abbey** at Capel-y-ffin where Father Ignatius, an Anglican clergyman who claimed to have seen a vision of the Virgin Mary in a nearby field, founded a monastery. It ceased to exist soon after his death in 1908 but was later the setting for a craft community led by Catholic sculptor and artist,

Sugar Loaf Mountain.

MAKING SENSE OF THE MOUNTAINS

The Brecon Beacons Mountain Centre opened in 1966 to a public not altogether convinced of the need for it. Today it attracts 160,000 visitors a year, so time has given at least one answer to the doubters, though not perhaps the one they had in mind.

The Centre is five miles southwest of Brecon on a stretch of wild moorland called Mynydd Illtud, about 1,100 ft (330 metres) above sea level. Critics said its very existence was a contradiction, that it was bound to damage the landscape the park was pledged to protect, bringing all the paraphernalia of cars, coach parties and crowds to a remote common once chiefly the haunt of lapwings, sheep and mountain ponies.

The Centre, established with help from the United Kingdom Carnegie Trust, achieves a balance between conservation, recreation and education with considerable success. The building itself, with its stone-faced and rough cast walls and stone slated roof, merges discreetly into its surroundings and its car parks are landscaped in plantations of native trees. Although there's a charge for parking, the Centre itself is free.

Inside, a large sitting room with chairs grouped around the windows offers vantage points for superb views of Pen-y-Fan and Corn Du, the high peaks of the Brecon Beacons. Maps, photographs and permanent information displays explain the flora and fauna, history, geology and local farming practices. An interesting little shop sells cards and small gifts and simple refreshments are available at a buffet counter. There's a lecture room, an indoor picnic room and covered picnic area with a preparation and wash-up room nearby.

Mynydd Illtud, meaning Illtud's Mountain, takes its name from the saint of that name who was a contemporary of St David. It borders Fforest Fawr, the Great Forest of Brecknock, a vast area of hunting ground reserved for himself by Bernard Newmarch, half-brother of William the Conqueror and first of the Norman lords of Brecon.

Sarn Helen (Helen's Causeway), the Roman road linking the old Roman fort at Brecon with Neath, crosses the existing Common road and on this lonely upland it does not take much effort of the imagination to hear those legions passing or to realise that, for these hills, today's legions differ only in degree.

The Brecon Beacons Mountain Centre.

Eric Gill. Westward over the hills is **Partishow** (or **Patricio**) **Church** whose early Tudor rood screen, beautifully carved from Irish oak, is one of the border country's chief glories.

Outlined on a map, the park resembles a miniature United States, with the Florida finger going down towards Pontypool, an enclave taking in a length of the 32-mile (51-km) **Brecon-Pontypool canal**, now navigable for the whole distance in a setting of the utmost rural charm, with the possibility of fishing and pleasant towpath walks.

Sooner or later, though, you come back to geology, as you always must in South Wales. On these southern fringes of the park you are in the limestone belt with its wooded ravines, its graceful lime-loving ash trees, pale escarpments and above all its caves. **Llangattock Mountain** is riddled with them—the biggest **Agen Alwedd**, is 18 miles (29 km) long—but they are open, only with permission, to members of approved caving clubs.

Travelling west along the Heads of the Valleys road, with the industrial valleys stretching away to the south, their scars now rapidly vanishing, you reach, north of Glynneath, the minuscule settlement of **Ystrad Fellte**. A few houses surround a well-kept stone church, sheltered by a set of magnificent yews, half-way down the valley of the **Mellte**, a little river with a great deal going for it.

Scoring deep into the limestone, the Mellte plunges from its source on the moor at **Fforest Fawr** into an impressive series of white cascades, from **Sgwd Clun Gwyn** (White Meadow Fall) to **Sgwd y Pannwr** (Fuller's Fall) with many another *swgd* as the wonderfully expressive Welsh word has it, on neighbouring rivers. The most remarkable is **Sgwd yr Eira** (Fall of Snow) on the Hepste, eastern tributary of the Mellte, where you can walk on a ledge and see the falls from behind.

Linked with the falls is another extensive cave system. The Mellte disappears into **Porth yr Ogof**, a cave with a mouth like a hungry giant, 2,000 ft (600

Summer cruising on the Brecon Mountains.

metres) long, from which the river re-emerges a quarter of a mile on. Ten miles (16 km) further west are the **Dan-yr-Ogof** show caves of the upper Tawe valley.

Searchers after solitude may well find the western reaches of the park more to their liking with quiet villages like **Bethlehem**, where people like to have Christmas letters stamped, and **Llandovery**, a delightful little market town (not actually *in* the park) whose public school is a friendly rival to Brecon's Christ College.

One of the greatest delights is to come across one of Wales's supreme visual experiences—the first sight of **Carreg Cennen Castle**, three miles southeast of Llandeilo. This is the ruined medieval fortress someone once described as "a castle like a rock upon a rock". Steep crags on three sides fall precipitously to the valley of the Cennen below, while on the other, two towers guard the approach. On the south side, a passageway, bored for 150 ft (45 metres) through solid rock, reaches a well that is supposed to have been the castle's water supply when under siege.

The present building may date from the 12th century but we are given more to conjure with in a British Museum manuscript that pinpoints the site as the stronghold of Urien, Lord of Is-Cenen, a Knight of the Round Table.

This is Welsh Wales and this is the language Urien would have spoken even though the Saxons might have been at the gate. It used to be said that the best Welsh was spoken in these southwestern areas and the best English, too, with the precise delivery and careful enunciation of those to whom it was a learned language.

The social map has changed markedly and perhaps irrevocably since the early 1970s when West Wales became the new frontier for city refugees in search of alternative lifestyles. A second wave of incomers is in progress in the latter half of the 1980s and the hill farms whose names identified the families who occupied them for generations—for instance, Teulu Beilidu, meaning the family from Beilidu

farm—have become almost rarities.

There are no very large hotels in the Brecon Beacons National Park, but many small guest-houses in and around Brecon, Crickhowell, Abergavenny, Llandovery and Llandeilo. The amount of farmhouse accommodation is on the increase; there are five youth hostels and, although there are not many official camping sites, farmers sometimes allow tents on their land.

The National Trust owns much of the open mountains and does not permit *ad lib* camping. Perhaps it's to individuals—the back-packer, the naturalist, the historian, the rider—that the park yields its chief treasures. Within its boundaries there are all those variations of the British landscape that sharpen one's appreciation of its sheer variety—wilderness to woodland, farmland to riverside, with all their plant and animal life, domestic and wild. What makes it even better is that it is part of the feast of Wales that stretches wild, beautiful and open to the free spirit for 100 more miles (160 km) to the north.

Below,
Maen Llia in
Forest Fawr.
Right,
Cradoc Golf
Course,
Brecon.

THE VALLEYS

From the top of the 2,000-ft (600-metres) **Mynydd Blaenrhondda** (the Blaenrhondda mountain), where the hang gliders use the escarpment to fly in some of the best air currents in Britain, it is possible to look due north and not see a vestige of habitation. If it were possible to walk in a straight line, the first signs of urbanisation would be met at Colwyn Bay, 110 miles (177 km) away on the North Wales coast.

Yet right behind is the **Rhondda**, most famous of the valleys that comprise the heart of South Wales. Cardiff may be the capital of Wales; Newport, Bridgend and Swansea may dominate the plain; but the valleys are the inner sanctum of Wales.

Here, in the village of **Pontrhydyfen**, above Port Talbot, the actor Richard Burton was born and brought up. Here, in **Tredegar**, Aneurin ("Nye") Bevan, creator of Britain's National Health Service and firebrand of British politics in the 1940s and 1950s, was born. Just down the road from Tredegar is the birthplace of Neil Kinnock, the Labour Party leader. In **Merthyr Tydfil**, Jack Jones, novelist author of *Off to Philadelphia in the Morning* and other works, was born.

Here, the great choirs and brass bands of Wales practise and play. Here, the coal and steel that once fuelled the industrial greatness of modern Britain was mined and smelted. Here is history.

The Blaenrhondda mountain is a perfect place to see just what a valley is. From the top, on the A4061 road, the visitor looks down on a perfect geological rift. Steep sides rise to perhaps 1,500 ft (460 metres) from a narrow floor that in places is not half a mile across.

The tops are plateaus, excellent for walking; the sides, deeply wooded higher up, have terraces of small houses lower down clinging to them like limpets. From the top, the view could be of South Africa's *veldt*, gently-waving long grass in the breeze turning to gold as autumn approaches. In the solitude the only sound is the sound of the wind.

Below, the river cuts a roughly straight path down to the coast. It will have originated just a few miles north, in the Brecon Beacons, the southern edge of the great plateau of Mid-Wales, a land where sheep outnumber people by 100 to one.

The rivers still run black, a legacy of the days of coal and the mendacious coal owners whose only consideration was profit and whose monuments, to be seen everywhere, are the tips, now grassed over like some enormous Roman burial grounds. But the rivers are being cleaned and the salmon are returning.

Boundary lines: The Valleys themselves stretch from Pontypool in the east, just over the border with England, to west of Llanelli. What is known as "the Valleys" is in fact the geological South Wales coalfield. The natural barrier in the north for much of the way is the A465 Heads of the Valleys road. Where the A465 turns south, at Glyn Neath, the geographic Valleys area

continues west to Ystradgynlais and Ammanford.

The southern line meanders irregularly west from Pontypool, home of ICI's giant fibre plant and a fine rugger team, following the plain of Gwent and the Glamorgans—once one county but now, for bureaucratic and political reasons, divided like Gaul into three. If there were a boundary it would pass through Cross Keys, Caerphilly, Llantrisant (home of the Royal Mint), Maesteg and Neath.

By the time the rivers have reached the plain they are running crazily like a snake on a snakes-and-ladders board through the soft alluvial soil of South Wales. The main ones run out in the big cities: the Taff into Cardiff, the Usk into Newport and the Tawe into Swansea.

But there are others. There are perhaps 20 valleys in South Wales running roughly north-south; it is difficult to be categorical because the rivers divide and sub-divide. One valley may be home to two or three "rivers"; the **Rhondda Fawr** (the Big Rhondda) and the **Rhondda Fach** (the Little Rhondda) join and become the Rhondda at Porth which then flow into the Taff at Pontypridd.

The "capital" of the Valleys is **Merthyr Tydfil**, named after St Tydfil the Martyr, daughter of the Welsh chieftain Brychan killed at the hands of marauders in the year 480. Merthyr is where an essential part of the Industrial Revolution started in the second half of the 18th century. It is here that iron ore and coal were first combined on a commercial scale to produce iron and then steel.

History forged: The cannon balls that sank Napoleon's fleets at the Nile in 1799 and Trafalgar in 1805 were made in Merthyr. So, too, were the railway lines that in the long era of peace after Waterloo were laid around much of the world—in France, Germany and the United States as well as throughout the growing Empire.

It was here, in Homfray's Penydarren iron works, that Richard Trevithick, a Cornishman, in 1804 built and ran the world's first steam engine whose

Bringing home the bottles in Merthyr Tydfil.

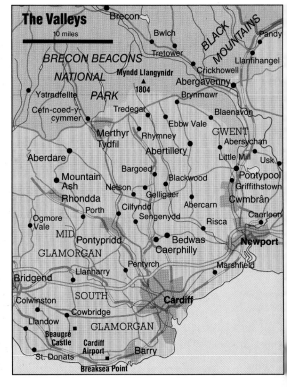

"train" carried coal and iron and 70 men for nine miles (14 km) down the valley to Abercynon, 21 years before the opening of Stevenson's pioneering Stockton-to-Darlington Rocket service.

The rails for the Stockton-Darlington line were actually made at John Josiah Guest's Dowlais works. Tramside Road in the town carries the name, and probably the route, of the Merthyr service. The tunnel along the route has recently been restored and may be inspected from the outside. The town contains a monument to the great railway achievement.

Bloody flag: Joseph Parry, perhaps the greatest of the 19th-century hymn writers, lived and died in the frontier-like town; and Dic Penderyn, in an 1831 uprising, raised the flag covered in blood that was to become the Red Flag of revolution around the world. Later, much later, Howard Winstone became boxing's featherweight champion of the world in 1968.

Today there are few signs—beyond the artefacts in the Museum in Cyfarthfa Castle—of the great iron works like those at Dowlais and Cyfarthfa that were so important in their day. Remains of some of the ovens in the Cyfarthfa works can just be seen alongside the Taff, and the engine shed for the Dowlais works has been restored; but the best view of what it must have been like when they opened the ovens and burnt the night sky red can be seen in a giant painting in the museum.

Parry has been more fortunate. His house has been restored and may be visited. The museum also houses artefacts of the coal industry, which has completely disappeared from the town. A century later, George Borrow, on his journey through Wales in 1854, was stunned by the glare of the iron furnaces, the dross shooting into the air like fireworks, the scorched and blackened appearance of the surrounding hills, the "low, mean" grey stone houses and "other remarkable edifices of a glowing, hot, Satanic nature."

Merthyr is far removed from this image now. The castle, built for the

Crawshay family who founded the Cyfarthfa works in 1825 as a private house, is part school, part museum. The Crawshays were reputed to have *droit de seigneur* over the local womenfolk and to this day there are those who will say it is possible to see the Crawshay features in many people in the town.

The greatest of them, Robert Thompson Crawshay, is buried in the little country church of **St Gwynno's** three miles (five km) outside the town in the hamlet of **Vaynor**. The top of his tomb carries just three words: *God Forgive Me*. This Crawshay was a particularly hard employer, paying low wages and employing very young children for long hours. His tombstone reflects a deathbed repentance. The same churchyard contains the graves of many young children, indicating the hard times they lived in.

Thomas Carlisle described Merthyr over a century ago as "the squalidist, ugliest place on earth". It no longer deserves that reputation, even though in the 1930s it vied with Jarrow as being the most deprived town in Britain. Hotels have been built, the tips have been removed, a ski run and leisure centre added and access to the immeasurably beautiful countryside improved.

The administrative boundaries of the town extend into the Brecon Beacons National Park. The Brecon Beacons Mountain Railway, one of several small railways in Wales, runs from **Pant** up into the park and to **Pontsticill Lake**, whose waters supply the people of Merthyr.

The railway, two miles long, is the brainchild of Tony Hills and his wife Jenny; he as tall as she is tiny. At the Pant end, which might loosely be called the terminus, the station shop caters for the tourist while Jenny Hills runs Shunters, one of South Wales's best all-day restaurants.

Elsewhere in the town, the Guest Memorial Library was built in 1863 at the instigation of Lady Charlotte Guest (who had translated the *Mabinogion*, the great Welsh work of the Middle Ages, into English), as a memorial to

A working man's club in the Valleys.

her husband Sir John Josiah Guest (now enshrined in the company Guest, Keen and Nettlefold) who had died a decade earlier. It was designed by Sir Charles Barry but is now a recreational centre.

Nearby are the remains of the Dowlais stables, the front being all that has survived the years. The stables were built in 1820 for the 200 horses used in Guest's Ivor iron works. The upper storey was the first school in Dowlais.

At either end of the town, Merthyr has three examples of the perfect art form of the Victorian engineer: the viaduct. Only one, in **Quaker's Yard**, still carries the trains down to Cardiff. The others have long since had their lines pulled up. The viaduct in **Cefn Coed**, to the north of the town, is perhaps the best example of the three because distance allows a better perspective. But the third, at **Pontsarn**, just before the church in Vaynor where Crawshay is buried, is the most used. Every Sunday, and on most days during the summer, parties of abseilers, ranging from members of the SAS to youth parties,

are to be seen climbing over the ramparts and descending earthwards at a dizzy, if controlled, speed.

Those wanting to go the other way—up—can be seen just across the river climbing the sheer rockface to **Morlais Castle**, started in about 1287 by Gilbert de Clare, one of the great Marcher barons. Morlais Castle was probably never completed and all that now remains is part of the curtain around the inner bailey, or courtyard, and two of the round towers.

King Coal: It is coal, though, not climbing, that has been the seminal influence on the valleys. Iron and other ores, especially copper, were smelted and large numbers worked in the industry. But South Wales is associated with coal like Bavaria with beer.

At its peak, in 1921, some 271,000 men worked in the industry. The record production, however, was in 1913, just before World War I, when 56.8 million tons were produced. Those numbers have been cut beyond belief: just 7,000 men are left in the industry now and,

where once pits were to be found on every street corner, only 11 remain. In the 1920s there were 66 pits in the Rhondda Valley alone. All have closed.

The best place to see a pithead and its dramatic-looking winding wheel is at **Abercynon**, just north of Pontypridd. There, the decaying remains of the **Lady Windsor Colliery** stand beside the A470.

Another good place is a little further north, in **Aberfan**, where the colliery is still operating. It was here, on the morning of 21 October 1966, just after school had opened on a desperately wet day, that the tip moved and slid down on the little village school, killing 116 children and 28 adults. The sad rows of headstones in the cemetery can be seen for miles across the valley.

The best place to get a feel of what it must have been like to work underground is the **Big Pit** in **Blaenavon**, closed in 1980. Visitors don a miner's safety helmet and ride down 294 ft (90 metres) in the cage the miners used to take. For an hour they can experience

the darkness and the stillness and get some idea of what it must have been like to work in the dank, humid conditions. Warm clothing and practical shoes are recommended.

There's also a range of colliery buildings, including the winding engine house, blacksmith's shop, pithead baths and pitman's cabin, with a gift shop and cafeteria in what was once the miners' canteen.

The drop in the cage was something few colliers welcomed, however often they did it. One, writing in 1925, recalled: "We sank rapidly down out of the daylight. The cage travels swiftly. About half-way down the engineman applies the brake. This checks the momentum and the queer sensation is experienced of coming back up again. Every miner experiences this. He knows, in fact, that the cage is still descending, but every physical sensation indicates that it is returning to the surface."Once down, the collier might still have a three-mile (five-km) walk to the coalface. It's not possible to recreate all this in Big Pit, but it still gives a good impression of the claustrophobia and inhumanity of working underground.

Explosions were frequent; roof falls, preceded by the sickening sound of the wooden pit prop giving way and then snapping, commonplace. The very worst explosions took a monumental toll on life.

On 18 October 1918, just before Armistice Day in the fields of Flanders, a massive explosion in the pit at **Sengenhydd**, then the nearest one to Cardiff, took the lives of 436 men. A quarter of a century earlier, on 23 June 1894, at the Albion colliery, **Cilfynydd**, near where the Lady Windsor now stands, 290 men and boys died. Edward Bennett, a 50-year-old ripper who lived not a stone's throw from the pit, left 12 children behind; Patrick Barrett, a labourer who was also 50, left 10. On eight other occasions more than 100 men died in separate explosions underground.

There is in the National Museum of Wales in Cardiff a record of these disasters. At the bottom are the lines:

Aberfan, scene of a slag-heap disaster.

A sudden change; at God's command they fell;
They had no chance to bid their friends farewell;
Swift came the blast, without a warning given,
And bid them haste to meet their God in Heaven.

Most miners worked in teams in those days and the collier, the prince of the profession, was paid a sum for what was cut, out of which he had to pay his assistants. Until 1842 these included women, more often young girls. Women were not barred from working above ground, in fact, until the 1920s. But long after women were banned underground, boys were still accepted.

It was common to start in the pits at about 10. "All the boys looked forward with longing to the day when they would be allowed to begin work," wrote one miner at the turn of the century. "They associated with big men and wonderful horses. They earned six shillings and nine pence *(34p)* every week. For me the prospect of going to work in the mine contained more glittering romance than if its black mouth were the entrance to Ali Baba's cave of gold."

Not everyone was as enthusiastic. "The job of the collier's boy was to gather the coal, cut by his mate, into the tram," states another contemporary account. "The boy had to be careful to pick only the lumps of coal as the collier was only paid for the large coal in the tram." This was his lot 12 hours a day, six days a week, for six shillings and nine pence.

Pits to park: The greatest valley for coal was the Rhondda. At one time it had 66 pits. They have all gone, though the **Heritage Park** being created on the site of the former Lewis Merthyr pit at Porth is a historical evocation of the industry that once dominated everything, even the **Parc and Dare Workmen's Hall** in **Treorchy**.

Workmen's halls were the "universities" of the valleys. They were funded by a voluntary levy on each miner of a penny for every pound earned, and were

Valleys children are no longer shielded from modern commercial pressures.

part social centre, providing a library and reading rooms; part health centre, providing doctors' surgeries; part educational centre, providing night-school classes; and part theatre.The Parc and Dare, named after two collieries in the town and built in 1903, now has a modern 800-seat theatre and an arts centre, but it is best seen as an example of the sort of Victorian architecture created by the workers of the area.

The Rhondda's most historic site is the **Shrine of Our Lady of Penrhys**, in Penrhys, which offers splendid views of the Rhondda Fawr. It was a place for pilgrims as early as the 13th century and originated as an outstation for the monks of Llantanarm Abbey in Gwent.

While working in the fields, the monks are said to have discovered a highly ornate statue of the Holy Mother grafted between the branches of a massive oak tree standing near a well. They built a chapel and shrine to house the statue and Penrhys soon became a centre of devotion. The shrine was destroyed in the dissolution and the statue

burnt by Cromwell but it remained a centre of pilgrimage and the present statue was put up in 1953.

Slightly older are the **Gorsedd stones**, erected to commemorate the holding of the National Eisteddfod, an annual festival to propagate the Welsh language, literature and music, in Treorchy in 1928. The National goes around Wales, rotating between North and South Wales each year. Each place where the Eisteddfod is held then marks the occasion by the erection of a circle of stones similar to Stonehenge—though much smaller in scale and scope.

What's missing: The one shortage in the valleys is castles. Wales has the greatest concentration of castles of any part of Britain but, because of the topography of the steep-sided valleys, there are few within the area.

Morlais, in Merthyr Tydfil, was the most important because it commanded the high ground in the area. **Neath Castle** is the only other of note, founded by Richard de Granville in 1129. The remains of the gateway and its flanking towers can be traced to the 13th century, although it is of interest more for the number of times it changed hands, rather than for its remains. Nearby **Penlle'r Castle**, at **Cwmgors**, 10 miles (16 km) outside Swansea, is a late 13th- or early 14th-century stronghold. The views are most impressive.

Far younger than the castles is the **Penscynor Wildlife Park** at **Aberdulais**, above Neath. Founded by Idris Hale, the centre has a fine collection of birdlife, many of them exotic species from around the world. This is not just a zoo but a place where many of the birds and animals can wander in a free environment. The parrots and parakeets are always a draw with children, but the greatest attraction is invariably the largest-known owl species in the world.

Giant trout (which can be fished at certain times), penguins, sealions, chimpanzees and monkeys galore inhabit the thickly-wooded hillside. It's perhaps a surprising thing to find in what is thought by many to be a centre of industrialisation—but then the valleys are a surprise to themselves.

Left, the BP oil refinery at Neath. Right, a farrier in the Rhymney Valley.

NEWPORT AND CAERLEON

It must be admitted, right at the start, that **Newport** is not high on most people's priority list of places to visit in Wales. When it comes to attracting tourists, the town is a poor relation to Cardiff and Swansea. Visitors usually turn a blind eye to Newport as they speed by on the M4, hardly captivated by the rather drab, urban skyline they see from the motorway as it skirts the town's northern fringe.

It's the same for those arriving by train. The railway runs through Newport's unprepossessing back yards before crossing the muddy, tidal banks of the Usk, the river that bisects the town.

But images and instant impressions can be deceptive. Although Newport, Wales's third-largest conurbation, doesn't have Cardiff's cosmopolitan confidence or Swansea's bright-and-breezy beside-the-sea charm, pockets of considerable interest are contained

within that bland coat.

This first becomes apparent as the train crosses the Usk, and a ruined castle comes into view on the riverbank. This medieval shell was built in the 14th and 15th centuries to replace an earlier hill-top motte and bailey fortification. Today it is an isolated misfit surrounded by road systems, shopping precincts, tower blocks and the large, modern Newport Centre leisure complex. Its scant remains display decorative touches—the windows, for example—which point to a castle that once had a residential as well as an important military role.

In the beginning: Newport's history began long before medieval times. **St Woolos's Cathedral**, on the top of Stow Hill (also the location of Newport's original castle), occupies the site of a fifth or early sixth-century religious settlement founded by Gwynllyw, lord of Gwynllwg (or Wentlooge, which became corrupted to *Woolos*—Wales is an etymological labyrinth). The cathedral has fine Norman nave arcades, though its most striking feature is a tall tower which was built around 1500.

Newport really came of age in the 19th century, because of its growth as an iron and coal exporting port serving the nearby industrial valleys. The Victorian boom-years are reflected in the architecture. A particularly fetching piece of Victoriana is the **covered market**, with its iron and glass barrel-vaulted roof, which has been restored to its original splendour.

The town's most infamous brush with history occurred on 4 November 1839, when thousands of ironworkers and coalminers marched to Newport in support of the Chartist cause for democratic reform of Parliament and the voting system. In the ensuing conflict outside the **Westgate Hotel**, troops fired on the crowd killing over 20 Chartists and wounding a further 50.

This episode has not been forgotten. The hotel still bears marks of the bullets fired, and there are heroic murals depicting this and other events in the Civic Centre's entrance hall. The town's excellent **Museum and Art Gallery** also contains material on the Chartist Rising, together with a noted collection of English watercolours.

The most conspicuous reminder of Newport's industrial past is the ingenious **Transporter Bridge**, its spindly framework dominating the view towards the docks. Built in 1906 to act as a "suspended ferry", this famous landmark is no longer operational.

An earlier example of engineering on an ambitious scale can be seen at **Rogerstone** on the northwestern outskirts of the town, where a huge staircase of canal locks—14 in all—are stepped into the hillside. The site, which boasts an interpretive centre and waymarked walks, has been imaginatively developed for visitors.

Newport is justifiably proud of **Tredegar House**, a splendid 17th-century mansion standing in a 90-acre (36-hectare) country park on the western approaches of the town. As a result of local initiative, it was rescued from extinction by the authorities in the 1970s and has since been refurbished to a high standard. This red-bricked mansion, regarded as the finest house of its kind in Wales, sums up the visible and the hidden sides of privileged life as visitors wander from gilded state rooms into functional servants' quarters.

Tredegar House can be seen as the flagship of a "new" post-industrial Newport: an unfairly maligned town situated on the doorstep of attractive, green countryside, a town with excellent communications at the western end of the M4 corridor, and a town which offers a quality of life absent in England's prosperous but beleaguered southeast. The official optimism seems to be justified. Ambitious redevelopment schemes are in the air, new high-technology companies have moved in, and major "white-collar" businesses have relocated here.

The promotional literature issued by the town authorities inevitably mentions Newport's proximity to Roman **Caerleon**. This is another site that, in the past, has been overlooked—which is strange because Caerleon, alias *Isca*,

Newport: once Wales's most important port.

122

was, along with the much more famous centres of Chester and York, one of only three Roman fortress towns in Britain, built to accommodate the elite legionary troops. But Caerleon's celebrity is on the up and up. This is partly due to the opening of an impressive excavated bath-house complex, the Roman equivalent of a modern sports and leisure centre.

Ideal camp: Caerleon's lavish Fortress Baths were built in A.D. 75. They were part of a huge 50-acre (20-hectare) camp that contained barracks, a headquarters, hospital, palace and amphitheatre, all laid out on an orderly grid-iron ground plan. It's still easy to appreciate the Romans' enthusiasm for the place. Caerleon is a neat and tidy little town in a favoured location. Standing among green fields above the looping River Usk, it must have been an ideal place to set up camp well away from the heathen wastes of an upland Wales populated by uncooperative natives.

The various excavated sites here paint an illuminating picture of life in one of the largest Roman military strongholds in northern Europe. The crack troops were well looked after. Apart from the hot and cold baths, the games and the wine enjoyed under cover at the bath-house, there was entertainment—which included bloody gladiatorial combat and animal baiting—at the 5,000-seat amphitheatre.

The amphitheatre's arena and grassy, circular banks are well preserved, as are the foundations of the troops' accommodation blocks, the only remains of Roman legionary barracks on view anywhere in Europe. Many of the finds unearthed at Caerleon can be seen at the town's **Legionary Museum**, a new museum which is already becoming recognised as having one of the foremost collections of Roman artefacts in the country. The exhibits, displayed in a bright, well-designed context, include life-size figures (a legionary, a centurion and a standard-bearer), arms and armour, mosaics, tombstones and a remarkable collection of gemstones found at the bath-house.

Caerleon: once one of the Romans' most important fortresses.

CARDIFF

Cardiff may be the capital of Wales but it is not much of a Welsh city. It's quite possible to find Welsh around: many of the streets in the centre have Welsh names alongside the English—*Heol y friennes* is Queen Street—and a lot of those in the suburbs have only Welsh names, like *Maes y Coed* or *Heol y deri*. A lot of other examples can be found, too: *Dynion* on the Gents, *Merchedd* on the Ladies. There's even a taxi with the spelling *tacsi*.

For all that, and for all the fact that this is a seat of government, with the Welsh Office conferring on Cardiff the same sort of status that the Scottish Office gives to Edinburgh, it is possible to spend a long time in Cardiff without actually hearing Welsh spoken. Anyone phoning S4C (Sianel 4 Cymru), the Welsh television channel, or the Wales Tourist Board, will be greeted in Welsh first, with the English version next. But these are the exceptions.

English feel: Cardiff is a very anglicised city: a city, its critics allege, not all that different from Gloucester or Bristol across the border—or, indeed, from Newport, 11 miles (18 km) east and even nearer England. Welsh is an advantage rather than a necessity in Cardiff, so very different in Swansea, Llanelli, Aberystwyth or Pwllheli, where it would be extremely unusual to go through the day without coming across Welsh being spoken as a matter of course as the first language.

But if the visitor comes across little Welsh directly, the pervading presence of the language is a lot stronger now than it has been for years, perhaps ever. As a city Cardiff (*Caerdydd* in Welsh) is a youngster, having nothing like the length of capital status enjoyed by the three other capitals that govern the United Kingdom. It was only designated as such in the 1950s.

At the start of the 19th century it was little more than a township and bore no relationship in importance to Merthyr Tydfil, 25 miles (40 km) to the north. But when the quantities of iron and coal being produced around Merthyr grew big enough to need an export outlet, Cardiff began to grow.

The important influence was the Bute family, who owned much of the land around the docks and saw the opportunities for creating a city based on *entrepôt* trade. They built the docks, bringing in labour from far and wide to undertake the construction work. In the nature of things, many of the immigrants married and settled in the area, so that by the second half of the last century Cardiff had a far more cosmopolitan population than the great northern citadels that had already outstripped it in size and importance.

The strongest influence came from the Irish; many of those who did not emigrate to America or find their way to Liverpool after the potato famine of the 1840s came to build Cardiff's docks and the canal and railways that linked the city to its hinterland. Cardiff had, and continues to have, a strong Roman

Catholic population, strong enough to warrant a Catholic cathedral alongside the Anglican one.

The Butes themselves are a leading Catholic family, which might be thought unusual in a country whose upper classes tended to be Anglican and whose working population were heavily Nonconformist. The Butes, a Scottish family, came to Cardiff in the 17th century, and the third marquess became a Catholic in the 19th century.

Signs of the Butes can be seen all over Cardiff to this day, especially in docklands which they virtually created. There is the famous Bute Street, Bute docks, a Bute Park and Butetown, probably better known as Tiger Bay. There is also a Mount Stuart Square, commemorating another of their titles.

They are not the only family whose ancestry is commemorated in the streets of Cardiff. Clare Road remembers a much longer established member of the nobility. The de Clares came over with William the Conqueror and Filbert de Clare, later Earl of Glamorgan, who died in 1292, did much to strengthen the defences of Cardiff by building the castle's black tower and rebuilding the Great Hall of the Keep. Memories of another Norman overlord can be seen in Despenser Street.

Much of Cardiff's (and later the Butes') wealth came from the Glamorganshire Canal that brought iron and coal down from Merthyr Tydfil, 25 miles (40 km) away to the north. The canal was built before the railway era; but, as iron gave way to steel and the new steelworks were built on or near the coast, the canal's trade was increasingly restricted to coal. Eventually all that, too, was carried by the Taff Vale railway (later to become part of the Great Western Railway) and gradually, section by section, the canal was closed.

The last section was shut down in 1942—even then, the canal was not being used in any economic form—and there are still many in Cardiff who remember it. A small section, perhaps no more than half a mile long, existed by the sea-lock for another nine years, but

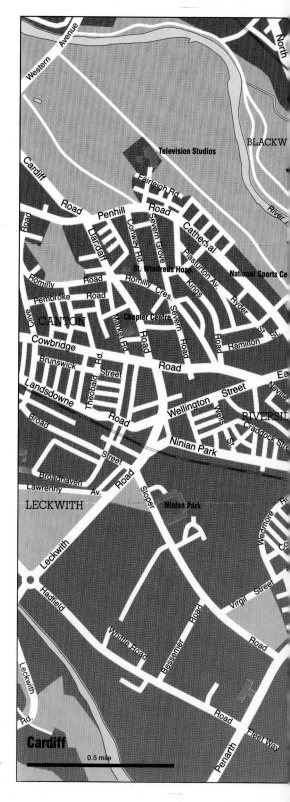

eventually a dredger hit the gate, broke the lock and all the water ran out.

There were other influences in the growth of Cardiff. Many men came from the border counties to work in the growing city. Gloucestershire, Somerset and Herefordshire supplied a lot while still others were attracted into the economic honeypot from Mid and West Wales. Until the 1930s the influence of the Welsh incomers could be seen in particular in the Welsh chapels.

Today, few remain. There are now only four which hold their services in Welsh, of which the leading one is Tabernacl, in The Hayes, bang in the centre of the city. Services here are at 10.45 a.m. and 6 p.m. on a Sunday. Another one nearby is **Ebenezer Welsh Congregational Church** in Charles Street, just behind Marks and Spencer's store and across the road from the Roman Catholic cathedral. There is one Church of Wales church, **Dewi Sant**, in St Andrews Place. These would have once been the tip of the iceberg.

Then there were the overseas immigrants. Cardiff always had a small but vibrant coloured community, one reason why it has to this day excellent inter-racial community relations. Originally, the coloured community came from the Lascars, often donkeymen on ships, the men who shovelled coal into the boilers. These men would be paid off, or jump ship, in Cardiff and stay in the city. The Lascars were in time supplemented by other races who found a home in the docklands area of **Tiger Bay**.

That coloured community was never large and mostly remained on the wrong side of the tracks, the then Great Western Railway line that connected London's Paddington station with Fishguard in West Wales.

Good community relations probably arose because the coloured population remained within its ghetto. But, whatever the reason, the vast majority in Cardiff always had a tolerant approach to the immigrants. Tiger Bay in its heyday was no place for the meek

East Bute Dock in the early 1920s.

and mild, though. In a much more law-abiding era it was said that the policemen always patrolled in pairs.

The area is bounded on one side by the railway line which runs the length of **Bute Street**, almost to pier head, from which the Campbell's paddle steamers would, in summer, ply their way across the channel to Weston, Clevedon and Ilfracombe in Somerset. The other boundary was the canal so that Tiger Bay was in effect a long rectangle stretching from the commercial and shopping heart of the city down to the waterside. It was tough and torrid, housing Cardiff's red-light area, some seedy cafés, and some even more seedy pubs.

But whatever its charms by night it was, by day a place of rectitude, a place where Cardiff's upright businessmen came to conduct their legitimate business, the sort of business that would have been amply regarded in Ebenezer or Tabernacl.

Service city: Cardiff was not then, indeed has never been, an industrial city. It could not hold a candle to those great northern monuments to Victorian wealth, Leeds, Manchester, Birmingham, Bradford and Sheffield. It was a service city. It existed to ship the coal and iron around the world. As in Liverpool, sometimes called the capital of North Wales since there were more Joneses there than along the Welsh coast, it oiled the wheels of trade.

At its centre was the **Exchange** in **Mountstuart Square**, in the very heart of Tiger Bay, the place where coal was traded as stocks and shares were traded on the stock market in London. The price of coal in Bremen or Buenos Aires would be set by what happened on the floor of the Exchange in Cardiff. A large, gaunt Victorian building, it is now being slowly brought back to life. The metamorphosis of the Exchange is reflected in a gigantic redevelopment in the whole of docklands that will turn this part of Cardiff into an exciting city for the 21st century. The life began to ebb out of Cardiff's dockland after World War I

Victorian dock building in Cardiff's harbour.

and, although it received a shot in the arm during World War II, a long decline began again in the 1950s.

By the early 1960s Cardiff's docklands were a shadow of their old self, and Tiger Bay was ripped apart as modern council flats and houses replaced the mean streets. The once torrid area became a place where the yuppies of the 1960s could come on a Saturday night to the Windsor pub, the first place in the city to serve decent French food.

Now a major multi-billion pound development scheme is taking place, culling ideas from the best around the world. Baltimore, Toronto, Vancouver, Boston and New Orleans have all been visited to see how a waterside community can be rebuilt. So, too, has London's docklands. What is happening in London is part-model for what is starting to happen in Cardiff.

Some steps have already been taken. New houses have appeared around the old East Bute Dock, which has been renamed **Atlantic Wharf**. The county

council, showing its faith in the area, built a new county hall slap-bang in the centre of the docks development. A marina has been opened under **Penarth Head** which has all the chutzpah of London's Wapping. Old buildings have been restored—one into a hotel, another into flats. Pubs have found they have space for a restaurant and are serving good food.

But this is only a beginning. At the heart of the whole development is a plan to build a barrage across the entrance to Cardiff Bay. This will create an inland lake of some 500 acres (200 hectares) of clean water around which a vast variety of new building will take place. Cardiff's inner harbour alone is larger than the whole dockside in Baltimore, and the rejuvenation of the American waterside is an international example of how such works can breathe new life back into a city.

As the building of Cardiff's docks was essentially the brainchild of one member of the nobility, the Marquess of Bute, so the present redevelopment is the brainchild of another, Lord Crickhowell. He wasn't Lord Crickhowell when the plan was launched: the Right Honourable Nicholas Edwards, PC, MP, to give him his original title, was Her Majesty's Secretary of State for Wales. A tall, spare, ascetic-looking man, he had become MP for Pembrokeshire in the early 1970s and entered government in 1979 when Margaret Thatcher formed her first Conservative administration.

Nick Edwards, as everyone called him, was an Anglo-Welshman, not a local at all. His father had been a leading figure in the London art world and he had been brought up more in the British capital than the Welsh one.

His early years as Secretary of State were dominated by the economic recession of 1979-81, which saw large parts of the two basic Welsh industries, coal and steel, wiped out. It wasn't until 1984 that he had the opportunity of looking to the future rather than fighting to put out bush fires in the present.

The Edwards vision was that if Wales was to prosper then it needed a capital

Cardiff harbour: low tide, high hopes.

that could lead the country. It was little use sustaining individual parts of the principality if the capital was falling apart. And the part that was so obviously disintegrating was docklands. So he drew up a plan to rejuvenate the whole area. But his plan was not just to do something about the one major run-down area; it was to link this redevelopment back into the city through a mall or boulevard that would run the length of Bute Street down to pier head and the inner harbour. Tiger Bay would revert to its former greatness.

That greatness was built on coal. It is frequently said that Cardiff was the greatest coal-exporting port in the world. The truth of that assertion is open to question: it all depends on the definition of Cardiff docks.

In 1914, when the industry was going full blast, 10,278,963 tons of coal were shipped through Cardiff. However, Barry, 10 miles (16 km) along the coast to the west actually handled 10,875,510 tons and so could claim to be the greater.

The rivals: In between Cardiff and Barry, though, lies a third port: **Penarth**. It is normally considered to be part of Cardiff, though the people of Penarth have always regarded it as separate from, and slightly superior to, the big city. Penarth handled almost four million tons in 1914 and if this is added to the Cardiff figure it would make it the greater exporter. But it is a subject of some debate—and not a little controversy—in Cardiff, which always likes to be thought of as the greatest.

Cardiffians also like to point out, with no little pride, what they consider to be the greatest civic centre in the Commonwealth. And, they say, they have royal backing for their assertion.

Cardiff has a perfect Edwardian civic centre, perfect in scale and scope. It was built in Portland stone around 1904 and most of the buildings put up since have been designed with an empathy for the whole. The buildings themselves enclose a large rectangle, within which wide, tree-lined avenues bisect **Cathays Park**. The Prince of Wales, in

Cardiff's Bute Street, around 1925.

recent trenchant attacks on modern architecture and its failure around the country, specifically omitted Cardiff from his criticism. He pointed to the way in which the architecture blended as a whole and the way in which everything was in scale.

In the inter-war years Cardiff won architectural commendations for its overall design. More important, it was copied as well as envied. Town planners and architects from the new Commonwealth that emerged after 1945 came to Cardiff and took away ideas, much as an earlier generation had incorporated bits of the city into places as disparate as New Delhi and Canberra.

The southern flank of the civic centre comprises the **law courts**, the **city hall**, dominated by its 194-ft (59-metre) campanile-type clock tower, and the **National Museum of Wales**. The eastern side has the **University College of Cardiff**, a constituent part of the federal University of Wales. The western flank comprises a number of buildings, including a county hall, and various university buildings. Its **Temple of Peace**, perhaps unique in Europe, ironically opened in 1938 just before World War II broke out. The northern edge is topped off by the **Welsh Office**. At the centre of this great rectangle is Wales's national war memorial.

The city hall contains a particularly fine collection of paintings. Among the portraits of the civic dignitaries who have graced its parlours and presided over momentous events is a particularly good one of Edward VII at the opening of the Queen Alexandra dock in 1909. John Glover's *The Bay of Naples*, first shown in the Louvre in Paris, hangs near it, as well as two paintings—*The Shadow* by E. Blair Leighton and *Winter* by Joseph Farquhanson—which have hung in their present position since at least 1925.

Statues honour the great names of Welsh life as well as those of the city, for Cardiff has always considered itself the first city of the principality and so

Left, City Hall clock. Right, a welcome in downtown Cardiff.

has never adopted the parochial approach to events that bedevils so much of Wales. David Lloyd George is here, for instance. He was not a native of the city, having been born in Manchester, but Cardiff treats him as an adopted son.

Another great politician, Nye Bevan, has a statue at the end of Queen Street, overlooking the castle which, to him, represented the privilege he so much wanted to overthrow.

History's heroes: Inside the city hall, there is Owain Glyndwr who led an uprising against the English in 1400; Llewelyn ap Gruffydd, the last prince of Wales before modern times, killed in 1282 for defying the English whom he had earlier befriended; William Williams, known throughout Wales as William Williams Pantycelyn and throughout the world as one of the great hymn writers, a man at the very cornerstone of the Methodist revival in the country; Harri Tewdwr, better known as Henry VII, born in Pembroke Castle, who overthrew the Lancastrian

line to the thrown and brought in the Tudors; Giraldus Cambrensis, the outstanding Welsh scholar of his age, another Pembrokeshire man, who made a historic journey around the country; and Boadicea, widow of King Prastagus, who, better known for her handsome defeat at the hands of the Romans, was also a Celt, like the rest of the Welsh nation to this day.

And, of course, there is Dewi Sant, St David, patron saint of Wales, founder of the cathedral that bears his name in the eponymous town. Cardiff's own sons and daughters comprise an elegant crowd, with the emphasis very much on their musicality or artistic ability generally. Shirley Bassey was born in the city and sang her way to fame in the clubs of Tiger Bay. The composer Ivor Novello came from a posher part of town and the house in **Cathedral Road** where he was brought up by his mother, who led the famous Royal Welsh Ladies choir, now has the obligatory plaque on it.

Howard Spring, whose novels

City Hall luminaries include Queen Boadicea.

include *Fame is the Spur*, was born here in 1899 at the very end of the great Victorian era, one of nine children; his ability as a wordsmith was honed on newspaper life in the city. Dannie Abse, poet and broadcaster, is of a more recent generation, as is playright Roald Dahl. Another novelist, Eric Linklater, was brought up in Cardiff during his formative years as a boy, though he never lost his Scottishness and looked back on Cardiff without much remembrance or affections. Jack Jones, who wrote *River out of Eden* and *Off to Philadelphia in the Morning*, was an immigrant from Merthyr Tydfil but Cardiff was as near as dammit home to him.

The **museum**, next door to the city hall, is a small, compact, interesting place. It is not cavernous and rambling, like London's Victoria & Albert, and can be seen "at a sitting", as it were. It is a "tidy" place, a Welsh use of the word denoting considerable approval. Although small, as museums go, it is in fact just the visible part, within the city

centre, of a much larger organisation, there being an industrial and maritime museum in Tiger Bay, next to Pier Head, and a world-renowned Folk Museum in St Fagans, one of the city's outlying suburbs.

At the heart of the museum's collection of paintings is the Davies Bequest, left to the museum by two Welsh sisters, Gwendoline and Margaret Davies, daughters of a notable coal-owner. The collection is not of Welsh painters, though, but of French since the sisters were among the first, in the early years of this century, to appreciate the Impressionists. The collection has been called "exceptional." Cézanne, Daumier, Manet, Millet, Monet, Morisot, Renoir, Pissarro and van Gogh are all represented.

This being a Welsh gallery, native artists are also represented, among them Frank Brangwyn, Cedric Morris, Ceri Richards and Kyffin Williams, as well as Augustus John and his sister Gwen who tended to remain very much in his

Two traditional faces: St Fagan's Folk Museum (left) and the Winter Smoking Room of Cardiff Castle.

136

shadow during his lifetime.

The **Industrial and Maritime Museum** is devoted to the development of industry in the principality, and the ground floor has nine major exhibits, ranging from a waterwheel to a turbo alternator.

The **Folk Museum at St Fagans** is devoted to heritage and has a vast collection of buildings showing just how people lived in the past. Of particular interest is a row of six cottages from Rhydycar in Merthyr Tydfil each of which shows how people were living at a particular time during the 150-year life of the houses.

St Fagans Castle, actually an Elizabethan manor house, was opened in 1948, having been presented to the museum by the Earl of Plymouth. The museum is not just a host of artefacts: it lives. The Denwen bakehouse, which came from Aberystwyth, produces traditional bread and bara brith, half cake, half bread, every day. Animals roam the grounds. A water wheel turns the grinding stones of Melin Bompren

flour mill, which came from Cross Inn in Dyfed, and a blacksmith is in the Llawryglyn smithy.

There is also a **tollhouse**, which was originally put up at Penparcau, Aberystwyth, in 1771. Treasures on display include a wide variety of cooking and dairying implements, musical instruments, including the Welsh *crwth* and *pibgorn*, and, of course, a large selection of Welsh love spoons.

The centrepiece of Cardiff, though, is not its museum but its castle, largely Norman in origin but with Roman traces still visible. **Cardiff Castle** dominates the city in a way few others do because it is part of the fabric of everyday life. Two of the main streets wind around it and the city fathers have ensured that it is not surrounded by high-rise modern buildings. So it's possible to see the battlements and walls from several directions and from a considerable distance.

The castle was originally a Roman fort, the Romans having arrived in A.D.

Cardiff Castle: proud as a peacock.

76. The fort, one of a chain across South Wales, was built on a strategic site alongside the river, the Taff, and intended to hold back the fiercely independent Silures.

The Normans rebuilt and enlarged the fort, something the Romans themselves had done at least once, and a keep, which still dominates the grounds, was added. William the Conqueror is said to have chosen the site in 1081 while on his way to visit the shrine of St David in Pembrokeshire.

During the civil war and Commonwealth, Cardiff was at first Royalist before succumbing to Cromwell's Parliamentarians in 1645. Subsequently the castle decayed badly, until the third Marquess of Bute appointed the imaginative William Burges in 1865 to undertake a major restoration; it was completed by 1872.

Rich tiles: Burges is not a household name among Victorian architects but his contribution to Cardiff Castle deserves to be known to a wider audience. He would be described today as a specialist in tiles, having been involved in the revival of interest in medieval tiles, and so his work in Cardiff is rich in this field. He created lavishly decorative interiors which today form the backdrop for many civic and other public functions.

The banqueting hall is particularly attractive, decorated with murals depicting the castle's history. There is also a Moorish room, a pleasant anachronism in a Welsh city, and a clock tower. Another interesting feature, often overlooked, is the tiled (and covered) roof-garden which again carries Moorish overtones.

The castle also contains the regimental museum of the Welch Regiment, now incorporated into the Royal Regiment of Wales, and 1st The Queen's Dragoon Guards, the Welsh cavalry regiment.

The grounds are now a public park, one of the many that grace Cardiff. For the statistically minded, there are 2,700 acres (1,100 hectares) of them, about a third the size of London's docklands.

Captain Scott's memorial in Roath Park.

The grounds of the castle, sometimes called **Bute Park**, stretch for two miles, almost to Llandaff Cathedral.

Roath Park is a mini-Kew, with the addition of a lake that once incorporated a swimming pool but is now restricted to boaters, who may take out a skiff. No motor boats or any such thing noisy and anti-social. See the memorial to Captain Scott, built like a lighthouse, at one end of the lake.

The top of the **Wenallt**, a stiff climb, affords a panoramic view of the city and offers nature trails; also, in severe winters, a place for tobogganing. Nearby **Parc Cefn on** is a jewel of rhododendrons and azaleas in spring.

Another jewel is **Llandaff Cathedral**, set (in some ways similar to St David's Cathedral) in a hollow. A religious community was established by St Teilo in the sixth century but a 10th-century Celtic cross, in the south aisle, is the only pre-Norman reminder.

Cromwell did his damnedest here, as in the castle, turning part into a beer house; but the cathedral survived his depredations, even though God and man has played nasty tricks with it. A storm in 1703 blew down the pinnacles of the north-west tower and caused them to fall through the roof; 20 years later the southwest tower collapsed. Then in 1941 German bombs severely damaged the whole edifice. Since it was rebuilt, the cathedral has incorporated the chapel of the Welch Regiment, the regiment most closely associated with the city, and Sir Jacob Epstein's *Christ in Majesty*, a contemporary sculpture which dominates the centre aisle and provokes strongly mixed views.

St John's Church, opposite the market, is the parish church; the present building dates from 1453, though a place of worship has been on the site considerably longer. Its main interest is an indirect connection: the tower was put up by Lady Ann Nevill, wife of Richard, Duke of Gloucester, who became Richard III.

Opposite is the great indoor **market**, one of the features of Cardiff life, a place not just of vegetables and pans but also a point for buying traditional Welsh foods such as lava bread, made from seaweed, and a host of Welsh cheeses. Nearby, too, are the arcades that are a prominent feature of Cardiff life. Long before atriums and covered shopping centres became popular, Cardiff's Victorian shoppers moved about under cover. Cardiff has more arcades than any other city in Britain and they are an important reflection on Victorian and Edwardian shopping patterns and architecture.

For the sports-minded, there is the finest rugby ground in the world in the **Arms Park**, opposite the castle, whose owns rugby museum is open to visitors. Soccer also has an international stadium at **Ninian Park**, home of the Cardiff City club, and there is a new **ice rink**.

Although Cardiff has been attacked by impassioned Welsh nationalists for being insufficiently Welsh, there is an understated sense of pride about the place. It's true that one seldom hears Welsh spoken in the streets; but on a rugby international day, there's no mistaking which capital you're in.

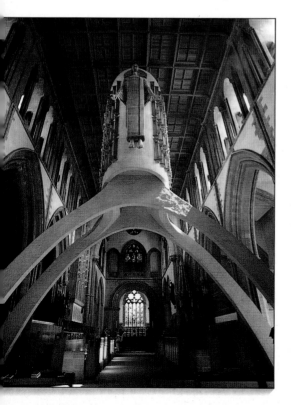

Epstein's controversial sculpture in Llandaff Cathedral.

GLAMORGAN'S HERITAGE COAST

It is claimed that South Glamorgan could once be found somewhere around present-day Bermuda. It is also said its inhabitants at the time, dinosaurs, basked in tropical sunshine. Perhaps it was when they moved to their new location that they became extinct, for surely no evolutionary invention has been so crucial to survival as the Wellington boot has been to this area.

For 14 miles (22 km), from the fairground smutty postcards, jellied eels and hotdog stands of **Porthcawl** in the west to the sedate tea houses of **Llantwit Major** in the east, the Glamorgan Heritage Coast displays an ever-changing, rugged beauty untouched by the juggernaut of tourism.

The mountainous **dunes** that stretch from the outskirts of Porthcawl and threaten to engulf all around them, are the second highest in Europe and the source of much of the history and legend of the region; lost villages, phantom funerals, spirit hounds and red goblins vie with relics of the Beaker People, Romans and Vikings.

Nowadays the dunes are frequented by athletes and ornithologists alike and are a more popular rendezvous with courting couples than the Bridgend cinemas. A walk across the dunes' switchback from **Newton Point** (the Heritage Coast's westernmost boundary) to **Candleston**, offers a profusion of unusual flora and fauna.

Commerce controlled: It would be fair to say Welsh buildings are not exactly the talking point of the architectural world. There are exceptions, of course, and a notable one is **Merthyr Mawr**, nestled behind the towering dunes just a mile inland from Candleston. The owners of the Merthyr Mawr estate have sensibly pursued policies that have discouraged pubs, tea houses and shops. Instead, there is a straggle of thatched cottages, a manor house, grey stone church, a red village telephone box concealed in a wall and a post office hidden inside someone's living room.

In the 19th century, cultural or even human conservation was not such a pressing public concern. At the nearby Dipping Bridge, the infamous Cap Goch (Red Cap), landlord of the New Inn and a fan of the French revolution, used to lighten the pockets of his guests in the name of income redistribution before disposing of their bodies in the river. Eighty years after he was hanged on a gallows beside the bridge, mass graves were still being found in the nearby woods.

The 14th-century Norman **Ogmore Castle** overhangs the River Ogmore like a discarded hunk of nibbled gorgonzola. Linking it to Merthyr Mawr are the stepping stones that were built, so legend has it, on the instructions of the mistress of the castle who feared her commoner lover's ardour might be dampened by wading the river.

The road continues climbing for a mile to **Ogmore by Sea**, the only coastal village along the stretch. Just 10 minutes by car from Bridgend or half an

Preceding pages: Nash Point Lighthouse. Left, dunes around Candleston Castle. Right, the Heritage Coast west of Cardiff.

hour from Cardiff, Ogmore is a nondescript ribbon of 1950s bungalows best passed through as quickly as possible if it weren't for its perfect location overlooking this great unsung coastline. The village boasts three shops, three pubs and a garage that doubles as an antique furniture showroom. The most notable building, and the best pub, is the mock Gothic Craig, a large friendly family pub with grounds overlooking Tusker Rock.

The coastal road hugs the cliffs snaking its way eastwards from Ogmore. The sea is often swollen here, perhaps angry at being channelled from the vastness of the Atlantic into the narrow funnel of the Bristol Channel. The tides are the second highest in the world, with a 50-ft (15-metre) lift and a notorious undertow.

At the Three Golden Cups, a mile and a half (two km) away, the owners have on display the Portuguese figurehead from a famous wreck. On another of the walls is a more recent piece of history: the autograph of Bob Dylan covered in perspex from a visit he made in 1986. Opposite the pub is the coastline's finest restaurant, Frolics, named after the passenger ferry that ran aground in 1832 with the loss of 40 lives.

Victorian folly: From Frolics, a descent to **Southerndown Beach** (also known as Seamouth) leads to the Heritage Centre with its useful guidebooks to walks, folklore and the history of the region. Here you can hire a bike or arrange guided "family" or "study" walks. All 56 surrounding acres (23 hectares) of natural parkland were only recently opened to the public. At present the Centre is engaged in landscaping what once was the Victorian folly of **Dunraven Castle**, supposedly destroyed in 1962 by the owner himself after a disagreement with the council.

There's a wonderful tale of nemesis concerning Robert Vaughan, an earlier owner of the castle who co-ordinated much of the wrecking along the coast and eventually lost his own favourite son, shipwrecked and dispatched in the

Gathering seaweed, used in making laver bread.

144

usual fashion by Matt the Iron Hand, the Lord's chief henchman. Locals lured ships (euphemistically referred to as "gifts from the sea") to their doom via lamps attached to sheep that grazed the clifftop. Once survivors had been butchered, the Wreckers disappeared into the night with their ill-gotten gains.

Above **Dunraven Gardens** are the defensive banks, ditches and burial mounds of an Iron Age promontory fort. The balcony (with Heritage Information board) offers a panoramic view along the coast and across the waters to Somerset. A descent to the wave-cut platform when the tide's out provides a splendid opportunity to view at close hand the teeming marine life: mussels and barnacles cling to rocks while shrimps and sea anemones shelter in the crevices and pools.

In the distance, you can see the lighthouse at **Nash Point** which is the starting point for a short but pleasant nature trail across streams and through woodland towards **Marcross**. The nearby manor has seen better days,

namely those when it auctioned off wrecking spoils. The Norman presence is clearly visible in the church here, as it is in those at Merthyr Mawr, Ewenny Priory and Newton. One of the most interesting features of this particular church is the "leper window" through which parishioners with contagious diseases participated in services.

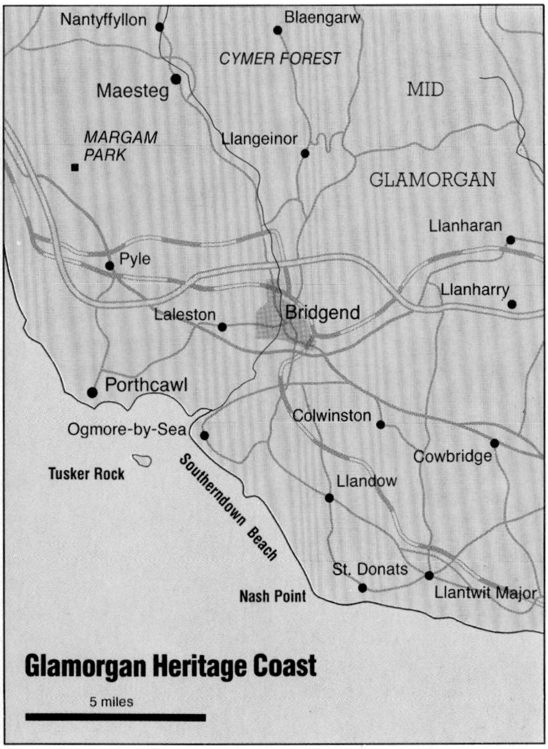

Perhaps the most famous church is that founded by St Illtyd at **Llantwit Major** in the fifth century. Here the practice of *Laus Perennis* (unending prayer), also practised at Old Sarum and Glastonbury, was introduced. Next to the Celtic stone crosses of local kings, an incongruous palm tree adds its exotic touch.

Llantwit is one of most ancient villages in Wales and many of the narrow lanes, dotted with tea houses and bed-and-breakfast establishments, are under conservation orders. During term time, its population swells with the influx of students from home or abroad who come to attend the world peace school of Atlantic College located in a fairy-tale opening in the forest high above the landscaped gardens of **St Donats**.

Once William Randolph Hearst's Welsh San Simeon, this extensive, wonderfully preserved castle belonged for 700 years to the poets, knights, wreckers and adventurers of the Stradling family. Said to be the most haunted house in Wales, it also hosts a lively arts centre.

To the east, the magnet for day-trippers is **Barry Island**, a bucket-and-spade resort complete with funfair and large outdoor pool. The town of **Barry**, a major coal-exporting port in the 19th century, is now sedately residential.

Fabulous walks: Because Glamorgan's 14-mile (23-km) heritage coast has largely been ignored, it has managed to retain all the most attractive, rugged features of an unspoilt British coastline. The only weather options may be presbyterian grey or bucketting rain, but the region offers fabulous coastal walks and enough pubs on the way to stop you feeling anything.

Glamorgan Heritage Coast

5 miles

Map labels: Nantyffyllon, Blaengarw, CYMER FOREST, Maesteg, MID, MARGAM PARK, Llangeinor, GLAMORGAN, Llanharan, Pyle, Llanharry, Laleston, Bridgend, Porthcawl, Colwinston, Ogmore-by-Sea, Cowbridge, Tusker Rock, Southerndown Beach, Llandow, St. Donats, Nash Point, Llantwit Major

SWANSEA AND ITS ENVIRONS

"I was born in a large Welsh industrial town at the beginning of the Great War; an ugly, lovely town (or so it was, and is, to me) crawling, sprawling, slummed, unplanned, jerry-villa'd, and smug-suburbed by the side of a long and splendid curving shore." Dylan Thomas's unsentimental hymn to his home town still evokes the essence of the place, despite recent refurbishment.

In the middle of the last century, **Swansea** was the metallurgical capital of the world, with 300 chimneys pumping their toxic gases into the Swansea Valley. Diseases included cholera, typhoid, and even an outbreak of yellow fever. There were 60 Beggars' Hotels and crime was endemic.

What was left of Swansea after poverty, disease and crime had taken their toll, Hitler's Luftwaffe tried to finish off in the 1940s. Then post-war planners began ripping out its barely beating

heart. With justification, it was said: "The only good thing to come out of Swansea is the road to Llanelli."

Swansea is Wales's second city. As there *are* only two, it's hardly surprising that it has in the past suffered a chronic inferiority complex. Although seemingly soulless (having its centre relocated half a mile away hasn't helped), Swansea is nevertheless a personable and personal city—it's the kind of place where someone honks a horn and everyone waves.

There are also unmistakable signs of a new-won confidence. Over the past 15 years 1,000 acres (400 hectares) of industrial wasteland in the Swansea Valley have been brought back to life to create one of Britain's largest urban forests, complete with pony trekking and river walks. The valley also houses an all-weather athletics track and Britain's first Enterprise Zone.

An £8 million barrage should further heal the industrial scars and provid yet more leisure facilities. As a sign of goodwill, the fish have returned to the **River Tawe**.

Indoor pursuits: A well-known Irish saying has been adapted to suit Swansea: "If you can see the hills of Somerset, it's going to rain; if you can't,it's already raining." Certainly, the city does seem to suffer an inordinate number of rainy days, but fortunately it does provide visitors with a number of options. The **Quadrant**, which opened in 1980, is the finest modern shopping centre in Wales. Alongside is a vast glass aircraft hanger of an **indoor market** (the largest in Wales) offering everything from ice cream to antiques and laver bread to carpets.

The other major development, the **Maritime Quarter**, got under way in 1982. The **Maritime Museum** houses a working woollen mill alongside other exhibits of the city's industrial and maritime past. Outside is a replica tram from the world's first passenger railway that trundled along the front from 1807 until 1960.

The **Marina** can accommodate 600 yachts alongside its floating exhibits— a tug, lifeboat and fishing smack (all

Preceding pages: Rhosili Head, Gower. Left, Swansea Castle. Below, on the Victorian boardwalk at Mumbles Head.

open to the public). A recent addition is the *Picton Sea Eagle*, a reconstructed man-o'-war, tamed into a tacky pub and restaurant. Also skirting the Marina is the Dylan Thomas Theatre, studios, steak house, disco, terraced cafés and 800 new homes festooned with carvings and sculptures that relate the city's maritime history.

Behind the museum is a **leisure centre**, as impressive inside as it is unimpressive out, offering indoor bowling green, spa pools, sauna, solarium and a pool with hydroslide and waves. Adjacent is the 1,000-seater open-air **Amphitheatre**.

Olden times: Not everything is modern. Swansea boasts the oldest **museum** in Wales (opened in the 1840s) with a marvellously eccentric pot-pourri of international and local exhibits (including a Welsh kitchen). Between the museum and the Marina is a small concentration of Victorian, Edwardian and Georgian streets (**Cambrian Place**, **Gloucester Place** and **Prospect Place**) under conservation orders.

There's also a nibble of **Swansea Castle** sandwiched between Castle Street and the High Street. For those seeking the little of the history that's left, the Information Centre in Singleton Street has leaflets on the **Morris Town Trail**, **Industrial Archaeology Trail** and the **Dylan Thomas Uplands Trail**.

Dylan Thomas's "Return Journey" to the **Uplands** leads to "the still house over the mumbling bay" in **Cwmdonkin Drive** where the poet grew up. Like many of the residential streets that clatter down the Uplands, Cwmdonkin Drive is as steep as Everest's final ascent and would drive anyone to drink.

From the commemorative plaque on his home, you can ascend a little further before entering Cwmdonkin Park— Thomas's "eternal park"—via a trodden-down fence that no doubt the poet assisted in accessing as a young boy. The view over the bay is spectacular.

A short distance from the Uplands shops is **Brynmill Park** with its small

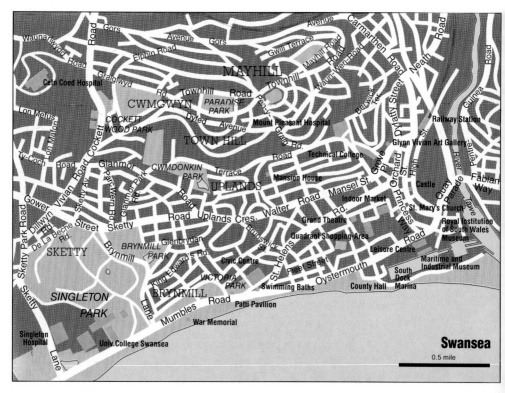

Swansea

0.5 mile

aviary beside the pond. The larger **Singleton Park**, with boating lake, nurseries and children's playground, connects with it and leads around **Swansea University** campus down to the front where locals do battle with bowls and tennis rackets in **Victoria Park**. Swansea is extraordinarily well endowed with grassland—no doubt courtesy of the 19th-century industrialists who realised they must have lungs if they were to survive their own pollution.

Garish panels: The eastern **Promenade** leads past **St Helen's Cricket and Rugby Ground** to the **Guildhall**, which contains the city's main concert hall as well as the garish **Brangwyn Panels** (the enormous canvases commemorate the British Empire and were originally earmarked for the House of Lords) and on to the Marina.

To the west, the tree-lined seawall continues skirting the four-and-a-half-mile (seven-km) bay to the 900-ft (275-metre) Victorian pier at the **Mumbles**. As the tide turns, the mudflats become populated by fishermen digging for lugworm. At **Oystermouth** (part of the Mumbles) a 13th-century castle overlooks the bay with underground passageways leading to the courtyard of the nearby hotel.

In the graveyard, among the tombs to lost sailors, is a memorial to the legendary Thomas Bowdler who had the zealot's small-minded arrogance to delete everything from 10 volumes of Shakespeare "which cannot with propriety, be read aloud to the family."

The White Rose pub is popular with younger locals, while the Antelope and the Mermaid stake their claim to posterity as old Dylan Thomas haunts. When the nights are balmy, cars cruise, roofs down, motorbikes roar along the silver slither of coast road and everyone seems to be drawn out of the city centre to this, the resort end of the bay.

The **Grand Theatre** (next to the Information Centre) combines the attractions bestowed by a £6 million facelift with an impressive track record in operatic and dramatic performances, and is well worth a visit, if only in order

to have a drink or a bite to eat.

There's also the **No Sign** wine bar at 56 Wind Street which some claim is the best pub in the world. There's sawdust on the floor, dust carefully preserved on the wine racks and antiques unselfconsciously littering the bars. Its checkered history has provided a marvellous riot of architectural styles that together create a charming harmony unmatched by any other public building in the city. If Dylan Thomas was drinking elsewhere, the man had no taste.

Opposite the No Sign, down Green Dragon Lane, is the **Hwyrnos**, where you may be equipped with a pair of clogs or have to serve the *cawl* (traditional thick vegetable soup) yourself. Along with the food and wine, three hours of entertainment is provided (harp playing, singing and clog dancing). If you're looking for a meal without obligatory entertainment, try **St Helen's Road**; it has more than 40 restaurants.

From the last week of September and through October, the city hosts the **Swansea Festival** (incorporating the fringe theatre festival). For those wishing to extend their Celtic experience, the Swansea-Cork Ferries will transport you to Ireland at reasonable cost.

Back to nature: Designated by the National Trust as the first area of Outstanding Beauty in Britain in 1956 and strangely defined as part of the actual city of Swansea, **Gower** is the real magnet for the visitor. It has three National Nature Reserves and 21 sites of Special Scientific Interest. It is both Swansea's dormitory and playground.

From the Mumbles, the Mediterranean switchback plunges and soars out of pine-clad limestone bays, dotted with occasional palms. **Langland Bay** is the nearest to town and popular with surfers. It's a safe family beach with rock pools for the kids to explore. The large old changing huts that line the upper reaches of the beach can be hired as virtual beach homes but overnight stays are forbidden. There are all-weather tennis courts, and Langland Golf Club is on the hill.

Looking over Swansea, towards Mumbles.

Caswell Bay has a fine deep bay but also a self-catering eyesore that arrived 20 years ago. Inland is the pretty village of **Bishopstown**. The Farmers Arms isn't a bad lunch spot; neither is the Beaufort Arms in nearby **Kittle**, which dates back to 1460.

Caves and castles: At **Parkmill** the coast road plunges under a leafy canopy through a valley suffused with garlic. **Parc-Le-Breos Burial Chamber** and **Cathole Cave** are located here. The 13th-century **Penrice Castle**, owned by the old Gower Methuen-Campbell family, comprises of a grand manor house and terraced water gardens that overlook **Oxwich Bay**; unfortunately these are not open to the public.

Barely visible in a grove overhanging the wide sweeping bay, backed by heather and woodland, is the ancient **church of St Iltyd**. The village itself is a quaint reminder of Cornwall, just across the water. The **Great House** behind Horton Bay, recently converted into a restaurant, was once the home of the 17th-century pirate and wrecker,

John Lucas, and is supposedly the oldest building in Gower.

Port Eynon Bay, like Oxwich, has a gently shelving sandy beach backed by dunes. **Culver Hole** and the **Salt House** are the main attractions here. The finest beach is at **Rhosili**, the westernmost point on Gower facing the Atlantic and Ireland. A four-mile (six-km) arching cuticle of sand banked by dunes provides a perfect surf. A few wrecks can be seen sticking out of the water and beyond them is West Wales's Pembrokeshire coast.

There's a large seabird colony here, a gaggle of homes, half a dozen bed-and-breakfast establishments, the Worm's Head Hotel and The National Trust Information Centre. Here, too, you may catch Gower's hangliding lemmings throwing themselves off the cliff edge 632 ft (193 metres) above the Atlantic.

Old mysteries: The nearby **Paviland Caves** are thought to be the oldest occupied site yet excavated in Europe, dating back 100,000 years. The skeleton of the Red Lady of Paviland (a man, actu-

Summer bathing at Mumbles Head. Overpage, cockle pickers at Penclawdd, Gower.

ally), neolithic burial chambers like **Arthur's Stone** at **Reynoldston** and spooky names like Druids' Moor, Devil's Kitchen and Hangman's Cross evoke the Celtic mysteries.

Meanwhile the cockle women of **Penclawdd** on the northern coast, who still traipse up to seven miles (11 km) a day across the mudflats to collect the cockles and laver bread, keep alive the region's more recent traditions. The northern fringed saltmarsh stretches eight miles (13 km) round to Carmarthen Bay and has a desolate beauty in marked contrast to the golden sands of the south.

Just as the Landsker Line divides Pembrokeshire's Northern Welsh speakers from the Norman south, so the high central ridge, **Cefn Bryn**, divides the Gower. Near Arthur's Stone, which is located on the high point of Cefn Bryn, is the **Gower Farm Museum** at **Llandewi** which charts 100 years of Gower family life. Also worth a visit for a meal or a stay is the country retreat of **Fairyhill**, with lake, trout stream and 24 acres (10 hectares) of woodland containing buzzards, badgers and even wild ponies.

Worth a visit: Within a radius of about a half-hour drive from Swansea are a number of other sights. **Afan Argoed Country Park** has a Welsh Miners' Museum and a Countryside Centre in densely forested hills. There are forest walks, cycle hire facilities and tours.

An 18th-century Orangery in **Margam Park** makes a visit worthwhile. The Tudor-Gothic Margam Castle, 12th-century Cistercian Abbey remains, and sculptures pepper the estate. Children are well catered for: there's a maze, pony rides and Fairytale Land with Three Bears, ogres, pea-green boats, and houses of straw with tape-recorded tales.

Aberdulais Falls in the Vale of Neath combines natural beauty and historic industrial remains.

Dan-Yr-Ogof Showcaves, in the Upper Swansea Valley, are the largest of their kind in Western Europe. Two-hour tours are run between April and October.

155

THE SOUTHWEST

According to the *Mabinogion*, the book of Welsh folklore, South West Wales was *Gwlad hud a lledrich*, "The Land of Mystery and Magic". In 1974 the new county of Dyfed came into being, subsuming Cardigan along with Carmarthen and Pembroke to become Wales's largest administrative area.

The new title may lack romance but every town still has its extraordinary tale and remarkable ancestor. **Carmarthen**, prosperous, sizeable and confident, may have been where Merlin dwelt, but tiny Aberbach is home to a man who captured a mermaid. Standing stones (*menhirs*) and great chambered Neolithic burial chambers (*cromlechs* or *dolmens*) dot the fields like mushrooms, White Ladies flit eerily about castles and fairies still visit town on market day.

Making myths: Tales of lost kingdoms gain credence when ancient submerged forests at Amroth, Manorbier, Newgale and Whitesands reveal themselves as the tide peels back. Romans, Vikings and Normans who came to tame the region have only added to its deep mystery, leaving behind them their castles, forts, people and placenames.

Alongside the romance is the beauty of one of Britain's finest coastlines. The **Pembrokeshire Coast National Park** is the only one of 10 such designated areas in Britain that is predominantly coastal. In southwest Wales, surrounded on three sides by the ocean, seafaring was a way of life long before tourists took to paddle boats. The Irish Sea was the major highway westwards both for copper and culture, with saints and pilgrims making their way to and from Ireland on the frailest of coracles.

The farmers who have tilled the land for thousands of years were equally dependent on the sea, always eager to supplement their income with a little fishing, smuggling, wrecking—or even piracy. Nowadays economic necessity has led them to turn outhouses into self-catering units and to nailing "Bed &

Breakfast" signs to their cottage doors.

The marriage of the region's two major industries of tourism and agriculture is doing little, however, for the sky-high unemployment figures around **Milford Haven** (23.7 percent compared to Wales's overall 14.7 percent). The town has never recovered from the decline of the fishing industry and the closure of the Esso oil refinery.

But the jobs drought is not county-wide. In 1985 the Centre for Urban and Regional Development Studies at Newcastle University named Carmarthen the only "boom town" in Wales. The twice-weekly covered livestock market is the largest in the country and its indoor market one of Wales's finest.

The city centre has a cluster of book shops, tea houses and bistros above the Roman amphitheatre in Priory Street. There's also a small museum housed in the former Palace of the Bishop of St David's on the outskirts at **Abergwili**.

The major tourist attraction in Carmarthen is the 1,000-year-old art of coracle fishing that is still practised on the banks of the **Tywi**. As only 12 families hold licences to fish the salmon, specimens may be hard to find.

"Little England": Guarding **Carmarthen Bay** to the south are the imposing castles of Kidwelly, Llanstephan and Laugharne. These are just three of the Norman castles dating from the 12th century that run in a straight line across the county through Llawhaden and Haverfordwest to Roch on the west coast. The **Landsker line**, as it is known, protected the Norman south from the war-like Celts in the north.

The division is clearly linguistic and cultural as well as military. Although people may no longer be ostracised for marrying across the divide, the villages to the north are more scattered, the small bellcoted churches showing their Celtic origins and the Welsh language dominant; to the south the villages gather tightly round the larger churches and the English language reigns (earning the region the soubriquet of "Little England Beyond Wales").

Kidwelly has packed its businesses,

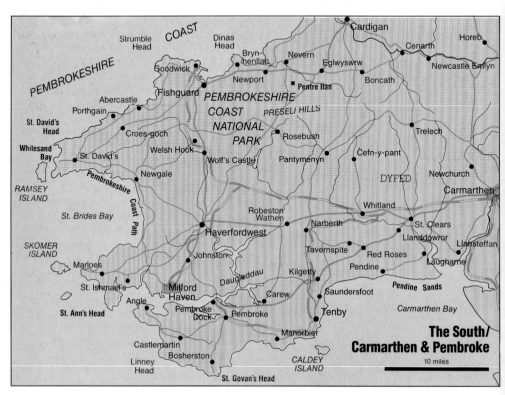

housing, industrial museum and an ancient church dedicated to St Mary on the southern bank of the **Gwendraeth Fach** river. This keeps the northern side clear, across the 14th-century bridge, for its showpiece medieval cobbled alleyways and remarkably complete 12th-century castle.

Llanstephan is a picturesque, uncommercialised coastal village with superb views from the 13th-century castle (built on a site 2,000 years older) round the headland to **Wharley Point** and across the River Towy to **Ferryside**. There, you might catch sight of the Swansea train trundling westward.

Dylan Thomas's "heron-priested shore" at **Laugharne**, overlooking the Taf estuary, is a real joy despite the tourist industry that has built up on the back of the tragic life of the poet. Georgian houses clatter down the hillside to the shore where the ivy clad 13th-century castle stands guard over the estuary's mud flats (the subject of a stormy Turner painting).

The Boathouse, where Thomas lived,

is open seven days a week from the Easter weekend through until 9 November (Thomas's deathday) and in the peak season receives 250 visitors a day. The views from both the Boathouse and the Shed where he worked are certainly inspiring. In July the town holds a festival celebrating the master's work.

Unlike some of the town's other establishments, Brown's Hotel ignores the cheap capitalisation of its most famous bar prop. There are a few faded photographs of the poet on the wall alongside rugby heroes, but it is an unsentimental place with atmosphere and lively conversation.

The less celebrated but equally accomplished poet Edward Thomas also resided in Laugharne. Clearly there must be something in the air that makes the imagination dance. It is claimed fairies still visit from their offshore enchanted islands to do their weekly shop. The ghost of a black dog lurks the streets at night and old Admiral Laugharne himself can be spotted occasionally rowing himself across the river

The boat shed at Laugharne where Dylan Thomas wrote.

DYLAN THOMAS: POETRY AND PASSION

Dylan Thomas, whose exhortation to his dying father to "Rage, rage against the dying of the light" is one of modern poetry's most defiant lines, failed to follow that advice himself. On 5 November 1953 he slipped into a final coma in a New York hotel room, following a heavy drinking bout.

His short life served as a blueprint for the modern rebel without a cause who feels it "better to burn out than to rust". Three-quarters of his poetry was written between the ages of 16 and 20, he was deemed unfit for military service, lived in a renovated boat house, wrote in a garage and died at the age of 39. The coroner's reported cause of death—"a massive insult to the brain"—fanned the flames of notoriety and romantic martyrdom. The 20th century's deification of those who die before their time, preferably of an addiction, and its conviction that great art is found only in the bed of possession and madness, ensured the poet's immortality.

Fortunately Thomas's works cannot be sentimentalised or diminished as his life has been: in the sepulchral silence of libraries his booming voice still declaims on records while his long, unrestrained lines of rich imagery overflow pages like waves breaking on the beach.

Thomas spent the first 20 years of his life in Swansea, the son of an English teacher with a love of words. He left school at 16 and had only one full-time period of employment (the 15 months he served as a junior on the *South Wales Daily Post*). He decided to be a poet almost before he was out of short trousers, dubbing himself "The Rimbaud of Cwmdonkin Drive".

Thomas's evocation of the passions and mysteries of childhood in his first three volumes of poetry were rooted in notebooks he kept between the ages of 16 and 20. Happy childhood memories of holidays spent around Carmarthen Bay, recaptured in *Fern Hill* and the short story *The Peaches*, led him back to Laugharne in the spring of 1938, though he was not to settle here until 1949. The Boathouse (bought for him by the first wife of the historian A.J.P. Taylor) appears to have been hewn out of the rock face and shares the same spectacular views across the bay as his workplace, "the Shed", 50 metres further down the hill.

At the Boathouse, Thomas lived with his wife Caitlin and their three children. In the Prologue to his *Collected Poems* he describes "the scummed starfish sands...the breakneck of rocks, tangled with froth, flute, fin and quill" and "shells that speak seven seas." Although he spent much time in the pubs and clubs of London, he could write only in Wales. It was here that he found fresh inspiration and his instinctive and elemental themes reached their final fruition.

His final work, *Under Milk Wood*, was also written at Laugharne. It was in his own words, an attempt "to write a sort of Welsh *Ulysses* where all the action takes place in 24 hours" and it revealed his sure eye for suburban pretensions. The real setting for the radio play may have been Laugharne but the fictional setting, Llareggub, when read backwards, displays Thomas's healthy irreverence for both the BBC (they changed the spelling) and propriety in general. However, it was the 1954 BBC recording with fellow Welshman Richard Burton that won the work instant acclaim.

Some accuse Thomas, in Nietzsche's words, of "muddying the water to appear deep"; others hail him as the greatest 20th-century British poet on the strength of a total oeuvre of little more than 100 poems. His paean to South Wales and his lyricism continued the long Welsh tradition for oratory and music. His own sonorous readings have been the single most telling factor in the growth of live and recorded poetry readings.

In *Twenty-four Years* Dylan Thomas says: "I advance for as long as forever is." Forever was not long coming. "Washed over by exhilarating waves of adulation," wrote Oscar Williams, "he crowded his threescore years and ten into the last four of his thirty-nine years of life." Dylan Thomas's body was flown back from New York for a simple but much photographed burial in Laugharne, and in 1982 a memorial stone was placed in his honour at Poets' Corner in London's Westminster Abbey.

in a coracle sporting nothing but his birthday suit. Perhaps it's something to do with the ale they serve here.

Mystery stones: To the northwest of Carmarthen are the **Preseli Hills**, the only large tract of hilly upland in Pembrokeshire; pretty rather than dramatic, possessing neither the austerity of the Beacons nor the grandeur of Snowdonia. Yet these gently sweeping hills are steeped in the mystery and history that gives meat to the bones of the folklore of the *Mabinogion*. It is from the southeast slopes that the blue stones came that make up Stonehenge's inner circle 200 miles away. Romantics claim the stones were moved on tree-trunk rollers, then transported on rafts; some even claim chieftains moved them through levitation. Hard-nosed geologists suggest that an Ice Age glacier handled the removal job.

The Long Barrow burial chamber at **Pentre Ifan** is said to be the finest Neolithic *cromlech* in Britain, dating back 4,500 years. Like some monstrous, double-trunked toadstool, the *cromlech* dwarfs everything round it. The vast capstone (16.5 ft/five metres long) rests on its tripodal perch 7.5 ft (2.3 metres) above the ground. This feat of engineering genius and sheer strength, together with its seemingly sculpted beauty, is awesome. The site offers uninterrupted views down to Newport Bay.

North of the Preselis, across the A478 main road from Fishguard to Cardigan, lies the elysian churchyard at **Nevern**. Skirting the horseman's mounting block in the lane outside St Brynach's, you enter a short shaded avenue of yew trees. One tree has become fabled as "the bleeding yew" because it produces a thick red sap. Beside the church is the fifth-century **Vitalianus Stone** which is thought to commemorate a Celtic soldier of the Roman legion. The inscriptions are in both Latin and Ogham (as is the inscription on another Celtic stone inside the church).

Nearby is the 13-ft (four-metre) 10th-century Celtic **Great Cross**, perhaps the finest in the whole of Wales. The

Pilgrims Path to St David's skirts the church and leads across a clapper bridge over a stream. A short way up the hill, pilgrims have cut a cross into the rock face and below it there is a recess with another small one incised.

A little further on, pilgrims' footprints have worn nine inches into the rock. Crosses appear in the heels of the steps where successive pilgrims made the sign. Overlooking the valley is a 12th-century motte and bailey castle.

Newport is just a few miles to the west along the A478. It is known for its craft and pottery (on Mondays there is a craft market in the Memorial Hall). The pubs, cottages offering B&B, book and gift shops are overlooked by the medieval castle and Iron Age Fort on Carningli Hill. The Boat Club is based on Parrog Beach.

Cwm Gwaun, separating the Preselis from Fishguard, is a fabulous deeply wooded valley full of sycamore, alder, blackthorn, wild cherry, hornbeam, hazel, wych elm—and no doubt dwarves and goblins. Gouged out by meltwater surging under the Irish Sea glacier 15,000 years ago, it is one of the last retreats of the otter and the Gregorian calendar. New Year in Cwm Gwaun (*cwm* means valley) starts on 13 January. This peculiar quirk of the people may have something to do with the home brew in the Duffryn Arms (better known as Bessie's) that offers instant oblivion.

Fishguard is the main shopping town of North Pembrokeshire, with a busy Thursday market in the Town Hall selling local butters, bacon and laver bread (made from seaweed). It is a Sealink ferry port, "the shortest sea route to Ireland". Outside the Royal Oak in the town's main square is a stone commemorating the signing of the Peace Treaty at the end of the last invasion of Britain in 1797. Inside is a copy of the treaty itself. A few doors down is the 19th-century parish church of St Mary's (built on a medieval church) where there is a gravestone to the great heroine Jemima Nicholas, who, if legend keeps on growing, will soon be hailed as having put down this shambolic invasion single-handedly. The true story is slightly less glorious.

Understandably enough, the invading French troops, consisting almost totally of convicts, felt no inclination whatsoever to fight the Welsh and instead spent the few hours of freedom they had, getting drunk. Jemima, meanwhile, rallied an army of women dressed in the local costume of tall pillar-box black hats and red flannel coats and marched round the headland. The drunken French, convinced the mighty militia were upon them, surrendered without a peep. Jemima managed to round up 14 recidivists singlehandedly with a pitchfork.

Lower Town, the older, more picturesque part of Fishguard, was a flourishing port in the past. It still has a healthy mackerel industry and has been the setting for a number of films; the most celebrated of these was *Under Milk Wood*—which, perversely, was not shot in Laugharne. Fishguard harbour opened in 1906, but World War I and the lack of an industrial hinterland

Fishguard: once had ambitions to be a transatlantic port.

164

killed off the dream of making Fishguard a great transatlantic port to rival Liverpool.

Coastal splendour: The **Pembrokeshire Coast National Park** was created in 1952. It extends from Poppit Sands (Cardigan) in the north to Amroth in the south; 160 miles (260 km) of truly spectacular coastal scenery. The only inland tracts in the park take in the Preseli's and Cwm Gwaun.

Although each of the coastal stretches has its own charm, the finest section starts at Fishguard, continues round the lighthouse at **Strumble Head** (one of Britain's finest sites for studying migrating birds and the nearest point to Ireland) and runs south round St David's Head and Ramsey Head to **Caerfa Bay**.

The coast road runs only a short distance inland with easy access to the hamlets and bays. The views over this rugged, untamed stretch from the youth hostel above **Pwllderi** and the layby a little before it, are quite breathtaking. Waves break over a thick gorse hump-backed promontory that juts out into the ocean hundreds of feet below.

Aber Mawr (the Great Bay) also once dreamed of becoming a great transatlantic port. Thankfully hubris struck, the dream died and Aber Mawr remains quite unspoilt with no facilities whatsoever.

Abercastle, once a coal, grain and limestone trading port, still has a lime kiln on view, and up on the hill at Longhouse is **Carreg Samson**, another dramatic *cromlech*. **Porthgain** has a long narrow harbour overlooked by the hoppers of an abandoned stone crushing plant. The "Scots Houses" (cottages where Scottish workers lived) have been converted into homes and the Alun Davies Art Gallery.

On the opposite side of the bay is the 18th-century Sloop Inn, a marvellously infectious good-time pub with a fine collection of photographs charting maritime and mining history. After the "Blue Lagoon" at **Abereiddy** (a flooded quarry) you get back to the wildness again at **St David's Head**, the

location of another *cromlech* and the fortified cliff site of Warrior's Dyke.

A less than gruelling detour will take you to the top of **Carn Llidi**, from which, on a clear day, one can see the peaks of Snowdonia and right across the Irish Sea to the Wicklow Hills. **Whitesands** is the most popular bucket-and-spade beach along the coast and a surfer's paradise.

From the lifeboat station at **St Justinian** you can catch boats to **Ramsey Island** to see the huge seal population. The ruins of St Justinian's medieval chapel stand on the hill. It was here that St David's sidekick walked across a fabled bridge to Ramsey, cutting it behind him with an axe as he went and thus creating the infamous wrecking rocks poetically named "The Bitches", through which the waters bubble like some witch's cauldron. His followers, tiring of his model asceticism, felt enough was enough and chopped off his head. The saint, undaunted, picked it up and walked back to the mainland.

The coastal path continues round **Ramsey Sound** where more seals and pups can be spotted. Offshore are the islands of **Skomer** (national nature reserve), **Skokholm** (Britain's first bird observatory) and **Grassholm** (one of Britain's few gannetries).

If it weren't for its cathedral, the most important ecclesiastical centre in South Wales, **St David's** would be just a pretty village instead of Britain's smallest city. A cluster of shops and restaurants surround the main square; there are a couple of hotels, a number of pubs, a few chapels (backs turned resolutely to the cathedral), and that's about it.

Apart from the cathedral, that is. St David, believed to have been born in a storm near the chapel dedicated to his mother, St Non, founded a monastery in the wooded Alun Valley in the sixth century. A vegetarian and teetotaller, David was clearly too good to be true as far as the wife of the local Irish chieftain, Boia, was concerned. Deciding to test the ascetic with a few pagan pleasures, she sent naked young girls to frolic in the nearby river and throw a few lewd

Surfing culture has taken root in the southwest coast.

suggestions across to the monks. Legend has it all succumbed but David.

It is believed that Patrick, patron Saint of Ireland, was born close to where the Cathedral stands. The monastic site became a major centre of pilgrimage for kings and common people alike. Two pilgrimages here was worth one to Rome and three were worth one to Jerusalem.

The striking grandeur of the purple-grey stone Cathedral is an ironic commemoration to the austere monasticism favoured by the saint himself. Inside the clarity and limpidity of light adds even greater majesty to the sublime interior. The floor rises sharply (some say deliberately to get the congregation nearer heaven) and the arcade piers splay outwards to the heavens to meet an intricately carved grey Irish oak 15th-century ceiling.

Inside Bishop Vaughan's Chapel rest the remains of St David and St Justinian; these were discovered during 19th-century restoration, bricked for safe keeping behind a wall. At the far end of the cathedral is the mausoleum of a local notary who used to spend her afternoons knitting, dog at her feet (it's still curled up there now in marble), keeping an eye on the artisans carving her vault. Occasionally she would raise herself and try it out for size at various stages in construction.

Beside the cathedral are the equally impressive ruins of Bishop Gower's Palace built in 1340. In the 16th century Bishop Barlow had the lead from the roof slowly stripped away as dowries for his five daughters. The lead was kept in the family: all five married bishops. The grounds are often used for Shakespearean or historical productions over the summer months.

Haverfordwest from St David's is 16 miles (26 km) and 17 hills away. The main A487 offers fine views across to **St Bride's Bay** where smuggling, piracy and wrecking were all popular pastimes. **Lower Solva** is the only memorable stop-off point—unless you take the coastal road south, calling in at **Little Haven** and the superb sandy

St David's: a grand tribute to an austere saint.

beach at **Marloes** (recommended by the *Good Beach Guide* as one of the best 23 beaches in Britain). There's a water sports mecca (and Fort Field Centre specialising in marine biology) at **Dale**.

Five miles (eight km) east of Haverfordwest is the Graham Sutherland Gallery at **Picton Castle**, housing the largest permanent collection of the artist's works.

Haverfordwest itself has a frightful one-way traffic system and is the main western railway terminus. It was a busy port before the railways arrived and is still the commercial, shopping and administrative centre of Pembrokeshire. The new shopping precinct, the Riverside Market, is located between the old and new bridges. A £15 million scheme to deepen the river into the town centre will allow the Haven rivercraft to reach it once more.

The town has a 12th-century castle (partly destroyed by Oliver Cromwell) which now houses a museum and art gallery. Few traces of this Norman walled garrison remain apart from the churches (St Mary's being the finest example on offer). The ruins of the old Priory are on the river beside the Bristol Trader Inn. Most of the town's little charm comes from its river setting and its elegant Georgian homes.

Mudflats and muntjac: The **Western and Eastern Cleddau** down to the Haven are also part of the National Park and have been getting plenty of attention. The oyster beds have recently returned after a lengthy absence, walks are being promoted along the river banks and cruises are operating out of Neyland and Hobbs Point along the mudflats through the steep oak-forested creeks to Llangwn. Keep your eyes peeled and you just might catch sight of the notoriously timid miniature muntjac, otherwise known as the Chinese barking deer.

To the east of the town and just five miles (eight km) from Pembroke Castle lies the Norman **Carew Castle** and corn mill, overlooking a tidal creek in the lower Daugleddau. Over the centuries it has been transformed from medieval

Pembroke castle: the most famous fortress in the area.

fortress to Elizabethan mansion. The impressive remains also house one of the three finest early Celtic crosses in Wales (the others are at Nevern and Maen Achwyfan in Clwyd).

Milford Haven, Europe's deepest waterway, fully tests Baudelaire's dictum that beauty can be true beauty only if it contains an element of ugliness. The industrial skyline can provide fabulous petro-chemical sunsets but most of the time the snaking pipes are ugly scars on an otherwise unblemished coast.

As a major oil port, Milford Haven is home to the mega-tankers. Built along with Pembroke Dock and Neyland in the 19th century, this region is southwest Wales's most populous and suffers the highest unemployment figures. The abandoned Esso refinery is a reminder for the unemployed of better days.

The fishing industry occasionally fizzles back into life at Milford Docks and new restaurants open up only to close a few months later. Understandably, the streets look depressing, the people appear poor and the air could do with some freshener. There are plans afoot to attract yachts and become a major marina.

Across the toll bridge is **Pembroke Dock**, whose sole distinction was that it was the setting for Britain's longest burning fire during World War II when the bombers hit the oil tanks at Llanreath. It's a shame they rebuilt it and, unless you're waiting for the ferry to Rosslare in Ireland, the area is best passed through quickly.

Pembroke is another story. Its main street is filled with chintzy cafés selling real coffee. It feels more prosperous and is certainly a lot more elegant. **Pembroke Castle**'s present limestone fortress with its 16-ft (five-metre) thick walls was built by the Normans between 1190 and 1245 on an older site and, like Tenby Castle, has the dubious distinction of having been attacked by both sides during the Civil War.

Bounded on three sides by a tidal inlet of the Milford Haven Waterway it is deservedly the most famous castle in southwest Wales and was the birthplace of Harry Tudor (Henry VII). There are also private museums: the **National Museum of Gypsy Caravans** and the excellent **Museum of the Home** (opposite the castle).

A detour westwards to **Angle Bay** and the peerless wild waters of **Freshwater West** is recommended before visiting the medieval world of walled gardens, orchards and fishponds at the Bishop's Palace at **Lamphey**.

A short hop from here is **Manorbier**'s Norman Castle—a particularly well preserved specimen—where Giraldus Cambrensis (Gerald of Barry) was born in 1145. Said to be Britain's first travel writer, he returned to the principality in 1188 with the Archbishop of Canterbury and kept detailed notes of his travels as he tried to drum up support for a third holy crusade. Eloquent and perceptive he saved his finest passage for his hometown: "Heaven's breath smells so wooingly... In all the broad lands of Wales, Manorbier is the most pleasant place by far."

Tenby is without doubt the major resort along Pembrokeshire's golden south coast and has been for the past 200 years. Though it's prosperous now, you could have bought the whole town and hinterland in 1348 for the princely sum of £38 8s 2d *(£38.41)*.

Its name is most readily associated with Pembrokeshire's own species of daffodil, renowned for its early flowering and its vibrancy of colour. The Tenby daffodil came close to extinction in just three mad years in the 1880s when half a million bulbs were dug up for export to London's flower stalls.

The idyllic **Harbour Beach**, like a child's bath full of brightly coloured bobbing craft, is overlooked by the hill castle and elegant pastel-coloured Georgian town houses. There are another three beaches, one of which, **South Beach**—banked with dunes and woodland and one and a half miles long—is quite superb. The esplanade high on the limestone cliff is graced with a succession of distinguished four-storey hotels and offers views along the beach to Giltar Point as well as to the islands of **Caldey**, **St Catherine's** and **St Margaret's**.

Tenby is justified in calling itself a historic resort because, apart from its seaside holiday facilities, the town itself is of significant historic interest. Its 13th-century medieval walls are mostly still intact, although only one of its five gates remains.

The walls encircle narrow labyrinthine lanes which make it easy to visualise medieval times. **Frog Street** is the most famous of these with its indoor market, adjoining cobbled mews, small pottery shops, tea rooms and crafts.

The mullioned windows of the gabled 15th-century Tudor Merchant's House project into the narrowest of alleys at Quay Hill. The community museum, run by volunteers and set inside what remains of **Tenby Castle** on St Catherine's Island, is thorough and informative with local exhibits dating back 12,000 years. Nearby is the Prince Albert memorial.

In St Mary's, the town also boasts the largest parish church in Wales. For something a little more modern, there's the De Valence Pavilion in Upper Frog Street: it provides a variety of entertainments from theatre to wrestling.

Tenby is the birthplace of Augustus John, and several of his paintings are on display in the excellent independent community museum and picture gallery. Perhaps a little parochially, he claimed of the town: "You may travel the world over, but you will find nothing more beautiful: it is so restful, so colourful and so unspoilt."

Commerce rules: No such claims could be made a few miles to the north at **Saundersfoot**, which has prostrated itself to the tourist god. The once pretty town is buried under fish and chip shops, Wimpy hamburger bars, noisy pubs and tat stalls. It's a holiday town, pushing fudge, rock candy and chips; but it's popular with younger visitors, who patronise the two discos.

At least one of Saundersfoot's shoe shops has—unlike the Welsh Tourist Board—accepted the realities of the Welsh seaside weather: it unabashedly displays in its window not the expected flip-flops but pairs of Wellington boots.

Tenby: narrow lanes hark back to its medieval beginnings. Right, shrine on Caldey Island.

THE MONKS OF CALDEY

Virtually closed to the world, yet barely three miles (five km) from one of Wales's most popular seaside resorts, a community of monks continues the timeless rigours of religious life on Caldey Island. The dozen or so—their numbers fluctuate as time vies with recruitment to maintain a viable population—are members of the Cistercian Order. Their routine is harsh, their devotions unending, their presence a reminder of eternal values.

Caldey can best be seen from Tenby's south cliff, a sweep backed by some of the resort's grandest hotels—the Atlantic, the Imperial, the Buckingham. It can also be visited from Whitsuntide to mid-September when a fleet of small boats runs to the island. For although Caldey is owned by the Cistercians it remains on the tourist beat. The monastery itself, the island's most imposing building, is inviolate except to carefully conducted parties which are allowed within its strict confines. Men only, though—women are not allowed into the monastery itself, although they can join the monks in prayer in the abbey church.

The island, one and a half by three-quarters of a mile (2.5 by 1.25 km) in area, is home to 20 other people, mostly retired, as well as the cowled monks. Their day begins at 3.15 a.m. summer and winter, when they rise for the first of seven services which punctuate a day ending at 7.30 p.m. when they retire for what is an unusually timed period of sleep. Three meals at 6.00 a.m, 12.30 p.m. and 6.30 p.m, break up the routine of work and prayer.

A largely self-supporting community, the monks work the land and gather raw materials for a unique industry which they established in 1953—the manufacture of perfume from the gorse and lavender which carpet the island. Caldey perfume is now internationally known, a stock line in scores of gift shops and available by mail-order. It is the worldly means by which an unworldly community keeps afloat. The monks have their own retail shop in Tenby town, hard by the harbour from which their own boat plies to

Caldey. Not that they ever leave the island, save for emergencies such as medical or dental treatment. The abbot, Father Robert, is excepted since he has to travel to meetings of the Order in Rome and elsewhere. Black-bearded and softly spoken, he remembers the 1960s when the community numbered 40. The roll dwindled and closure was contemplated.

But a quiet campaign of monastic public relations pulled 100 inquiries. In 1988 five candidates were selected for a five-year programme culminating in the taking of their final vows.

Novices are allowed to communicate during day-time hours, but the routine forbids "unnecessary" conversation and periods of silence lasting 12 hours form part of the probationers' training. It is an unyielding round of hard work and inflexible rules to winnow out all but the most firm of purpose.

The monks possess a remarkable tranquillity. Their life occasionally takes an odd turn in deference to the demands of the 20th century. In 1986 a second-hand fire engine was flown to Caldey by helicopter, thus providing some insurance against a repeat of the fire which in 1940 damaged the abbey church. Three monks joined half-a-dozen of the island's other inhabitants to form a fire crew trained by professionals from the local brigade back on mainland Wales.

Such worldly contacts are rare—but it has always been so on Caldey. Like many of the islands off the west coast of Britain, it has long been inhabited by monks. The first recorded there is said to be a hermit called Pyro who lived a lonely life in a simple cell 1,300 years ago.

How he survived, or whether he did at all, is not known. Perhaps the abundance of fish and wild berries sustained him through the cold winters. The gorse and the lavender were probably there all those centuries ago, splashing their colours across the island long before the science of perfumery was refined.

At night the beam from Caldey's lighthouse (which is operated automatically) sweeps sea and island to the delight of children watching from Tenby's elegant seafront. To go to Caldey is to experience, however briefly, another sort of illumination.

MID-WALES

Motorways, creeping remorselessly over virtually every tourist map in Europe, have yet to put in an appearance in Mid-Wales. In the south, the M4 offers a speedy run from London into the heart of rural west Wales; in the north the A55 is being rapidly improved at enormous expense to provide quick access to Wales's north coast resorts and the Isle of Anglesey. But Mid-Wales lacks such expressway connections and that helps to explain its unspoiled charm.

A somewhat arbitrary definition of the area would be the oblong from the mouth of the Teifi in the south to the mouth of the Dovey, with boundaries running east to meet the wayward England/Wales border. It contains the administrative district of Ceredigion (formerly Cardiganshire), a good slice of Montgomeryshire, Radnor and slivers of Brecon. Don't worry too much about the names: concentrate on the scenery, which ranges from lonely rounded mountains to secret beaches hiding away at the end of narrow lanes.

The **River Teifi** stands guard at the southern edge of this seductive territory. **Cardigan**, a town with agricultural and seafaring connections, is the lowest crossing place. A crumbling castle overlooks a fine arched bridge. Huge baulks of timber shore up the castle's outer walls which rise from a public street.

The sailing ships for which Cardigan was once famous are long gone—hounded to near-extinction more than 100 years ago by the railway; ironically Cardigan lost its rail link after World War II, and today the motor car is noisily supreme in the town's narrow streets. Market day—usually a Saturday—is worth taking in. The covered Guild Hall makes an imposing venue for displays of local produce—and for the itinerant traders' stalls piled with merchandise ranging from jeans to digital watches.

Cardigan Island, offshore, is not inhabited, though a flock of sheep was ferried there to try out the grazing.

The A484 winds inland from Cardigan close to the banks of the Teifi. Upstream, **Cenarth** survives as a centre for coracle fishermen. The flimsy craft, looking for all the world like overgrown walnut shells split in two, are made of calico stretched over a wooden frame. A competent coracle maker is said to be able to construct one in less than 24 hours. Working in pairs with a net stretched between them, the coracles float down the river to catch salmon on their way upstream. Then the fishermen carry the craft on their backs to the starting point for another sweep.

Newcastle Emlyn is a friendly town serving a wide area where farming predominates. The castle, built on a loop of the Teifi, is not outstandingly spectacular. Markets bustle with talk of fatstock prices and forecasts of wool clip. The town is the home of one of Wales's most successful cooperatives which are reviving small-scale rural industries. The woollen mills of the Teifi valley, famous 100 years ago for their vitality,

Preceding pages: hill farm near Llandrindod Wells. Left, Cenarth Falls on the River Teifi. Right, Rhayader publican.

may yet make a comeback.

Twenty miles (32 km) further east, on the A475, **Lampeter** (pop. 2,000) unassumingly plays host to several hundred students at one of Britain's smallest seats of learning—St David's College, a constituent of the University of Wales. Many people, of all ages, anxious to learn Welsh attend crash courses at the college.

Danger Zone: From Cardigan the A487 leads north, sometimes swooping down to a seaside settlement, but mostly staying a couple of miles inland. An airstrip and a cluster of buildings laid out with military precision stand above the little resort of **Aberporth**. Mysterious aerials and similar impedimenta are sited on the cliff-top. There are occasional bangs, signifying the testing of missiles. A large area of sea is out-of-bounds to civil craft.

The military's targets floating on the Irish Sea swell sometimes break loose and end up on beaches miles up the coast; as they are often redundant motor cars, painted white and fastened to rafts,

their liberation causes some amusement. Locally it is known as "the white Cortina syndrome"—an endorsement the Ford Motor Company might not entirely welcome.

Tresaith and **Llangrannog** have good sandy beaches, a scattering of houses and, except at the height of the season, an air of having been ignored by 20th-century bustle.

New Quay, like Cardigan, once boasted important shipping connections. The last ship was built there in 1898, and now yachting holds sway. The huge curved quay is delightful, just the place for sitting in the sunshine and dreaming. A privately-run hospital for sea birds and marine creatures is one of New Quay's more recent claims to fame. Commercial fishing concentrates on skate, plaice and sole. Lobsters and scallops are a major catch, most of them being hauled away by lorry to customers in England and the Continent.

A list of harbour dues, a venerable piece of Victoriana, tells of a time when a ton of ivory could be landed at a cost

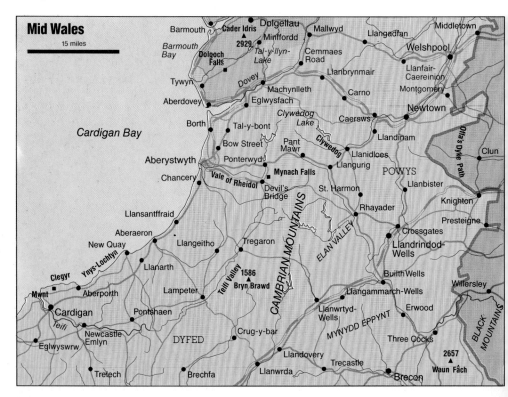

of 2s. 6d. (12.5p.). Cliff walks are rewarding, bringing into view colonies of sea birds. A boat trip gives an even better insight into the Cardigan Bay coast's teeming wildlife.

The A487 winds north through **Llanarth**, an inland village in a steep valley. Horse lovers home in on Llanarth Stud every October for the annual sale which attracts buyers from all over the world.

Aberaeron is a cheerfully busy town. A yacht club and a handsome public house, the Harbour Master, face one another across the harbour entrance. Many of the houses are Georgian in character, brightly painted and the object of much loving attention by their owners. One of the grandest is the home of Sir Geraint Evans, the famous opera singer. The beach is uninspiring. An aquarium and the ice-cream parlour next door are much visited.

The **Vale of Aeron** runs back to Lampeter, a drive through some of the most relaxing countryside in Wales. **Llangeitho**, a bastion of Welsh culture,

is a quiet village. The sermons preached by Daniel Rowland, one of Wales's most charismatic evangelists, attracted thousands to the village in the 18th century.

No town can better the claims of **Aberystwyth** to be considered the capital of mid-Wales. Others, inland, towards the English border, may dispute. But Aber, as it is affectionately called, wins the vote. To describe the town as the terminus of British Rail's line from Shrewsbury and the sea-end of the narrow-gauge Vale of Rheidol railway, as train buffs tend to do, is to ignore its many charms.

Aber is a university town, a commercial centre, a popular holiday resort and a handy base from which to explore the haunting hinterland of sheep walks and lonely lakes. It is also the headquarters of the Welsh Language Society, which has offices next to a Chinese restaurant on the promenade.

The original university buildings on the front (still in use) date from the mid-19th century; the 20th-century addi-

Aberystwyth: a magnet for Mid Wales day-trippers.

tions, including a magnificent arts centre, are located on a hill a mile away. There are numerous outstations of learning, notably college farms and pastures where agriculture is studied by undergraduates from many parts of the world. A College of Librarianship and the National Library of Wales are located on the sloping campus.

Town and gown mix freely. Commerce, too, gives Aber a somewhat unusual flavour for what appears to be a resort town populated (in term time anyway) by hordes of young men and women. Plans are afoot to build a marina at the harbour which has seen better days. Coupled with a revival of the modest fishing fleet—a revival now gaining pace—it could make a big impact on the town's economy.

An interesting investigation into the habits of the local lobster population is also under way. Baby nippers are tagged and then carefully lowered onto suitable off-shore sites; catches are examined to see how they develop. Finding the best home for a growing lobster is a task of some importance.

Aber has a rather grand funicular railway which leads up to a camera obscura, one of the town's latest acquisitions.

The **Vale of Rheidol narrow-gauge railway** is steam-operated. By far the best way of seeing the lovely valley, the line opened in 1902, linking the coast to Devil's Bridge, 12 miles inland. British Rail used to own it, but it has passed into private hands.

The countryside at **Devil's Bridge** so inspired the poet Wordsworth that he composed verses praising its beauty. The name is said to be derived from legend, not unknown elsewhere in Europe. An old woman's cow had strayed across the gorge; a monk appeared, and said he would build a bridge if she promised to give him the first living creature to cross it. She gave her word, the bridge was built, and the monk beckoned her to cross. But she spotted his cloven hoof, called her dog, and threw a crust across. The dog followed, and she told the devil he could keep it.

Left, tower on the University of Wales. Right, Aberystwyth's inviting bay.

Another legend—some say an absolute truth—concerns the people of **Cardiganshire** (known as Cardis) and their reputed caution in matters financial. They are said to have deep pockets and short arms; in other words, they're held to be mean. Joked about by their compatriots, Cardis are sometimes unnervingly hospitable and only occasionally reluctant to come forward when it's their turn to buy the drinks. But legends die hard.

Just how the village of **Bow Street**, a few minutes north from Aberystwyth on the A487, came by its very English name remains a mystery. Housing estates are beginning to sprout, signalling the creation of a dormitory serving Aber itself. **Borth**, the next place of any size, is hidden from the sea by high breakwaters. Inland, **Borth Bog** is of great botanical interest. It contains many rare plants and is zealously guarded by conservationists.

Extensive saltings back the coast further along, where the Dovey joins the Irish Sea. A small shipyard is located at the river mouth; it has pioneered a regeneration of sail, constructing small steel-hulled clippers sufficiently streamlined to enable the wind to supply steerageway in the open sea.

Tal-y-Bont (there are many Tal-y-Bonts in Wales, incidentally), a straggling village back on the A487, has rival chapels and rival pubs. One chapel is Gothic in design, the other Classical. The pubs' differences are starker—one's the Black Lion, the other the White Lion—and they stand cheek-by-jowl overlooking the village green. A satirical magazine is published in the village every year in time to sell out at the National Eisteddfod.

A side road from Tal-y-Bont climbs into the mountains where the gaunt ruins of lead mines, long since worked out, testify to West Wales's forgotten industrial muscle. If you venture a closer look, beware of the old shafts.

A gigantic water wheel stands by the bridge at **Furnace**, an elongated village. In the mists of the past it—rather its predecessor—powered machinery

Water stop on the Vale of Rheidol railway.

whch was used to refine silver; later, a blast furnace produced iron from ore shipped from northwest England. The wheel fell into disrepair and was eventually restored in the early 1980s.

A track alongside the stream winds up **Artist's Valley**, an appropriate name for a vale which has engaged the talents of colourists for many years.

The road north follows the edge of marshes fringing the River Dovey. On the landward side, wooded hills rise steeply. The climb through trees to the open mountain brings a rich reward: the view over the river to the outriders of Snowdonia beyond is superb. At sunset, when the golden ball sinks into the sea, it is particularly entrancing.

Machynlleth is as decidedly Welsh as its formidable name suggests. It's a name which causes panic among monoglot English broadcasters who are sometimes called on to pronounce it. *Ma-hunk-cleth* would be a approximation; locally, "Mach" suffices. The town boasts wide airy streets and a prominent clock tower erected in 1873 which provides a focal point where young people congregate on warm summer evenings.

The town has a special significance for Welsh nationalists. Owain Glyndwr, a rumbustious prince who played cat and mouse with English armies, held a parliament there in 1404. Precisely where is a bit of a mystery— but it is probably not on the site of Mach's Parliament Building, a young-ish construction which was substantially rebuilt early this century. Sheep, not familiar with the cry "fore", roam the local golf course at their peril.

Many walks, ranging from leisurely strolls to quite tough treks, start at the town's edge. The Dovey is one of Wales's leading salmon rivers, and anglers line the banks at the height of the season. Floods can close the bridge over the Dovey just north of Mach. Don't ignore the warning notices which police, through long experience, erect in good time; many a motorist has ended up stalled and glad of a tow from some obliging tractor driver.

How to count sheep and stay awake.

The road inland, the A489, joins the north-south highway, the A470, at **Cemaes Road** five miles from Mach. Much criticism levelled at the A470 is explained by geography. Twisting and turning round mountains, swooping under (and over) the railway which connects Shrewsbury to Mach and beyond, it is a route to test a driver's skill. But don't be deterred—just remember that in mid-Wales the pace of almost everything is low-geared.

Carno is a kempt village, as befits somewhere with a Laura Ashley factory. Hundreds of machinists, cutters and office staff travel to work in the modern, glass-fronted complex. A helipad nearby underlines the company's wide-ranging activities. Whoever gave the village of **Clatter** its name must have been a joker—it is very, very quiet.

The commercial and industrial jewel of mid-Wales is **Newtown**. The town is the headquarters of Mid-Wales Development (MWD), a government agency set up in 1976 to revive the economy of a rural sweep covering more than a third of the land area of Wales, populated by fewer than one-tenth of its 2.5 million people. MWD is headed by an energetic Scot, Dr Iain Skewis, who earlier helped to boost his native Highlands. New factories, housing estates and a theatre have brought the town into the front rank of new towns.

Once a centre of the flannel industry, Newtown is remembered by today's entrepreneurs as the home of the world's first mail order business, founded there in 1859. The town's most famous son, Robert Owen, who started the co-operative movement, was buried near the River Severn which flows majestically through the town.

Soon after the A470 swings south, a riot of flowers in carefully manicured front gardens announces **Llandinam**, a frequent winner of Wales's best-kept village competition. It was the home of one David Davies, a self-made millionaire who started on the road to riches in the middle of the last century by buying a tree for £5, sawing it up and selling the pieces for £80. He went on to develop

Furnace Falls, near Machynlleth.

ALTERNATIVE LIVING

Some may consider the trend as the modern alternative to Welsh mysticism. Others may see it as a kind of back-to-the land revivalist movement. But organic farming and alternative technology have gained a strong foothold in the rough hill country of West Wales.

Led by a band of quintessential English refugees from the rat race of London and the southeast shires, these born-again farmers have formed a growers' cooperative and set up shop on an industrial estate in Lampeter. A market town since 1284, Lampeter has become the UK's largest centre for the preparation, packaging and distribution of organic fruits, vegetables and dairy products.

Some of the exotic fruits and vegetables, raised without the boost of chemical fertilisers or the protection of potentially harmful pesticides, are imported. But an increasing amount of the seasonal produce is home-grown on abandoned farms and small holdings (about two dozen at last count) within a 100-mile (160-km) radius of Lampeter.

Many of the growers are new farmers, like Oxfordshire-born Giles Bowerman, who manages the Organic Growers West Wales cooperative. Tired of city living and with a desire to become self-sufficient, he and a girlfriend emigrated to Wales six years ago and found a small holding to rent just south of Camarthen. While he now looks after the cooperative growers, his partner tends to the crops: 10,000 heads of little gem lettuces, five acres (two hectares) of carrots, an acre of courgettes, hoop houses filled with cucumbers and tomatoes and an experiment in raising Chinese leaf.

Nick Rebbeck, a film director-turned farmer who was born in West Sussex and became captivated by Wales while on holiday there in the mid-1970s, is now a partner in Bwlchwernen Fawr, an organic dairy farm near Lampeter. In between film engagements, he oversees the herd and, as a first-time organic vegetable farmer, suffered his first unarmed bout against a swarm of predatory caterpillars which had infested the 90,000 red cabbage plants he had contracted to raise for the cooperative.

Bwlchwernen Fawr's milk is processed into cheese at Welsh Organic Foods, a new dairy cooperative run by Australian-born, London-bred Dougal Campbell. A veteran Swiss-trained cheesemaker, Campbell and his Cambridgeshire-born wife, in wellies and shorts, churn out 10 tonnes a year of their own label "Tyngrug", a rough unpasteurised farmhouse Cheddar/Caerphilly cross they sell from their 120-acre (48-hectare) hill farm near Lampeter.

Their surplus milk, along with milk from other organic member dairy farms, is bought by the cooperative at twice the price the government-regulated Milk Marketing Board pays farmers. At the modern Lampeter dairy cooperative plant, the milk is processed into "Pencarreg", a soft pasturised brie-type, and two other Welsh brands of organic cheese, which are sold to UK supermarkets.

West Wales has a long tradition of cooperative and organic farming. In the old university town of Aberystwyth, 23 miles (37 km) northwest of Lampeter, the University of Wales has just begun offering a full-year course in organic farming. It is the first university in the UK to do so.

Further north, just off the A487 three miles (five km) past Machynlleth, lies an unusual microcosm of what some see as tomorrow's world: the Centre for Alternative Technology. Built on the foundations of an abandoned slate quarry, the Centre is both a museum and a real-life application of techniques which save resources and eliminate waste and pollution.

It runs not on mains electricity but on renewable energy sources: windmills, water turbines, solar energy and biofuels. Cottages are built of recycled materials and heated by solar power and wood stoves. Even human sewage, provided by visitors using the Centre's public lavatories, is recycled into organic fertiliser for the organic vegetable garden. Transport of people and materials is confined to non-pollutant bicycles, water turbine-charged electric vehicles and a hand-operated steel track site railway.

The Centre, open daily from 10 a.m. to 5 p.m., also offers short residential courses on alternative energy, low-cost building and organic gardening.

mines in South Wales, and even built Barry docks, through which he exported coal all over the world.

The **Gregynog Estate** includes a magnificent house with a vast library and a marvellous collection of paintings. A private press publishes highly prized limited editions, using traditional printing methods, rapidly being displaced elsewhere by computers and similar wizardry.

Llanidloes, a market town, located almost at Wales's geographic centre, is not to be missed. A timbered market hall in the middle of the town dates from the early 17th century and looks as though it has been built specially to frighten road users. Lorries have difficulty negotiating the historic chicane.

Unspoiled and unsophisticated, it is a friendly place, with a good selection of shops and a splendid wholefood café. A pleasant riverside walk along the banks of the Severn is recommended for those with a taste for strolling. For the more energetic, the surrounding hills are invitingly open.

The **Clywedog Valley** is within easy reach, offering angling and sailing on the waters trapped behind a massive man-made dam, one of the tallest in Britain. A mountain road winds waywardly back to Machynlleth, passing one of Wales's remotest pubs, the Star Inn, which lurks behind a copse. A curious feature of this remote area is the message painting on the road, with white-washed protestations of love vying with political slogans.

The next town of any significance on the way south is **Rhayader**. It guards the entrance to the Elan Valley where in the 19th century the canny burghers of Birmingham built reservoirs to supply water to the thirsty city. Pony trekkers and bird watchers, as well as tourists, can be spotted among the wooded slopes and deep ravines. Ornithologists have a special interest in the area for the red kite, once down to fewer than 50 breeding pairs, is making a comeback in this remote—and hence relatively safe—fastness. The dedicated members of the Royal Society for the Protection

Left, solar-powered house at the Centre for Alternative Technology. Below, feeding time at a Llanwrthwl farm.

of Birds guard the nesting sites with the vigilance of Horatio. Nest robbers are severely dealt with by the courts.

Rhayader is remembered by generations of war veterans as the base from which they sallied forth to fight imaginary foes in the inhospitable mountains. It is also recalled for the high quality of its fish and chips at the end of soggy days spent slogging through bog and bracken in preparation for real combat.

To the east, **St Hermon**—more a straggle of farms than a defined settlement—has the dubious distinction of being one of the coldest places in Britain; at least it always feels that way on a winter morning when the snow clouds come scudding in and the sheep huddle behind the windswept hedges.

The source of the **River Severn** is a bog up in the **Cambrian Mountains**, accessible from several sides for those prepared to trudge across the boggy approaches. **Plynlimon**, the highest peak, stands in the centre of a lofty plateau. The summit is topped with a sizeable cairn which is added to all the time by walkers following the tradition of tossing a stone, however small, onto the pile. This is remote territory, little visited outside summer, but home to hardy sheep farmers who claim it to be one of the most peaceful places on earth.

New lifestyles: The road east from Rhayader, the A44, heads towards the English border 30 miles (48 km) away. The countryside becomes progressively softer. Black and white timber-framed houses begin to appear. Place names become decidedly un-Welsh. Off the main road there are tiny valleys which seem to want to hide themselves away. But discovered they have been— by young people, seeking an alternative lifestyle. Some try to support themselves by subsistence farming; others engage in rural crafts, selling their carvings, weavings and embroideries at markets on both sides of the border.

Penybont, a handsome village, was once renowned for its market. Now it is notable for its trotting races, an activity seemingly as much appreciated by the horses as by the knowledgeable crowds.

Studying form at Machynlleth sheepdog trials.

Knighton, a thriving market town, is right on the border; its train station, in fact, is in England. Streets climb steeply to the inevitable clock tower, and the church, which has a remarkably squat tower, is particularly handsome. Many buildings are being renovated and some are being converted from warehouses into flats. In the 1990s, one suspects, Knighton will be a commuter town, daily despatching executives to their desks in the Midlands.

Ten miles (16 km) south, **Presteigne** also stands sentry on Offa's Dyke, the ancient earthwork separating Wales from England. The town is famous in Wales for its annual festival of music and theatre. Its leading hotel is a fine example of black-and-white architecture. Once an important coaching town between London and Aberystwyth, it was, until recently, the site of an assize court—a legal distinction withdrawn when in the 1970s Britain opted for a more centralised judicial system.

Much of the borderland is heavily forested—conifers, planted by both the Government's Forestry Commission and private interests concealing many unexpected streams, ponds, and tiny valleys which older folk remember as positive features of the landscape.

One of mid-Wales's gems, the spa town of **Llandrindod Wells**, has an air of Victorian splendour. Tall houses, once owned by the wealthy, mostly converted into flats, look down on broad streets. Above the town an artificial lake beckons strollers, anglers and standers-and-starers. The fish may be too domesticated for real sport—they tread water inshore, waiting to be fed by visitors. A short step away, the local golf course offers a hilly challenge to would-be Faldos and Lyles.

The pump room, down in a wooden glen across town, has been lovingly restored, reviving the atmosphere of 100 years ago when thousands came to Llandrindod Wells to take the waters. Health-giving water is still dispensed there. There's a choice of three—and plain ordinary tea or coffee.

A glass (or a cup) can be taken while

watching chess matches being fought out with Grand Master concentration on a giant board in the courtyard. Splendid public gardens abound and the bowling green, on which international tournaments are held, is the smoothest of the smooth.

Llandrindod's annual Victorian week, held in September, returns the town to the leisurely days of hansom cabs, top-hatted railway staff, frock coats and mutton-chop whiskers. The high point is a grand ball at which appropriate dress is obligatory. Local tailors and dressmakers are skilled at kitting out party-goers.

Ten miles (16 km) south of Llandrindod is another Wells: **Builth Wells**. The Royal Welsh Agricultural Society's showground, on which one of Britain's premier farming jamborees is staged, stands on one bank of the River Wye—the town on the other. The annual show is a fine shop window for rural Wales.

Prize bulls, home-made jam, equestrian displays, scores of firms selling everything from tractors to toffee—it's a free-ranging mixture jollied along with outdoor brass band and jazz concerts. Builth itself boasts a fine tree-lined walk along the River Wye and an enterprising arts centre, which stages films, plays and concerts.

Just south of Builth on the A483, a huge stone by the roadside marks the spot where Llewelyn the Last, a 13th-century prince, was slain by English soldiers. Occasionally bards in their enveloping robes gather there for memorial meetings, their Volvos and Fords cluttering the landscape.

Two other Wells come next: **Llangammarch**, where Victorians congregated to drink water containing barium (recommended for scrofulous cases according to hucksters of that era), and **Llanwrtyd**, a bigger place where the favoured flavour was sulphur. A large woollen factory is one of the town's contemporary attractions and pony trekking is a major activity.

There are unresolved arguments about Llanwrtyd's status—the weight of opinion believes it to be a small town rather than a large village. Whatever the definition, it is a pleasant place—and the jumping-off point for a spectacular journey over rugged mountains to Tregaron 15 miles (24 km) away.

The road discourages anyone in a hurry; the views are breathtaking, but drivers should concentrate on the way ahead. Some gradients are said to be one in four, but often seem steeper. The area is almost uninhabited. Sheep speckle the vast hillsides, an occasional shepherd can be seen, birds on the lookout for a meal circle warily. It is a slightly scary journey when the weather turns wet, as it can do unexpectedly.

Tregaron has the air of a frontier town. A workmanlike place, it considers sheep more important than tourists. The ruins of a Cistercian Abbey at **Strata Florida**, north of Tregaron, lie beside meadows carpeted with seasonal flowers. The abbey dates from the 12th century and was once a renowned centre of culture. Mid-Wales's 20th-century centre of things cultural and commercial, Aberystwyth, is 16 miles (25 km) distant across the mountains.

Left, traffic-jams of horse-drawn caravans have been known. Right, a male redstart.

BIRDWATCHERS' WALES

In summer, there are few lovelier places from which to watch birds than the hills of Wales. The rocky hillsides are vibrant yellow with gorse, the melancholy calls of curlew drift across sheep-nibbled valleys and the hanging oakwoods, stunted, gnarled and dripping with lichen, burst with birdsong.

As well as the resident woodland birds—woodpeckers, nuthatches, tits and treecreepers—these woods hold thousands of summer visitors from Africa. There are pied flycatchers, the males dapper individuals with contrasting black and white plumage. Wood warblers fill the woods with their shivering, vibrating song. Redstarts—the most colourful of all—flit between mossy branches, tails shimmering fiery-red in sun-dappled clearings. Tree pipits, garden warblers, siskins and crossbills are some of the other interesting woodland birds that can also be seen.

Above the woods, on the open hillside, quite different birds are found. Wheatears skim low across the rocky ground and sing their rattling song from lichen-studded rocks. Among heather and gorse, where knuckles of rock clench tightly and bulge from the rocky ground, ring ouzels, stonechats and whinchats nest. Higher still, rocky crags provide nesting ledges for ravens, buzzards and peregrines.

On vast windswept stretches of open moorland, curlew, redshank, golden plover, dunlin, snipe, lapwing, red grouse and black grouse nest on the ground among rough grass and heather. And on the lakes and reservoirs, goosanders dive deep for fish while common sandpipers forage at the water's edge.

In the skies above these hills, it seems that there is always at least one buzzard circling and mewing, spiralling upwards with its broad wings held stiffly in a shallow V. However, in mid-Wales, not all soaring birds of prey should be dismissed as buzzards; this is the heart of red kite country. The red kite, found nowhere else in the British Isles, can often be seen wheeling above the hillsides of central Wales, coaxing the gusty air currents with its long, crooked wings and rufous, forked tail.

Countless places offer good opportunities for birdwatchers. Some are reserves where entry is by permit only; others have completely open access. Among the more famous areas are the Gwenffrwd and nearby Dinas, Ynis Hir and Lake Vyrnwy (reserves owned by the Royal Society for the Protection of Birds), Cors Caron, near Tregaron (National Nature Reserve), the Elan Valley area, the Brecon Beacons and Snowdonia.

The hills of Wales are also home to two birds in decline. The merlin, a beautiful and dashing falcon, is fast disappearing as large expanses of heather-clad upland are "improved" for agriculture or converted into conifer plantations. So, too, the dipper, a dumpy, action-packed little bird of fast-flowing mountain streams is fighting a losing battle as the acid level of the water rises, killing the insect larvae upon which the dipper depends for food.

Countless places offer good opportunities to see these moorland and woodland birds amid lovely scenery. Some are reserves where entry is by permit only; others have completely open access. Among the more famous areas are the Gwenffrwd and nearby Dinas, Ynis Hir and Lake Vyrnwy (reserves owned by the Royal Society for the Protection of Birds), Cors Caron, near Tregaron (National Nature Reserve), the Elan Valley area, the Brecon Beacons and Snowdonia.

Around the Welsh coast are some of Europe's finest seabird breeding colonies. Among the most important are the islands of Grassholm, Skomer, Skokholm and Ramsey. Breeding birds include gannets, puffins, razorbills, guillemots, storm petrels, Manx shearwaters, kittiwakes, fulmars and choughs. In spring and autumn, rare migrants regularly turn up at some of these coastal sites but it is in winter that the coast of Wales holds the greatest number and variety of birds. In sheltered estuaries and harbours, from October, there are huge numbers of waders, many thousands of duck, including common scoters velvet scoters, eider and mergansers, divers, grebes, Greenland white-fronted geese and whooper swans. Birds of prey can also be seen hunting in winter: merlin, peregrine, hen harrier and short-eared owl.

SNOWDONIA

Half a million people walk on **Snowdon** every year—which means that one mountain has done more to attract visitors to Wales's greatest national park than any advertising agency could ever have managed.

There's more to **Snowdonia National Park**, however, than the mountainscape centred on Snowdon. At nearly 850 sq miles (330 sq km), it runs from near Conwy on the north coast all the way down to within a few hundred metres of Machynlleth in the south. On its western edge it is bordered by the A487 Porthmadog-Caernarvon road. Bala sits on its eastern boundary.

Although the highest point in Snowdonia is a modest 3,560 ft (1,085 metres) above sea level, you can still get the feeling of being very alone in the surrounding wild country. The area around **Llanberis** especially gives the impression of being in the midst of a major mountain range—even though the landscape suddenly becomes tame just a few miles down the road. Hilaire Belloc wrote: "There is no corner of Europe that I know which so moves me with the awe and majesty of great things as does this mass of the northern Welsh mountains."

Such sentiments are not exaggerations—although there's an accompanying assumption, unfortunately, that if you stray as far south as Harlech you have left the "good bits" of the national park behind. This isn't true.

As well as being out of doors, you're likely to be out of breath: walking, skiing, orienteering, pony trekking, fishing, canoeing, sailing and water skiing are all pursued with equal vigour. There are more than 1,500 recognised rock climbing routes in Snowdonia National Park. And each winter, more and more mountaineers visit Snowdonia to climb on snow and ice. Names like the **Carnedd Range**, the **Glyder Range** and the **Hebog Range** get climbers' adrenalin flowing.

Southern approach: There are hints of the landscape to come a few miles north of Machynlleth. As you approach the small community of **Corris**, steep pine-clad slopes suddenly and self-consciously mimic a sort of mock-Alpine landscape. No longer does the land undulate gently. Things have changed.

A few minutes beyond Corris, as you negotiate a bend in the road, the sudden bulk of **Cader Idris** looms into view. At 2,927 ft (892 metres), it's an imposing sight; you'd be excused for missing the small roadside sign which officially announces your arrival in Snowdonia National Park.

This mountain takes its name from a seventh-century warrior killed in a battle against the Saxons. Appropriately, this means that the Park begins and ends with mountains called after national heroes: the northern counterparts of Cader Idris are **Carnedd Dafydd** and **Carnedd Llewelyn**, each more than 3,400 ft (1,040 metres) high.

Despite the fact that Cader Idris doesn't make the 3,000-ft mark, its accessibility means that it comes a close

second to Snowdon in popularity. There are several routes up to **Pen-y-Gader**, the summit, from Dolgellau and Tal-y-Lyn lake. The two highest glacial lakes—**Llyn Cader** to the north and **Llyn Cau** to the south—are favourite destinations.

A very prominent geological feature in this vicinity is the **Bala Fault**. This 12-mile (19-km) crack in the earth's crust originates on the eastern side of Cader Idris and is responsible for the lakes at Tal-y-Lyn and Bala.

For railway enthusiasts, this quiet southwestern corner of Snowdonia has one claim to fame. The **Talyllyn Railway** has the distinction of being the first of the Welsh narrow-gauge railways to be saved. Like most of the "Great Little Trains," the Talyllyn line has its origins in the slate quarries of the 19th century. Slate mining opened up in 1847 near Abergynolwyn and packhorses were used to transport the slate to Aberdovey. In the 1860s, the narrow-gauge railway was built down to the connection with the mainline railway at Twyn.

When the line was re-opened by enthusiasts in 1951, it carried less than 16,000 passengers; today, during the summer months, it carries many times that number. Its story and that of other narrow-gauge railways, is told at a museum at **Wharf Station** in **Twyn**.

Nearby, in the small village of **Llanfihangel y Pennant**, can be traced the origins of an international religious organisation. In 1800, so the story goes, a girl called Mary Jones, having saved for six years, set out for the village of Bala to purchase a Welsh Bible from the minister, Thomas Charles. On her arrival, she found that the last Bible had been sold. Moved by the young girl's disappointment, the minister gave her his own. It was this incident which prompted Thomas Charles to found the internationally known British and Foreign Bible Society.

Since then, the Bible's fortunes have been assiduously promoted in the society's London offices. Mary Jones's Cottage has fared less well: it's a ruined building marked by a plain memorial.

Gold from the Clogan mine, near Dolgellau, is used to make wedding rings for the Royal family.

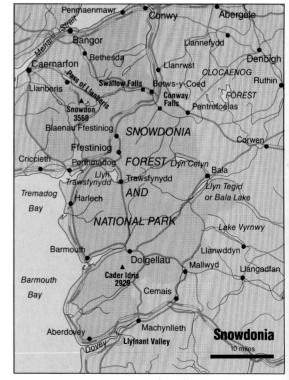

Snowdonia

10 miles

Little remains of **Castell y Bere**, a short distance away. It is one of the few castles in Wales which owes its origins to a Welsh rather than an English sovereign. While this site may not be worth visiting, it is at least worth pondering its location. The presence of a cormorant nesting ground at nearby **Craig yr Aderyn** (Bird Rock) suggests that the sea was at one time much nearer; it is possible that Castell y Bere was not far from a navigable marine channel.

The administrative centre of Merioneth has shifted since this shire was created in 1282. Harlech was the county town originally. Bala took over at one point in history. Today, the principal county functions are conducted in **Dolgellau**.

The town gets its neat and tidy look from the local stone which has been used to build the sturdy three and four-storey Victorian houses and in summer it attracts more than its fair share of visitors. But Dolgellau's bridge, dating largely from the 17th century, is no match for the traffic volume and the

town's quaint streets can turn into a slow-moving jam. A riverside woollen industry once thrived here, but today Dolgellau makes its living from farming and tourism.

To escape from the busy roads, you could try travelling up the Welsh coast by train. From Tywyn, the main British Rail line (**Cambrian Coast Line**) runs right next to the sea as far as Barmouth.

The old railway bridge which carries the line across the **Mawddach Estuary,** just out of Fairbourne Station, only adds to what Wordsworth called a "sublime sight" when he came here in 1824. Try catching the estuary at low tide at sunset and, as you gaze across the wide sand and mud flats to the Cader Idris Range rising in the background, you'll see what Wordsworth meant. If you want to spend more time walking by Mawddach Estuary, ask for directions to the **Panorama Walk**, which runs for more than three miles (five km) along the estuary.

Railway enthusiasts take a trip on the **Fairbourne to Barmouth Steam Rail-**

The Cambrian Coast Railway at Barmouth.

way—voted in 1988 best minimum gauge railway in Britain. Its northern terminus is at **Porth Penrhyn** at the entrance to the Mawddach Estuary.

Despite being one of the most scenic spots in Wales, the town of **Barmouth** lies just outside the official boundary of Snowdonia National Park. That doesn't stop people coming here in the summer months. Having grown up as a resort in the 19th century, this very English-looking seaside town (it does have a Welsh name: **Abermaw**) owes its livelihood to its wide sandy beaches.

Just 10 miles (16 km) further up the coast, **Harlech** is an altogether different coastal community. In the 13th century, it was dominated by Edward I's sturdy castle, built between 1283 and 1289. Seven centuries later it's the same story. This is still only a small community and **Harlech Castle** still dominates everything around it. The only thing that has changed is the proximity of the sea. At one time, Harlech stood at the water's edge; today a golf course occupies land from which the sea has retreated.

Harlech Castle played a key role in the events and incidents of the uprising led by Owain Glyndwr in the early 15th century. Harlech's capture, together with that of Aberystwyth Castle (both after long sieges) in the spring of 1404, gave Owain authority over central Wales. Harlech became the residence of his court and, with Machynlleth, one of two places to which he summoned his parliament. Five years later, Harlech was retaken by the English after a long siege and heavy bombardment.

Sixty years later Harlech played its part in the Wars of the Roses when it was held for the Lancastrians by Dafydd ap Ivan. Asked to surrender, he replied: "I have held a castle in France until every old woman in Wales heard of it, and I will hold a castle in Wales until every old woman in France hears of it!" It was this siege which is traditionally supposed to have given rise to the song *Men of Harlech*.

Western approach: A natural port of call for many travelling into north Wales is **Bala** and a particularly dra-

Harlech Castle.

matic approach road is the B4391. As the road leaves the village of **Llangynog**, it climbs until it runs precipitously along the steep-sided glacial valley of the Eirth.

Militir Gerig Pass marks the end of this ascent and leads out onto wide open moorland. From here on, the B4391 marks the westernmost boundary of Snowdonia National Park and, fittingly, there is usually a fine view most of the way down into Bala of the northern highlands of Snowdonia in the distance.

Dubbed the "Centre of the Welsh Lakes" by the Welsh Tourist Board, Bala certainly lives up to its name and attracts some energetic visitors. As Wales's largest natural sheet of water, **Bala Lake** is an established inland sailing centre, hosting major events in the yachting calendar. Bala is also a major windsurfing and canoeing centre.

The presence of so much water, however, has had its drawbacks. The **River Dee**, which flows out of Bala Lake to the sea at Chester, was prone to frequent flooding. In the 1960s exten-

sive works were undertaken to control the flow of the river water to the lower parts of the valley. This system was devised in conjunction with Llyn Celyn to the north of Bala, a man-made lake created by flooding the Tryweryn valley and submerging the village of Capel Celyn. Llyn Celyn supplies water to Liverpool; when necessary, the river can be diverted into Bala lake to reduce the volume of the Dee.

The dam at the southern end of Llyn Celyn has not dampened the ardour of canoeists. In 1981 the World Slalom and Wild Water Racing Championships were successfully staged on the River Tryweryn and it is now established as a leading European canoe slalom course. You can watch and/or participate by going to **Canolfan Tryweryn**—the National White Water Centre—just two miles (three km) out of Bala.

Water sports comprise the most modern chapter in Bala's history. Before the Industrial Revolution, the town was an important centre for the woollen industry, being the market outlet for

The mountain road from Lake Vyrnwy to Bala.

THE STORY OF SLATE

To learn about Wales's once great slate industry is to learn about Wales itself not just about its economy but also about its religion, its culture, politics and education.

In the heart of mountainous Gwynedd, which was the centre of the slate industry, the scars left by the quarries, mostly now silent, are the most significant feature of the landscape. But the great jagged tears in the blue-grey hills are more than just scars. The sunlight reflected from the blasted rock has a sombre beauty of its own, and the giant mounds of waste are the residue of a famous past.

At Llanberis, Bethesda and the Nantlle valley, in the old county of Caernarfon, and around Corris, Abergynolwyn and Blaenau Ffestiniog in the old county of Merioneth, 16,000 men once toiled, practising skills of a higher order in harsh and hazardous conditions. A practised quarryman (*chwarelwyr*) could tell how well a piece of rock would split even before it was blasted, and how many slates of what size he and his gang—often a family group—could extract from it. It was a skill on which the gang's livelihood depended.

The skill of slate-splitting is still demonstrated at Llechwedd, near Blaenau Ffestiniog, which was one of Wales's few slate mines. It is now a major tourist attraction; visitors are taken underground by rail to view the giant caverns where men clung to the rock walls like flies and worked by candlelight to prise out roofing tiles for the world.

Many of the little ports of Gwynedd—such as Porthmadog, Port Dinorwic and Aberdyfi—owed their origins to the industry which, in its heyday in the late 1800s, transported thousands of tons of slate on narrow-gauge railway lines for shipment to destinations all over the world.

The workmen's cabins on the quarry floor served not only as shelter but also as chapels and classrooms, where brighter youngsters could be started on a route that might eventually lead them to university. And in those same cabins there must have been sown the seeds of revolt which led to an heroic struggle that captured the attention of the whole of Britain. A dispute between the infant Quarrymen's Union and autocratic quarry-owners over minimum pay resulted, in 1900, in a lockout which lasted for three long and bitter years.

There was frequent violence, but the dispute ended in a crushing defeat for the workers. The hardships of those times have been told and retold in prose and poetry, not least by Kate Roberts, whose writing has been compared to that of Katherine Mansfield and Chekhov, and some of whose work has been translated into English.

The lockout was the beginning of the end for Welsh slate. By the time it finished, not only was there a depression in British building but new types of roofing material had arrived on the scene, as well as tiles from the United States. The resulting departure of whole quarrying families to South Wales to seek work in the coal mines is poignantly described by Alexander Cordell in *This Sweet and Bitter Earth*.

Though the culture of the quarrymen and their villages survives, most of the major quarries closed down after World War II. The names that litter the history books—Oakley, Dorothea and others—are no more.

The exception is Dinorwic, at Llanberis, no longer a quarry but the biggest pumped-storage electrical generation plant in Europe. Behind the grand quarry face, engineers constructed a cathedral-like cavern housing turbines powered by water cascading from an artificial hilltop lake to another on the old quarry floor.

A few small quarries are still working in Gwynedd but employ between them no more than 500 people who produce roofing slates by mechanical means. Small craft workshops fashion bits of slate into ornaments and nameplates to tempt tourists, who form the mainstay of the economy in the former quarrying districts.

The old *chwarelwyr*, who knew little of leisure and even less of affluence, might not altogether approve of that. But they would certainly look with favour on the success of the Llechwedd slate museum and other quarry tourist attractions. There, the story of their proud craft and the conditions under which they practised it are told to a generation that knows little of such things.

garments knitted in the area. It is said that George III wore Bala stockings when he suffered from rheumatism. The introduction of machine-made garments led to the decline of Welsh wool just as quickly here as in other parts of Wales.

Religion has also figured strongly in Bala. Thomas Charles, the minister who gave his own copy of the Welsh Bible to Mary Jones of Llanfihangel y Pennant, is commemorated by a statue in Tegid Street (just off the high street). Another local clergyman who made a name for himself was Michael Jones. In 1865, he took more than 150 people to Patagonia to set up a nonconformist colony on the Chabut river (now part of Argentina). The settlement survives to this day, its inhabitants speaking Welsh and Spanish.

If you prefer a more sedate prospect of Bala Lake than the one canoe and sailing enthusiasts enjoy, you can take the 25-minute train journey along Lake Bala's southern shore. The **Bala Lake Railway** is a "remnant" of the Great Western Railway standard-gauge line which opened in 1868 and ran from Ruabon (near Wrexham) to Barmouth, skirting Lake Bala. Closed down in 1965, the line was partially resurrected in 1971 in the form of a 23-inch narrow-gauge railway which by 1976 ran four-and-a-half miles (seven km) from Bala to Llanuwchllyn.

It's tempting to wonder how Victorian slate entrepreneurs would react to today's environmental lobbyists. Just a few miles from Llyn Celyn, **Blaenau Ffestiniog** is the kind of monumental blot on the landscape that is matched in Wales only by the slag heaps of the old mining communities in the south. The scenic route traced by the B4391 across open moorland provides little warning of the astonishing grey wasteland that lurks just a few miles away.

The effect is the same if you take the **Ffestiniog Railway** up from Porthmadog; picture-postcard views of the Vale of Ffestiniog quickly fade from mind when you arrive at the terminus. More than a century of slate mining has covered the surrounding slopes with thousands of tons of grey waste.

Blaenau Ffestiniog is not technically part of the Snowdonia National Park. It sits there in the middle of things rather like a Black Hole, the park boundary skirting cautiously around the town and its immediate vicinity.

Slate was to North Wales what coal was to the south. At its peak in 1898, the North Wales slate industry employed 16,766 men, of whom a quarter worked in the mines and quarries in and around these hills. Ffestiniog Parish had a population in 1801 of just 732—a figure which had risen to 11,433 in 1901. At the turn of the century the town of Blaenau Ffestiniog had 22 taverns (compared with six today) and no less than 37 places of worship. Other towns too—**Porthmadog** is one example—owe their origins entirely to slate.

Llechwedd Slate Caverns (a mile out of Blaenau Ffestiniog) have received more than three million visitors since 1972. You can choose one or two (or both) tours through the 19th-century mines. The Miners Underground Tram-

Left, slate workers. Below, tourism at Bala Lake creates jobs—for traffic wardens.

way enters the side of the mountain through an 1846 tunnel leading to a succession of enormous chambers.

The Deep Mine tour takes you underground via an inclined railway, after which you follow on foot a guided tour that unfolds the story of a typical slate miner. Back on the surface, there are craft demonstrations and a **Slate Heritage Centre**.

Directly opposite Lechwedd is **Gloddfa Ganol**, which bills itself as "The Largest Slate Mine In The World." The menu here is less imaginative than at Lechwedd but includes a museum of the slate industry as well as three cottages furnished in period style.

Just three miles (five km) further along the road towards Betws-y-Coed, **Dolwyddelan Castle** is said to be the birthplace of Llywelyn the Great. It is more likely, however, that he was born elsewhere in the area and that it was Llywelyn himself who built Dolwyddelan's first Keep in the early 1400s.

Northern Snowdonia: Draw a line from Betws-y-Coed to Beddgelert and you mark a rough-and-ready boundary for what many people call Snowdonia proper. In this northeastern corner of Snowdonia National Park there are 14 peaks over 3,000 ft (900 metres).

Betws-y-Coed is rather a tame first stop if you are approaching North Wales from the east. Sitting sensibly along the banks of the **Llugwy River**, it is deliberately quaint—the sombre grey Welsh buildings here enlivened by white ornate garden railings and pretty porches. You can hear the sound of the river in the picturesque high street—but only in the early morning or late evening when the busy traffic has receded.

Betws-y-Coed is Snowdonia at its most touristic. There are the usual craft shops selling pottery, brass, woollens and other souvenirs, but the commercialism is tempered by the all-pervasive "great outdoors". Next to the bridge over the Llugwy River is Climber and Rambler, a store that sells just about everything the aspiring trekker and mountaineer requires and reminds everybody who visits it that there is more to

The River Conwy at Betws-y-Coed.

life than being a day-tripper. The railway station has somehow managed to squeeze on to its platform the Station Wool Shop, the Alpine Coffee Shop, Dil's Diner and Cosyfeet Crafts. Nearby are the **Snowdonia Water Life Centre**, the **Motor Museum** and the **Railway Museum**.

The **Snowdonia National Park Information Centre** provides an excellent introduction to the National Park and has maps of walking routes waymarked by the Forestry Commission in the Gwydyr Forest woodlands surrounding Betws-y-Coed.

"Real" walkers, however, head for **Capel Curig**, a small village a few miles further along the A5. North Snowdonia is a centre for rock climbing and trekking and the National Centre for Mountain Activities provides training for these and a range of outdoor pursuits, including skiing, orienteering and canoeing.

Snowdon is not only the highest, but also the most distinctive of all the Welsh mountains. Along with one or two other peaks in the Glyder Range, it even boasts a plant species—the Mountain Spiderwort—which can be found nowhere else in the British Isles.

Although in height Snowdon beats Carnedd Llewelyn, to the northeast, by just 75 ft (23 metres), the unobscured outlook alone places it at the top of the league. One reason Snowdon is so popular is that you don't have to be one of the serious breed of climbers to reach its 3,560-ft (1,085-metre) summit.

Snowdon was popularised as a walking destination in the 19th century. In 1892, Britain's former prime minister William Gladstone—at the age of 83—opened one of the main ascents and walked as far as what is known as **Gladstone's Rock** where, in front of a crowd, he saw fit to make a speech on freedom for small states.

Decades of tramping later, Snowdon is suffering severe erosion and a programme of footpath restoration work, the Snowdon Management Scheme, is in progress.

If you want to take on Snowdon, you

On the summit of Tryfan.

have a choice of six main walking routes: **Llanberis Track**, **Miners' Track**, **Pyg Track**, **Snowdon Ranger Path**, **Watkin Path** and **Rhyd Ddu Path**. The Snowdonia National Park advises all walkers to wear appropriate footwear and clothing and to check the weather forecast before setting out.

If you prefer to ascend Snowdon less energetically, you can try **Snowdon Mountain Railway**, Britain's only public rack-and-pinion railway. On the day it opened, 6 April 1896, an accident occurred, closing it for a year while the rack system was modified. It has operated safely since then—the round trip from Llanberis to the Summit and back lasts two hours, including 30 minutes on the top to enjoy the view.

Llanberis sits at the very foot of Snowdon (though just outside the park). On a cold, wet day the Llanberis Pass can look distinctly forbidding; on a warm summer's day it is a magnet for the many tourists meandering through Snowdonia's glaciated landscape.

There are good reasons to come here

all the same. The **Welsh Slate Museum** occupies the workshops of the **Dinorwic Quarry**, which stopped work as recently as 1969. A short distance along the Caernarvon Road, the **Llanberis Lake Railway** runs along the north shore of Llyn Padarn. **Padarn Country Park** tempts visitors with lakeside picnics, woodland walks and craft shops.

Between Llyn Peris and Llyn Padarn, **Dolbadarn Castle** survives from the 13th century.

Before the wide estuary of the Glaslyn was reclaimed by the construction of the embankment at Porthmadog, boats could come as far inland as the bridge at **Pont Aberglaslyn**. Overland routes from here to Caernarvon and Bangor allowed ships to ply their trade without having to navigate around the Lleyn Peninsula. A short distance north of Pont Aberglaslyn, **Beddgelert** was able to operate as a medieval seaport.

A Celtic monastery, ranking second only to the one on Bardsey Island, was established here in the sixth century. This was superseded by an Augustinian priory, in the late 12th or early 13th century, of which Beddgelert's parish church is the sole surviving building. Beddgelert—which means "Grave of Gelert"—is as quiet as its name suggests. But the tiny village does a good trade in postcards which tell the story of the legendary wolfhound, mistakenly killed by Prince Llywelyn after it had saved his baby son from a wolf.

Beddgelert doesn't really need gimmicks like that to attract people. There's more than enough magnetism, wherever you go in Snowdonia National Park, to guarantee a continuing flow of visitors. But that carries danger. When the Queen Mother listened to Sir Clough Williams-Ellis outlining in 1943 his vision of a national park in Snowdonia, she is reported to have said: "It's fine your preparing this splendid countryside for the people, but are you doing anything about preparing the people to make proper use of it?" The damage caused by the half million people who trample the slopes of Snowdon each year suggests—maybe—that not enough has been done.

Left, Snowdon Mountain Railway. Right, Bala Lake barnyard.

THE LLEYN PENINSULA

Long before tourist boards perfected hyperbole, the **Lleyn Peninsula** was exercising its own subtle charisma on visitors. In the 1930s, one writer, reading up on Lleyn the night before setting out from Caernarvon, was informed that this "Cornish-like arm which thrusts itself westward below Anglesey, is one of the last provinces of Arcady." Aberdaron was "a remote wilderness 17 miles from a railway station" whose inhabitants "live in happy ignorance of this modern world."

Centuries earlier, Gerald of Wales, while on his celebrated tour of 1188, also succumbed to the peninsula's sense of mystery. He wrote of Bardsey Island: "Either because of its pure air, which comes across the sea from Ireland, or through some miracle occasioned by the merits of the holy men who live there, the island has this peculiarity, that no one dies there except in extreme old age, for disease is almost unheard of. In fact, no one dies there at all, unless he is very old indeed."

Just 16 miles (25 km) long and between three and 10 miles (five and 16 km) broad, the Lleyn Peninsula still trades today on its sense of being "different" to other parts of Wales. Shaped uncannily like Cornwall, it boasts of being the Land's End of Wales.

Star attractions: The coastline alone, designated in 1956 an Area of Outstanding Natural Beauty, attracts a good proportion of Lleyn's visitors. Inland too, however, there are small communities which do indeed have a sense of peace and remoteness that give the region its own character. And, depending on where you mark the geographic starting point of Lleyn, the peninsula boasts the star attractions of Caernarvon and Portmeirion.

Few who visit Wales for any length of time miss out **Caernarvon**. The Romans certainly didn't. The name Caer-yn-Arfon is ancient; there has been a castle on this spot for centuries.

The castle and town walls built by Edward I between 1285 and 1322 were successors to a strategic Roman fortification built in the vicinity more than 1,000 years earlier. Taking its name from the River Seiont, Segontium was garrisoned by the 20th Augustan Legion. Its foundations can still be seen.

The fortification that stands today, **Caernarvon Castle**, is part of the most ambitious military construction project of the Middle Ages—spawned by two 13th-century conflicts with Llywelyn ap Gruffydd, prince of the ancient kingdom of Gwynedd. Caernarvon is part of a network of fortifications that includes Conwy, Rhuddlan, Denbigh, Flint, Ruthin, Hope, Harlech, Aberystwyth and Builth.

How it all came about is explained in an excellent permanent exhibition within the castle walls. There's also a multi-slide show on the history of all the North Wales castles. In the northeast tower another display explains the long and complex history of the many Princes of Wales, the most famous of whom is the present Prince Charles. His

Preceding pages: the Lleyn Peninsula. Left, Caernarvon harbour. Right, Caernarvon Castle.

Investiture was held in Caernarvon Castle in 1969.

In the 19th century, when Caernarvon's military importance had long declined, it became a thriving port exporting slate to all parts of the world. Urbanisation accompanied this and the town's population more than doubled in the first half of the 19th century.

The castle and town were originally built as a single structure, though when the town walls ceased to serve their original purpose as a defence, the ditches were filled in to become roads and new archways were added in the 18th and 19th centuries to ease the flow of traffic. The town also began to spread along the banks of the Seiont and by the end of the 19th century it was three times as large outside its walls as within them.

Despite this, Caernarvon has kept its simple grid pattern of medieval streets and it is this feeling of compactness and enclosure that gives the old part of the town its character. Caernarvon's connections with the British Royal Family mean that this town looms much larger in the mind than in real life.

The Roman garrison at Segontium stood guard over what in medieval times came to be called Watling Street, a line of communication of great strategic importance. Evidence of an outlying fort, guarding the approaches to Watling Street, can be seen at Dinas Dinlle. But it's an uninspiring sight.

A more exciting spectacle is provided by a Snowdon Pleasure Flight. This is the brainchild of Snowdon Mountain Aviation, which operates a 1934 De Havilland Rapide out of Caernarvon airport, which adjoins the sandy Dinas Dinlle beach.

But if you don't have a head for heights and like your ancient sites to be more substantial, you should visit St Bueno's Church at **Clynnog Fawr**. This unspoiled 16th-century Tudor relic is dedicated to the second most important saint after St David. St Bueno is said to have visited Clynnog Fawr in A.D. 635.

The three-peaked mountain over-

Caernarvon Castle was begun 700 years ago.

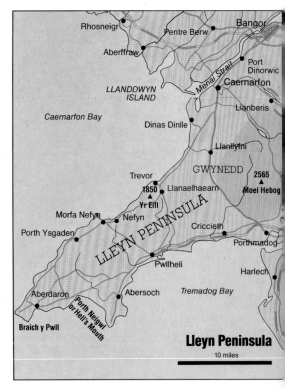

GWYNEDD

Lleyn Peninsula

10 miles

looking Trefor and Llanaelhaearn is called **Yr Eifl**, though this name has been anglicised into The Rivals. The easternmost "summit" (accessible from the B4417) is the site of Tre'r Ceiri, a hillfort-village thought to date from the second century.

Old wounds: While Lleyn is rightly praised for its scenery, the lure of slate in the 19th century has left its scars on the landscape around **Trefor**. The quarry here closed years ago and Trefor is a quiet, run-down backwater. The steep quarry tracks zig-zagging up the mountainside behind this village are still visible from a distance.

There are good beaches along this coast. The sand runs uninterrupted for more than a mile near **Morfa Nefyn**, culminating in the quiet village of **Porth Dinllaen**.

As the B4413 leads down to **Aberdaron** and a wide panorama of Cardigan Bay opens up, it's tempting to think of medieval pilgrims journeying to the Abbey of St Mary on Bardsey Island. For them, Aberdaron was the last stag-

ing post on their journey. They stayed in the small cottage of Y Gegin Fawr, today a cafe.

This building, however, isn't the only remnant from that time. The small church nearby dates from the 12th century. Aberdaron's hump-backed bridge is thought to be the original medieval structure.

Today **Bardsey Island** is a lonely nature reserve. Its Welsh name, Ynys Enlli, translates as Island of Currents or Island of Tides but its strong religious association has given it another name: the Island of 20,000 Saints. From the fifth century onwards, it was an important ecclesiastical centre and a major place of pilgrimage. It is said that two pilgrimages (some think three) to Bardsey could be reckoned as the equivalent of one to Rome.

The first monastery was founded here in A.D. 429. In the early part of the seventh century it was a refuge for monks fleeing the destruction of the monastery at Bangor-Is-Coed.

The sense of the ancient fades away in

Aberdaron: once a staging post for pilgrims.

Abersoch, a small and smart resort with a leisurely and distinctly nautical atmosphere. Boats are very much in evidence, whether bobbing around colourfully in the harbour or parked in private front gardens with For Sale signs prominently displayed. Add a sprinkling of sporty cars topped by surfboards, and on a good summer's day there's an air of ease and affluence that seems a thousand miles away in a small village like Trefor.

If this makes Abersoch a little too crowded in the summer, there are other diversions near here. Less than two miles (three km) away, the 15th-century church of **Llanengan** is thought to be the oldest in the Lleyn Peninsula. Midway between Aberdaron and Abersoch is **Plas yn Rhiw**, a 17th-century Welsh Manor House overlooking Porth Neigwl (Hell's Mouth).

You can take a boat to the **St Tudwal Islands**, east of Abersoch. Sir Clough Williams-Ellis purchased them in 1934 to save them from development.

A few miles along the coast is another

of Lleyn's resorts: **Pwllheli**. There is little of Aberdaron's neatness and tidiness here. Pwllheli may have a noble past, having received its first charter in 1355 from the Black Prince, but today it is the unashamed commercial centre of Lleyn's tourist trade. The old town of Pwllheli is overshadowed by the seaside suburbs of South Beach and West End offering pony rides, adventure playgrounds, crazy golf, ninepin bowling and a craft centre.

Premier citizen: It would be interesting to know what Lloyd George, one of Britain's most gifted prime ministers, would have made of Pwllheli's seaside-resort incarnation. He was brought up just a few miles from here along the coast at **Llanystumdwy** in a cottage called Highgate—he was born not in Wales but in Manchester—and was educated at the church school at the west end of the village. He died here, too, in 1945 in a house above the Criccieth road called Ty Newydd.

A writer visiting **Criccieth** in 1932, just two miles (three km) along the road, noted: "The ruined castle and Mr Lloyd George are the only 'sights' in Criccieth. Those who visit in the summer are not happy until they have seen Mr Lloyd George and even, perhaps, thrust their cameras through the gate."

That total of two sights in Criccieth is today reduced to just one. Lloyd George bought a house in 1939 back in Llanystumdwy. **Criccieth Castle**, built around 1230 but sacked and burnt in 1404 after it was captured by Owain Glendower, is still ample reason for stopping by.

On the south side of Lleyn, the staging point for the peninsula is **Porthmadog**. In the early years of the 19th century this small town didn't exist. It owes its origins to William Alexander Madocks, who in 1798 acquired land near here in order to reclaim it from the estuary. Following bigger projects, the community of Tremadog was born and by 1811 the great embankment of The Cob had been completed.

Meanwhile Madocks had been exploiting the infant slate industry in Snowdonia and there was soon a need

Abersoch beach: standing room only in summer.

for a port for shipping slate. Porthmadog was opened in 1824 and rapidly became a bustling port and an active shipbuilding centre, producing between 1891 and 1913 a total of 33 elegant top-sailed schooners known as Western Ocean Yachts. They sailed the world, carrying out slate and returning with every conceivable cargo.

Few go to Porthmadog today other than to board the Ffestiniog Railway. But if you want to see how the fledgling sea port looked in the 19th century, visit the **Maritime Museum** near the Porthmadog terminus of the railway. It's a downmarket exhibition area, to say the least, but it houses some fine enlarged photographs that capture a sea port in the making. The sight of so many tall ships moored in a harbour populated by today's modern but unremarkable small craft, is enough to recreate just that sense of romance, of time gone by, and conjure up the charisma that has attracted people to Lleyn since Gerald of Wales first related his modest knowledge of a modest peninsula in 1188.

Fantasy village: If you ever thought that warnings over architectural insensitivity and bad taste were a symptom of the 1980s, spend a day in **Portmeirion**. Sir Clough Williams-Ellis, its gifted creator, was hammering home the same message in the 1920s.

He built this quirky Italianate village as a "living protest in wood and stone against the havoc being wreaked by so-called development" and renamed his cherished site Portmeirion ("port" because of its natural harbour and "Merion" after the old county of Merioneth). Suspecting that most people did not readily appreciate architecture and landscape, he presented them with a "light opera approach".

Portmeirion grew gradually and not to a preconceived plan. Built round a central courtyard flanked by the Campanile and Dome, this colourful community of buildings was originally inspired by the Italian town of Portofino.

But Portmeirion amounts to more than the often-used label of "Italianate" implies. Knitted into its architectural

Left and right, Portmeirion Italianate village.

THE MAN WHO BUILT PORTMEIRION

For the hard-pressed tourist out "to do the sights" of North Wales, it would be easy to see the fantasy village of Portmeirion as nothing more than just another attraction—slightly eccentric perhaps, but undeniably beautiful. Of course, Portmeirion was conceived as a visual entertainment; but at its heart lies a much more serious purpose which the day-tripper can overlook.

In 1925, a successful architect, Sir Clough Williams-Ellis, bought the site—a headland near Porthmadog—with the intention of building a complete miniature seaside town. Sir Clough said that he had first had the dream of building "such a place to my own fancy" when he was just five years old and it never left him. "Throughout the years of my war service abroad [*in World War I*] I had to dream of something other than the horror, destruction and savagery—and what more different than to build with whatever serenity, kindness and loveliness one could contrive on some beautiful unknown site, yet to be miraculously discovered?"

Portmeirion was to be a demonstration that "one could develop even a very beautiful site without defiling it and indeed, given sufficient loving care, that one might even enhance what nature had provided as your background". His aim was to show that "architectural good manners can also mean good business".

Taking his inspiration from Portofino in Italy, and from buildings he had seen while travelling in Austria, Sir Clough gradually built up Portmeirion using odds and ends of houses rescued from demolition ("the home for fallen buildings," he called it). In its construction, he developed what he described as his "light opera approach to architecture" to produce what he hoped would be "beauty without solemnity".

An example of this rescue process is the village's town hall. After seeing by chance that a Flintshire mansion, Emral Hall, was to be demolished, he hastened to the house sale where he bought the Hall's ballroom ceiling for £13: there were no other bidders for "so awkward and speculative a lot". With considerable effort—and vast expense—the 17th-century ceiling was brought back to Portmeirion in 100 different pieces to form the centrepiece of the Hercules Hall.

Sir Clough was chairman of the first of Britain's New Towns, Stevenage, and his ideas on sympathetic town planning were a radical force. Without the economic depression of the 1930s and the coming of war in the 1940s, one wonders what Sir Clough might have achieved on a national scale.

Portmeirion remains, however, as a fitting tribute. When Sir Clough died in 1978 there were fears that the dream of Portmeirion might die with him. The buildings were mostly of lightweight construction, not designed to last. When the Portmeirion hotel was completely destroyed by fire in 1981, there seemed reason to believe that the whole village might also fade away.

Sir Clough conceived the hotel as the economic generator for the whole project: attracting holidaymakers who would contribute to the place's upkeep. He wrote: "I had little interest in any hotel, large or small, as such—but only as a nucleus feeder and *raison d'être* for the village." However, under the direction first of Sir Clough's daughter Susan Williams-Ellis, then of his grandson Robin Llywelyn, the Portmeirion Foundation has been engaged in a long-term project to ensure the village's preservation.

In 1988, the Portmeirion hotel reopened: it has been handsomely and elegantly restored, and should once again take its place as one of the leading hotels in the country.

Since its creation, the artistic imagination of Portmeirion has provided inspiration for others. Noel Coward wrote his play *Blithe Spirit* while on holiday in the village.

But, curiously, Portmeirion is best known as a backdrop to the cult TV series *The Prisoner* which was filmed there during the 1960s. The labyrinthine complexity of the *The Prisoner*'s surreal plot has defied most efforts at comprehension (efforts not helped by one British TV company which carelessly transmitted several episodes in the wrong order). It ought not to be surprising that Sir Clough found this rather baroque TV programme entirely to his taste.

fabric is a complicated thread that includes Georgian houses, a Jacobean country hall, ornate Victorian facades and even gilded Burmese dancers on Ionic columns. And you don't have to pencil Portmeirion in as a day-trip either because it even manages to incorporate a secluded hotel, recently refurbished following a fire in 1981.

Construction began in 1925, the Campanile being one of the first buildings to pop its head up above the surrounding countryside as a portent of things to come. A second phase of building began in 1954, following the end of post-war restrictions.

Building work often resembled the putting together of a jigsaw puzzle. Many of the features and structures had earlier lives and Portmeirion owes as much to one man's inspirations as it does to other men's demolitions. The Town Hall, one of the first buildings to go up, earned Sir Clough Williams-Ellis the reputation for having established what he called a "Home For Fallen Buildings".

Portmeirion is an architectural jigsaw puzzle.

This particular edifice was once Emral Hall, a Welsh mansion that Clough Williams-Ellis had visited in his youth and which boasted a unique barrel-vaulted 17th-century sculptured ceiling. In the 1920s, on reading in *Country Life* magazine of its impending demolition, Williams-Ellis bought up as much of it as he could afford and moved it to Portmeirion.

Few visitors are prepared for the elegant and compact dreamscape they find as they walk through Portmeirion's gates. As they explore the stairways and passageways, investigate the grottoes and courtyards, listen to the soothing sound of fountains, and ponder the "centuries-old" external paintwork, expressions of amazement are everywhere to be seen and are just as entertaining as the buildings themselves.

But it's surely what Sir Clough Williams-Ellis eccentrically intended: that even after his death, the thousands of visitors who pass through Portmeirion every year still hear his rallying cry to the cause of sympathetic architecture.

ANGLESEY

Some visitors to Wales don't bother with **Anglesey**. It's flat and featureless, they've heard. There's not much there, they've been told. And how can it compare to Snowdonia?

The Druids would certainly have welcomed such apathy. Nearly 2,000 years ago the Romans made every effort to cross the narrow stretch of water of the Menai Strait. Paulinus Seutonius, in the reign of Nero, arrived in A.D. 61. He sent his infantry across in boats and had his cavalry ford the shallows. On the far shore the Druids and the Britons were lined up ready for battle, but it was an easy victory for Rome.

Yet the lure of Anglesey didn't last long and Paulinus Seutonius cut short his stay on receiving news that Boadicea was marching on London. Some years later Agricola arrived. Not content to mess around in boats, he had trained a special corps in swimming and it is said they could fight in mid-stream. The Druids were beaten once more and this time nearly exterminated into the bargain.

Ancient remains are, however, not difficult to find. Anglesey was populated in prehistoric times and the legacy of ancient settlements and burial chambers is plain to see. One of the best-known ancient sites is **Bryn Celli Ddu**, a burial chamber in the southeast of the island which is thought to date from as far back as 2,000 B.C.

Facing the Menai Straits, the village of **Brynsiencyn** was once a Druid settlement. Close by is **Bodowyr**, another prominent burial chamber. There's a long list of similar sites scattered around the island.

Since the 19th century, Anglesey has received far more welcome visitors than the Romans. It was Telford who first bridged the Menai Strait when his Menai Suspension Bridge was completed in 1826. Stephenson increased the flow of traffic with his railway bridge in 1850. The original Britannia Bridge was originally built by

Stephenson too, being completed in 1850, but was damaged by fire in 1970 and replaced by a new structure.

Despite decades of being connected to the mainland of Wales, many visitors to Anglesey are just passing through—the Holyhead ferry service to Ireland ensures that. Anglesey has never escaped the charge that it doesn't have much going for it.

This was certainly so in the time of Gerald of Wales in the 12th century, whose verdict on this island was: "an arid stony land, rough and unattractive in appearance." However he was charitable enough to recognise its fertility, telling his readers that Anglesey was known as the "Mother of Wales" because: "when crops have failed in all other regions, this island, from the richness of its soil and its abundant produce, has been able to supply all Wales."

Appropriately enough, this northernmost point of Wales can also claim to be fertile ground for the Welsh language. An English travel writer visiting in the 1930s said: "Anglesey is entirely Welsh-speaking. In the remote parts of the island there are still old people who could not carry on a conversation in English."

Ironically, Anglesey's undulating low hills make this island seem extremely un-Welsh. **Beaumaris**, especially, is regarded by the real Welshman as an English town. Beaumaris Castle was the last of Edward I's Welsh fortifications but today it is often the first place visited by tourists. Beau Marais (Beautiful Marsh) was named after a nearby marsh that was drained by the castle's moats.

The town grew up around the castle, which, though declared defensible in 1298, was never finished. These days it is a yachting resort and the short main thoroughfare of Castle Street is a tidy line of pastel-coloured Regency and Victorian houses which give the street an upmarket look.

The town boasts much older buildings. Tudor Rose, one of the oldest houses in Britain, is said to have been

Preceding pages: Menai Suspension Bridge; Beaumaris Castle, Anglesey. Below, the Marquis of Anglesey.

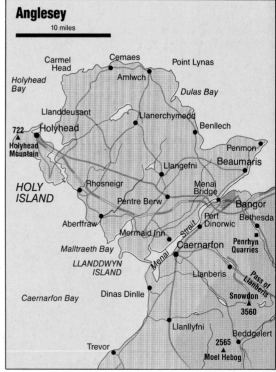

Anglesey

10 miles

Carmel Head
Cemaes
Point Lynas
Holyhead Bay
Amlwch
Dulas Bay
Llanddeusant
Llanerchymedd
722 Holyhead
Benllech
Holyhead Mountain
Penmon
Llangefni
Beaumaris
HOLY ISLAND
Rhosneigr
Menai Bridge
Pentre Berw
Bangor
Aberffraw
Port Dinorwic
Bethesda
Mermaid Inn
Caernarfon
Penrhyn Quarries
Malltraeth Bay
LLANDDWYN ISLAND
Menai Strait
Caernarfon Bay
Dinas Dinlle
Llanberis
Pass of Llanberis
Snowdon
3560
Llanllyfni
Beddgelert
2565
Trevor
Moel Hebog

built around 1400. It was restored by Hendrik Lek, an artist who died in 1985. His son, Karel Lek, has inherited both the house and the talent of his father and exhibits oil paintings, water colours, drawings and engravings.

Nearby are three more historic buildings: the **George and Dragon Hotel**, dating from 1410; the **Court House**, built in 1614 and unchanged since the 18th century; and the **town jail**, a 19th-century building which provides insights into past punishments.

The Beaumaris **Museum of Childhood**, which lies on the other side of the road from Tudor Rose, has assembled a collection of antique toys and games that includes oddities such as Polyphons, Zoetropes and Praxinoscopes. This studious museum might have little to tell you about Anglesey but it certainly adds to the charm and interest of Beaumaris.

Dominated by such a venerable castle, it's not surprising that Beaumaris is big on history. A much-

advertised attraction is the Timelock, an audio-visual show "hosted" by the Roman historian Tacitus. Slide projectors rush you through the centuries of Anglesey's "exciting and sometimes cruel history". This is family entertainment Anglesey-style, with the emphasis firmly on entertainment.

Rich veins: Once you've wandered around Beaumaris, keep wandering. Your reward will be to stumble across quiet coves like **Red Wharf Bay** or **Benllech**, which are especially fine at low tide.

Amlwch exercised its own attraction in the 18th century, but not through any scenic virtues. While the Romans had worked copper mines near here, it was in 1768 that some especially rich veins of copper ore were tapped. Amlwch became the most populated part of the island and a port was built here in 1793. The source of the ore, Parys Mountain, was eventually exhausted and this small community is overlooked by its scarred remains.

Further along the northern coast at

Sailing in the Menai Straits.

Cemaes Bay, secrecy was an ingredient for success for smugglers who used its secluded beaches. The secrets today take the form of Wylfa nuclear power station which, in a desire to keep its public relations sweet, invites the public on educational tours of the plant.

For visitors to Wales, **Holyhead** is the end of the road; for those bound for Ireland, it is just the beginning. There are records of passenger boats between Anglesey and Ireland as far back as 1573. In 1801, Holyhead became the official crossing point and the opening of the road bridge (1826) and the railway bridge (1850) at Menai ensured the London-to-Ireland route's future.

Ireland became much more accessible in 1965 when the first car ferry service was introduced. After decades of so much passing through, Holyhead these days offers a generally unattractive townscape of dockyard gantries, railway sidings and run-down back streets.

The only interesting remnant of the past is the **parish church of St Cybi**.

The churchyard takes the form of rectangular walls which are part of a Roman fort built in the third or fourth century. In the sixth century St Cybi set up his oratory within the protection offered by these Roman walls. Today's church dates from between the 15th and 17th centuries.

In the summer, those visitors who are not just passing through make their way up **Holyhead Mountain**, which at more than 700 ft (210 metres) can provide fine views of Snowdonia, Ireland and even the Isle of Man. These slopes were a natural choice for ancient inhabitants and hillfort ramparts are still visible. The signposts to the Irishmen's Huts refer to the remains of a large Celtic settlement that thrived between the second and fourth centuries.

Tongue-twister: The village with the world's second longest name (a New Zealand hamlet is even more prolix) is famous only for having 58 letters. In 1988, Gwynnedd County Council, conscious of how long the name took to type, grasped the nettle and shortened

The railway station with the longest name in the world.

218

Llanfairpwllgwyngyllgogerychwyrndrobwllllantysiliogogogoch on its documents and maps to a more manageable Llanfair Pwllgwyngell. "It would be impractical to use the full name on road signs," argued the council chairman. "Each sign would need its own bypass." The full name does have a meaning, translating as "St Mary's Church in the hollow of white hazel near the rushing whirlpool and Tysilio of the Red Cave's Church".

Sign-writers at least have earned a good living from the name. It is writ large—more than once—on James Pringle's woollen store which dominates the unassuming railway station (on the line between Bangor and Holyhead). The station itself sports a nameboard 15 ft (4.5 metres) long, supported by five steel posts. The name is repeated on the wall of the Penrhos Arms and, just a few yards up the road, the Ty Gwyn Hotel.

Plas Newydd, as well as having a much more manageable name, has much more to offer. Administered by the National Trust, this 18th-century mansion has opulent interiors, fine furniture and paintings, and stately gardens. Plas Newydd's Rex Whistler Exhibition contains the artist's largest wall painting.

The Cavalry Museum devotes one room to the First Marquess of Anglesey, an officer whose stoicism has gone down in history. Losing his leg while on horseback at the Battle of Waterloo, so the story goes, the Marquess (at that time he was the Second Lord Uxbridge) announced solemnly to Wellington: "By God, sir, I've lost my leg!" Back came the stiff-upper-lip reply: "By God, sir, so you have!"

In **Brynsiencyn**, Anglesey Sea Zoo, a fish farm that breeds trout, oysters and lobsters, bills itself as the island's top attraction. Undeniably, it receives a rush of visitors. Its aquaria display a variety of species—including conger eels, sea rays and dogfish—all of which are native to Anglesey's waters. The adjacent Sea Catch & Carry sells fresh seafood whose reputation has travelled.

South Stack Light, Holyhead.

NORTH COAST RESORTS

The 30-mile strip from Bangor to Prestatyn is no riviera—the best Welsh beaches are in the west. In summer, though, it manages to draw enough of the populations of Liverpool, Chester and the Midlands to create a summer-long traffic jam. Wider roads were a long time coming and, when completed, are more likely to add to the congestion rather than dilute it.

This small stretch of coast has been working hard to attract visitors since Victorian times, and the emphasis has always been on family holidays. The British seaside town comes brashly into its own on the north Wales coast, with Colwyn Bay, Llandudno, Rhyl and Prestatyn each trying to forge its own inimitable version of what a day by the sea should offer.

The fare that they dish up is surprisingly varied, with Prestatyn putting its money on Edwardian seaside elegance, while Rhyl goes for the Coney Island approach—complete with roller coaster. On a warm summer's day in any of these towns, amid the ice-cream, the candy floss, the weary children, and the fish and chips, it's difficult to believe that just a few miles away there are agile and adventurous souls busily clambering around Snowdonia.

Sober start: If you are setting off from **Bangor**, however, you should be prepared for something much more sober. This city, a place of learning and an ancient religious centre, has a serious atmosphere that won't appeal to those solely in search of seaside amusement. The word Bangor has its origins in a word meaning great circle or wattle enclosure—a reference perhaps to the wattle fence which surrounded the monastic community founded here in the sixth century by St Deiniol. The cathedral, originally constructed in the early 12th century, received its most damaging assault at the hands of Owain Glyndwr in 1402 and lay in ruins until 1496 when repair work began. Today's building dates from a restoration by Gilbert Scott begun in 1866.

Bangor is best known for its university; but it's not the kind of ancient institution found in England, Scotland or Ireland. Even though the idea of a Welsh university was one of Owain Glyndwr's dreams in the Middle Ages—letters in which he wrote about this are preserved in archives in Paris— it wasn't until five centuries later that it became a reality.

Bangor College was established in 1883—although at that time, along with colleges at Aberystwyth and Cardiff, it was not allowed to confer degrees. In 1893 all three colleges were incorporated as the University of Wales, and were later joined by colleges in Swansea and Lampeter.

Bangor was by that time well established on the north Welsh map. In the early 19th century the Penrhyn slate quarries inland at Bethseda were producing riches for Liverpool entrepreneur Richard Pennant, and the port of **Penrhyn**, to the east of Bangor,

developed quickly. The construction from 1815 of Telford's road (today the A5) marked Bangor's coming of age. One good place to investigate all this is the **Museum of Welsh Antiquities**. Exhibits help build up a picture from prehistoric times, through the Roman era and on into the Middle Ages and Victorian times. There's an art gallery downstairs.

Some of the profits from the Penrhyn slate quarries went into turning a neo-Gothic house just outside Bangor into **Penrhyn Castle**, a vast mansion said to represent "the masterpiece of the Norman Revival in Britain."

The man behind this lavish residence was George Pennant (a cousin of Richard Pennant's sister), who in 1820 commissioned an architect called Thomas Hopper. Penrhyn Castle was described in 1844, shortly after the project had been completed as "stately, massive and stupendous." Those words barely do justice to the intricate interior woodwork and masonry let alone the furniture and decor.

Conwy owes much to successful engineering. In 1824 Thomas Telford displayed architectural good manners when he started work on the elegant suspension bridge across the Conwy Estuary. Its towers match those of **Conwy Castle**, itself a fine piece of medieval engineering, so that the two structures not only blend together but even enhance each other. Local residents hope that this century's contribution—the road tunnel under the Conwy Estuary—will be just as beneficial to the town.

The much celebrated Conwy Castle is another link in the network of fortifications erected by Edward 1. Conwy's town walls, nearly a mile long and with 22 towers and three original gateways, are among the most complete anywhere in Europe. The town itself, however, was for a long time less important than the strategic defences: records from the late 16th century show that there were just 60 houses here.

The coming of the railway helped the town expand and gave rise to the need

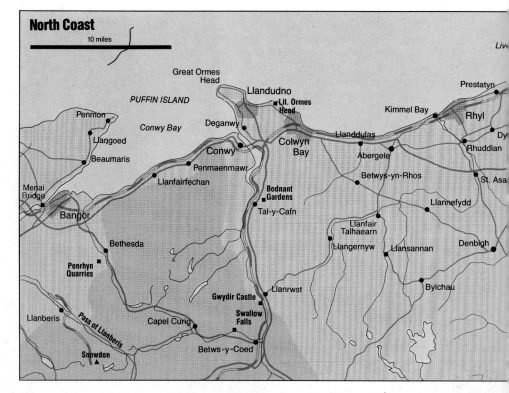

for a second bridge across the Conwy Estuary—this one built by Robert Stephenson in the mid-19th century.

Conwy has retained much evidence of its past. One of the 60 Elizabethan residences is **Plas Mawr**, built between 1577 and 1580 and open to the public. Remains of the Cistercian abbey of Aberconwy, built between 1172 and 1187, have been incorporated into **St Mary's Church** nearby. A gravestone on the floor of St Mary's states that Nicholas Hookes died in 1639, the 41st child of William Hookes and himself the father of 27 children. **Abercony House** is a stone and timber building that some claim is the oldest house in Wales. **Ty Bach**, tucked away by the quay, has been dubbed the smallest house in Britain.

You'll see more than one advertisement in Conwy or Llandudno for a bus tour of the **Vale of Conwy**, billed as "a Swiss Alpine scenery tour." Alpine the vale is not, though the choice of words says much about how North Wales would like it to be perceived.

Edward I moved the Cistercian monks of Conwy into the Vale of Conwy at Maenan, north of Llanrwst, in 1283, where they remained until Henry VIII's dissolution of the monasteries in 1536.

The Conwy River's source is just a few miles northeast of Blaenau Ffestiniog and its swift run down to the sea has carved out a formidable tourist route: the B5106 runs for 14 miles (22 km) along its west side and the A470 returns you to the coast via its eastern flank. Excursion coaches busily lap each other between Conwy and Llanrwst all summer long.

Change of scenery: The Vale of Conwy more or less marks the eastern border of Snowdonia National Park, as if to point out that the really rugged territory is not to be found here. The Vale is in fact rather neat and tidy.

At **Bodnant Garden**, just before the village of Tal-y-cafn, the landscape has actually been carefully manicured. Laid out in the late 19th century by Lancashire industrialist Henry Pochin and then added to by later members of

Conwy Castle and town.

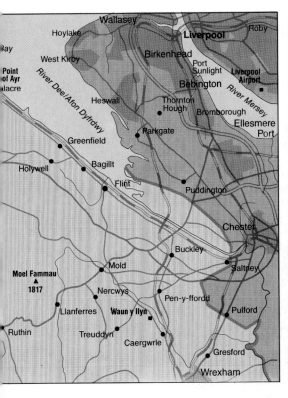

his family, this is a celebrated piece of landscape gardening that makes imaginative use of conifers, rhododendrons, yews, roses, water lilies and many rare varieties besides. This 70-acre (28-hectare) garden is one of the best in Britain.

At the top of the Vale of Conwy, **Llanrwst** has actually declined rather than grown in the past 100 years. In the middle of the last century it was home to twice the population of today, an industrious town that made its living from wool, malting and tanning. An early resident was William Salesbury, who translated the New Testament into Welsh in the 16th century.

The Wynne family, one of the most important in the Vale, has left its mark in the form of **Gwydir Castle**, over on the west side of the river. This Tudor mansion was burnt out in the 1920s but was restored by new owners after World War II. The Wynnes built two impressive chapels that still stand. In Llanrwst, **Gwydir Chapel**, dating from 1633, may have been designed by Inigo Jones. Near Gywdir Castle, **Gwydir Uchaf Chapel**, dating from 1673, retains an elaborate 17th-century painted ceiling.

Jewel in the crown: In anybody's books, things begin to look increasingly worn out the further east you go. Not so, however, at **Llandudno**, the principality's largest resort. For more than 100 years it has been the jewel in the north Wales crown.

On a sunny day, the Victorian houses lining the bay on the North Shore are a picture of gleaming white symmetry. For once, the tourist office brochure has got it right. Llandudno can indeed "lay strong claims to be the most beautifully situated resort in the whole of the British Isles."

Lying on a wide gently curving bay between the headlands of **Great Orme** and **Little Orme**, in the mid-19th century Llandudno was little more than a collection of fishermen's cottages. It was the Mostyn family that stood behind and helped finance the town's growth. Mostyn Street, Mostyn Avenue

Llandudno's Victorian look lingers on.

and Mostyn Broadway are the most visible legacy of the town's benefactors. The family also gave its name to the **Mostyn Art Gallery**, North Wales's major public art gallery.

A century of growth has allowed Llandudno to dominate the headland; with Great Orme separating the wide beaches of the North Shore and the quieter West Shore. Llandudno's earliest known visitor, St Tudno, made Great Orme his home in the sixth century. Today, the ancient Celtic church of **St Tudno's**, from whom the town takes its name, has become one of Llandudno's great attractions and a cable lift transports visitors to the top for open-air services.

The **North Shore** offers just about everything the seaside has ever dreamed up. Its pier, all 2,296 ft (700 metres) of it, was said by Sir John Betjeman to be one of the finest examples of a Victorian pier in Britain. The fact that the pier is now home, in the summer months, to an amusement arcade, candy floss, an aquarium,

Professor Peabody's Play Palace, advertisements for boat rides and coach rides and still more entertainments for young and old has not detracted from it. Down on the beach there are donkey rides and a Punch and Judy show.

On the **West Shore** is a memorial, portraying Lewis Carroll's White Rabbit, unveiled by Lloyd George in 1933. During frequent stays in Llandudno, the author would walk with Alice Liddell, the little daughter of his friend Dean Liddell. She is said to have been the inspiration for *Alice In Wonderland*.

The growth of Colwyn Bay as a resort was more recent than that of Llandudno and can hardly hope to compete. In the 1940s it was just a village. Today the four-mile (six-km) stretch between Llandrillo yn Rhos, Rhos-on-Sea and Old Colwyn is a continuous built-up area liberally sprinkled with guesthouses. The promenade is around three miles long and offers, among much else, bowls and tennis.

Overlooking the bay is the **Welsh**

Gardener at Bodysgallen Hall, Llandudno.

Mountain Zoo. Best known for its birds of prey displays, it's an enterprising collection that aims to show its animals in natural surroundings. The semi-circle of hills to the south and west of the town protect it from rain and wind. Local people claim that Colwyn Bay has its own "local climate"—one reason, perhaps, why this resort continues to be so popular, even in winter.

Just two miles inland at **Llanelian-yn-Rhos** a story is told of the potent cursing well of St Elian. The eponymous sixth-century saint is said to have prayed for water here—at which point a well sprang below his feet. The saint asked God to grant the wishes of all who came to it with faith in their hearts. In time, however, the wishing well was looked upon as a wicked well. A woman called Sarah Hughes is said to have earned £300 a year both from people who came to curse their enemies and from the cursed ones who paid to have the spells removed.

Another famous well-keeper was John Evans who in the 19th century turned the well into a good business. Whenever somebody came to curse another, Evans would write the name of the enemy on a piece of paper, put it in a piece of lead and tie it to a slate with the initials of the curser and throw the whole package into the well, reciting the curse as he did so. His business plan depended on telling the person who had been cursed, who would come to pay for its removal. The well-keeper would then read out Psalms and Scriptures, retrieve the leaden box and place the curse in the hands of the person at whom it was aimed. The well is said to have been eventually drained by a local clergyman who wanted to dissuade his flock from casting spells on each other.

Rhyl is surely a lesson in how not to develop a seaside resort. As one drives in from the west, the first sight to catch the eye is the huge amusement park, dominated by its roller-coaster and the "Crazy Octopus". From then on, however, Rhyl seems content to be average. Its long promenade is

Family at leisure on Black Rock sands.

uninviting and gimmicky, relying on attractions like the Arnold Palmer Putting Course—a quite ordinary crazy golf course.

The amusement park and extensive beaches are about the only thing that Llandudno, Colwyn Bay and Conwy can't compete with. Its only other selling point is the Sun Centre at the eastern end of the promenade, a kind of indoor beach resort that combines under one roof a swimming pool, surfing pool, monorail, sunbeds, a 200-ft (60-metre) water slide and Tropical Bar.

Old battles: A few miles inland the story is a little different. **Rhuddlan Castle** is one of the most important locations in the battle for Welsh independence; it was here in 1284 that Edward I announced the formation of the government of the conquered principality. Rhuddlan Castle was the second to be erected as part of Edward's strategic chain. The River Clwyd was diverted so that the castle could be supplied by sea and Rhuddlan was a port right up until a century ago.

Just three miles (five km) south of Rhuddlan is **St Asaph Cathedral**, a building that makes this small community a city. Both city and cathedral are Britain's smallest.

Prestatyn is another resort that leaves a lot to be desired, and the building of a long concrete promenade hasn't done much for it. The town was once the site of a castle held by the Prince of Powys. Following three major victories as they repelled three invasion attempts by Henry II in the 12th century, Welsh leaders missed a unique chance to unite against the English.

History fades, however, as you follow the coast road east. The caravan parks around Rhyl and Prestatyn soon give way to the dockyard cranes and factories of the approaching industrial landscape. This was the way Henry II came in his first attempt to invade Wales. It's the way many visitors come now as they are siphoned on to the A548 and A55 from Lancashire, Cheshire and the Midlands. The English are more welcome these days.

The boating lake at Colwyn Bay.

THE NORTHEAST

This corner of Wales, mainly the county of **Clwyd**, is a strange hybrid. In the remote, thinly populated moors and mountains to the west, you'll find the small, grey-stoned villages typical of traditional Wales. In parts of the east, where England meets Wales, the flat landscape is filled with busy roads, bleak industrial estates and anonymous, this-could-be-anywhere towns. So potent are the cross-border influences that speakers in parts of Clwyd can sound as if they come from Liverpool.

Northeast Wales is a cultural amalgam. There's the mainstream traditional Wales of the rural hill communities; and, in complete contrast, there are the industrial and urban incursions into the flatlands around the Dee Estuary and Wrexham which have brought with them an anglicised culture.

Wrexham, the biggest town in these parts, is a rather plain place. Its main source of interest is the **Church of St Giles**, with its 16th-century tower ("Wrexham Steeple", one of the so-called Seven Wonders of Wales). East-coast Americans make a pilgrimage to this spot, for the church contains the tomb of Elihu Yale, the benefactor of the eponymous American university, who died here in 1721. Look out for his long epitaph, part of which reads:

Born in America, in Europe bred,
In Africa travell'd, and in Asia wed,
Where long he liv'd and thriv'd;
at London dead.

Don't miss **Erddig**, on the outskirts of Wrexham. This 17th-century house, in the care of the National Trust, is not the usual opulent country mansion. Its individuality comes from the vivid insight it gives into "upstairs, downstairs" life in a country house of old. The well-preserved kitchen, laundry, bakehouse and smithy are as important as its decorative finery and period furniture.

Erddig's well-rounded character is partly a reflection of the benevolent attitude the Yorke family, who lived here from 1773 to 1973, had to their staff. The relationship, by all accounts, was an untypically happy and equitable one, the Yorkes even decorating their walls with specially commissioned portraits of their servants.

The landscape around Wrexham bears plentiful evidence of past and present industrial activity. More recently, this has been a coalmining area, though iron was the speciality in early industrial times. At **Bersham**, just west of Erddig, ironmaking took place from 1670, reaching its peak in the 1780s. Those interested in industrial archaeology can seek out the remnants of this pioneering enterprise—parts of the old furnace, workers' cottages and so on—in and around Bersham.

Mold, a small town to the north of Wrexham, is noteworthy as the home of Theatre Clwyd, a large, modern arts complex. At **Flint**, on the Dee Estuary, you'll have to search for the town's important historical landmark. This was the home of the first castle built—

Preceding pages: Valle Crucis Abbey. Left, Ruthin Castle, now a luxury hotel. Right, Erddig.

7—by the all-conquering King ...ard I in his campaign to subdue Wales. Edward's sturdy fortress—the harbinger of even greater castles constructed at Caernarfon, Conwy, Harlech and Beaumaris—is hidden away behind the very ordinary facades of the town centre.

Indecent exposure: Just up the coast at Holywell, there's a cluster of places worth mentioning. The little town has yet another of those Seven Wonders: the **holy well of St Winifride**, dating from the seventh century and possibly the most famous healing well in Britain. The much-travelled Dr Johnson was offended when he visited this "Lourdes of Wales" in 1774; he noted disapprovingly that "the bath is completely and indecently open: a woman bathed while we all looked on."

The **Greenfield Valley Heritage Park**, leading down to the coast, has been developed on a site where textiles, copper and brass were once produced. At the estuary end of the park is **Basingwerk Abbey**, a monastic ruin founded in 1131.

Holywell's most unusual place of interest is an underground military museum, the **Grange Cavern Museum** which contains a veritable invasion force of military vehicles, all housed in a chilly two-acre (one-hectare) cave scooped out of the hillside.

The **Clwydian Hills**, which run northwest to southeast above the Vale of Clwyd, are the first natural upland barrier between England and Wales. These hummocky, rounded hills—an officially designated "Area of Outstanding Natural Beauty"—rise to 1,821 ft (554 metres) at **Moel Famau**.

From the spectacular little mountain road that cuts through the hills between Ruthin and Mold (the main road, the A494, takes a southern loop through lower terrain), a number of paths lead to this windy summit, which is crowned by the ruins of the Jubilee Tower, built in Egyptian style in 1810 to commemorate the Jubilee of King George III. Go to the top to wonder not

Ruthin, a pretty market town.

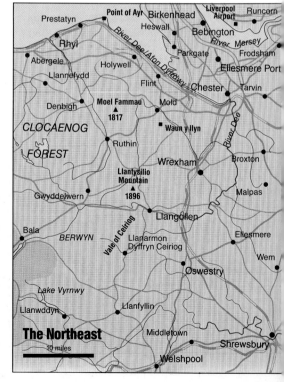

The Northeast

10 miles

only at the views (you'll see Snowdonia and Liverpool on a clear day) but also at the profligate enthusiasm, so typical of 19th-century Britain, which inspired the construction of a 115-ft (35-metre) tower on top of a weather-lashed Welsh hill.

Spread out beneath Moel Famau is the fertile Vale of Clwyd, a rich farming area. **Ruthin** is a pretty market town, "unique in north Wales for its number of timber-framed buildings" according to the Council for British Archaeology. Its architecture—a delightful black-and-white half-timbered jumble—is indeed irresistible, which is more than can be said for the so-called "medieval banquets" held at the Ruthin Castle Hotel (an otherwise commendable establishment which incorporates into its fabric parts of the town's original medieval castle).

Denbigh, further up the vale, is another fine medieval town. It has grown up around its hilltop castle—ruined, but with a most impressive Great Gatehouse—and boasts a well-preserved, and almost complete, circuit of town walls.

When you leave the fertile, sheltered pastures of the Vale of Clwyd and head westwards, you are entering the *real* Wales, the harsh, marginal uplands of economic value only to the hill-sheep farmer and—more recently—the forester. The empty, exposed moorlands between the vales of Clwyd and Conwy are bleakly beautiful, resembling a Scottish moor when the purple heather is out.

In this century, man has radically altered the southern part of this lonely plateau. **Llyn Brenig** is a massive, man-made reservoir, completed in 1976 to accompany the smaller Llyn Alwen, built in the early 1900s. Casting aside, for a moment, the concerns often expressed by conservationists, the construction of the reservoir has at least given the public access to this previously untravelled upland. Overlooking the dam there's an excellent visitor centre which explains the local history and ecology, and also

Waitresses burst into song at Ruthin Castle's medieval banquets.

serves as the starting point for a number of lakeside footpaths.

Conservationists have particularly strong feelings about the spread of the ubiquitous, conformist conifer. The **Clocaenog Forest**, Wales's second-largest commercial plantation, covers much of the southern moor. Along with the water authorities, the Forestry Commission is nowadays acutely aware of its public image and makes efforts to welcome visitors to its woods. The Commission's recreational focal point here is **Bod Petrual**, an old gamekeeper's cottage off the B5105 which has been converted into a visitor centre.

The **River Dee**, which flows eastwards from Bala to Llangollen, is a convenient dividing line between the northern and southern halves of northeast Wales. Whereas the north is a mixture of moor, vale, hill and urban and industrial areas, the south presents a much more consistently rural picture. Centred around the bulky Berwyn Mountains, the south is an area of green, steep-sided valleys, remote mountains and undulating border country, dotted with unpronounceable villages like **Llanfihangel-yng-Ngwynfa** and **Llansantffraid ym Mechain**.

Llangollen, on the fast-flowing Dee, stands at one of the most dramatic entry points into Wales. Driving westwards along the A5 (the route pioneered by that extraordinary Victorian engineer, Thomas Telford), the wide borderland vistas are suddenly replaced by a form of tunnel vision as the road funnels into the claustrophobic, cramped **Vale of Dee**. Llangollen, guarding the entrance to this narrow, severe valley, is a pretty town famous the world over as the home of the International Musical Eisteddfod.

Welsh *eisteddfodau* can, frankly, be a bit of a disappointment for non-Welsh speakers. Conducted in Welsh, and for the benefit of a Welsh-speaking Welsh culture, these festivals of the arts make few concessions to outsiders. Llangollen's event, held each July, is different. Taking the traditions of the

Llangollen Railway, one of Wales's "great little trains".

236

eisteddfod and applying them to a world stage, the event is a colourful, extrovert, outward-looking celebration of international fraternity. Started in 1947 to help heal the wounds of a world ravaged by war, it has grown into a major event attracting thousands of musicians and dancers from all corners of the globe.

Llangollen's **Plas Newydd** is a fine "magpie-style" black-and-white mansion (those cross-border influences, once again) which was the home from 1780 of the town's most unconventional inhabitants, the "Ladies of Llangollen". The ladies in question were Lady Eleanor Butler, her companion the Honourable Sarah Ponsonby and their maid Mary Carryll, who established an eccentric, gossipy household visited by the likes of Wordsworth, Byron and Shelley.

An eerie drive: There's a stiff climb from the town to the stump of **Castell Dinas Bran**, a ruined fortress perched on a magnificent vantage point 1,000 ft (300 metres) high. If you're lazy, you can drive much of the way to the top, past an eerie line of cliffs (which would not look out of place in a spaghetti western).

Another interesting drive through the narrow, steep lanes north of Llangollen will take you to **World's End**, a secluded, spectacular spot. For easier motoring, stick to the A542, which passes the ruins of the Cistercians' **Valle Crucis Abbey** and the ninth-century **Eliseg's Pillar** before climbing in a great loop along the Horseshoe Pass.

The easiest, most relaxing travelling of all is by boat along the **Llangollen Canal** which runs east from the town, though you'll need a head for heights as it crosses the Dee Valley by Telford's superb 120-ft (37-metre) high **Pontcysyllte Aqueduct**, the longest in Britain.

Chirk is another gateway town—and has the gateway to prove it. The approach to Chirk Castle is protected by wrought-iron entrance gates, made in 1719-21 by the Davies brothers of

Pontcysyllte, the longest aqueduct in Britain.

Bersham, which display remarkable intricacy, finesse and painstaking detail. The castle, a National Trust property, is not what you might expect judging by its name. Although it began life as a rough-and-ready border fortress, over the centuries Chirk evolved into a stylish stately home embellished by neo-Classical and neo-Gothic influences. Its fabric is a reflection of its record, unique amongst north Wales castles, of continuous occupation from medieval times.

To get to **Glynceiriog** from Llangollen, you can either drive via Chirk (the easy but long way around) or hold your breath and take an as-the-crow-flies route direct over the mountain on narrow, steep country lanes. Either way, this out-of-the-way village merits a visit, if only for the surprising evidence it displays of past industrial activity. It once played a minor role in north Wales's great slate-mining industry, as is revealed at the **Chwarel Wynne slate cavern**, an old mine open to the public.

The village stands at the entrance to the **Vale of Ceiriog**, a popular pony-trekking and walking area. This narrow valley ventures into the obscure **Berwyn Mountains**. Although not, in statistical terms, monumentally tall (they rise to around 2,500 ft/750 metres), precious few inroads have been made into this often-ignored corner of Wales. There are few villages, few facilities for visitors; and few ways of getting to grips with the area other than on foot or horseback, for it does not lend itself to relaxed car touring, the topography having thwarted the efforts of the road-builders.

But its shortcomings are also its strengths. This tranquil backwater is peace and quiet personified. It's worth making the effort to get to **Pistyll Rhaeadr**, the tallest waterfall in Wales, which plunges 240 ft (74 metres) into a rocky, wooded valley. The fall can be found right at the end of the road which sidles into the Berwyns northwestwards from **Llanrhaeadr ym Mochnant**, a village whose place in Welsh history is

Welshpool: a quite prosperous border town

assured through its 16th-century associations with Bishop William Morgan, translator of the Bible into Welsh.

Lake Vyrnwy is also mountain-locked, though a little more accessible. This reservoir, built at the end of the 19th century to supply Liverpool with water, can hardly be criticised on aesthetic grounds. Its location, surrounded by thickly wooded mountains, is superb, its inky-black waters adding a sense of extra drama to a powerful backdrop of peaks.

Perhaps the reservoir's dramatic personality also has something to do with the period in which it was built. The Victorians, never renowned for doing anything by halves, brought an architectural embellishment to Lake Vyrnwy's twin-spired water tower that owes much to the Gothic excess which also inspired Bram Stoker's *Dracula*. Call in at the **Vyrnwy Visitor Centre**, located in a converted chapel near the dam, if you want information on the rich wildlife in the woods around the lake.

Welshpool is a handsome, prosperous border and market town of tall buildings, a wide main street, and pleasing half-timbered and Georgian architecture. There's an interesting local museum and, for steam-train enthusiasts, the chance to ride on the narrow-gauge **Welshpool and Llanfair Light Railway** which runs on a scenic route through the hills to **Llanfair Caereinion**, eight miles (13 km) away.

The town's most significant site lies a mile to the south. The mellow red walls of **Powis Castle**, an opulent National Trust property, rise above a magnificent series of terraces. The castle's links with Clive of India are reflected in its Clive Museum.

Rivalling the exotic grandeur of the castle itself are the gardens, a series of four grand terraces of Italianate design. Created between 1688 and 1722, they are horticulturally and historically important because they are the only formal gardens of this date to survive in their original form.

Powis Castle: an opulent National Trust property.

ANATOMY OF AN EISTEDDFOD

One of the world's most spectacular cultural gatherings? An excuse for a week of maudlin sentimentality? The occasion for celebrating a way of life essentially Welsh and totally separate from other parts of the United Kingdom? The Royal National Eisteddfod of Wales is labelled all these and many more.

But first, a necessary word about Welsh words. An eisteddfod is a public meeting at which contests in literature and music are held. Poetry and singing predominate. Hundreds of eisteddfodau (Welsh plurals take *au*, not *s*) take place every year in towns and villages throughout Wales. Some of the smaller gatherings are as highly regarded for their cultural content as the National—the eisteddfod at Llangwm, a remote village a few miles off the A5 trunk road near Bala in the north, is one such star in the Welsh firmament.

There's an eisteddfod for pensioners, one for South Wales miners, another for the Urdd (the Welsh League of Youth). Most schools enter the lists. Not everyone understands the language—only 500,000 of Wales's 2.5 million people speak Welsh—but the spirit is widely shared.

The National is simply the star at the top of the pyramid. There the honours are the greatest. The ambitions and the strivings of every competitor in a sprawling network of eisteddfodau focus on the National—perhaps to be awarded the Bardic Crown or the Bardic Chair, the two highest honours in a land where achievement in things cultural is highly valued.

Rules of the game: Much of what goes on at the National does not require the visitor to know the language. Arts and crafts competitions, music and ceremony stand unaided. But a lot does. It takes something of a mental gymnast to comprehend the precise rules of Welsh poetry and the intricate patterns of penillion singing. More popular forms are widely known, even beyond Wales—few

Preceding pages: horses in Snowdonia National Park; a National Eisteddfod. Left, procession at a National Eisteddfod and (right) at an International gathering.

Welsh men and women admit to being unable to sing the national anthem, even though they don't understand the words.

The language of the eisteddfod field (the *maes*) is Welsh. That doesn't mean that other tongues are not heard; far from it. To help non-Welsh speakers, HTV, Wales's commercial television company, lends out handheld receivers through which an English commentary can be picked up.

Welsh is the language spoken in the main pavilion where the major events are staged

with boundless brilliance. The building seats upward of 5,000. On the huge stage the bards in their ceremonial robes stare out across the footlights; the cuter members of the audience play "spot the bard"—a game in all conscience difficult enough in the cavernous surroundings and one made even harder by the costumes' ability to make every bard look alike.

They are there for the big ceremonies, the Crowning and the Chairing. Two events of greater theatricality are hard to imagine. In theory, the winners are not supposed to know in advance. A name is called out, a spotlight sweeps the audience and lights on the successful competitor who is led on to the stage amid thunderous applause. Oddly, the winner invariably seems to be wearing a neat suit.

In a kingdom not as united as its title supposes, the National offers scope for social and political comment. The chaired Bard at the 1988 festival caused controversy for attacking nuclear power in his winning ode. Elwyn Edwards, a careful man, took the opportunity to point his literary finger at Trawsfynydd nuclear power station, an incongruous pile in the middle of the Snowdonia National Park, blaming it for cancer cases in his home area. Revealingly, the Central Electricity Generating Board re-

the eisteddfod's ruling body open to charge of being bought. Like much of Wales's establishment, the National is run by men—a few statutory women are thrown in—who are quick to proclaim their Welshness. But, when the militant Welsh Language Society holds a rally on the *maes*, their embarrassment replaces national pride. He who pays the piper seems to call the tune.

A moveable feast: The National is peripatetic, a restless culture fest which roams around Wales without a permanent home. It comes to rest for a week every August, one year in the north, the next in the south. The cycle is as predictable as the rising of the sun: a different location each year and new traffic

acted angrily, starting a debate which will not go away.

Outside the main pavilion hundreds of stalls promoting everything from Welsh lamb and Celtic fashions to wood carving and harp repairing, line up like some eastern bazaar. Fat cats such as the Wales Tourist Board, presided over by Mr Prys Edwards who is reckoned to be one Wales's sharpest dressers, inhabit huge glossy stands. In a remote corner, a tiny tent extols the virtues of an early Welsh radical called Nicholas Glais.

Culture never comes cheap. The National cost more than £1 million to stage. The Government stumps up about a quarter, laying

problems for a different set of perspiring policemen.

Rows about the need for a permanent location occur regularly. The Royal Welsh Agricultural Society's splendid show ground at Builth Wells is slap in the middle of Wales and would be a happy choice. Monotonously, the National's governing body votes for the open road, citing the need to involve local communities. It is a well-founded argument—as proved by the heroic fund-raising undertaken in the chosen areas.

Commercial sponsors, including financial institutions and industrial companies, have increasingly come to the aid of the National.

Their influence is certain to grow and perhaps the day will come when logos will be emblazoned on the bards's robes.

If that does happen, it will follow to its logical conclusion the canny footwork of one Iolo Morganwg, the bardic name of Edward Williams, an 18th-century Glamorgan stonemason whose influence on the festival persists to this day. Although the first eisteddfod is believed to have been held at Cardigan more than 800 years ago, the cunning Iolo invented the Gorsedd of Bards (the Bardic Circle) and forged documents to support the story he was the sole surviving member of the ancient Druids.

Today Wales is littered with circles of

represented, Patagonia predominating. In recent years South African Welsh have not been welcomed because of that country's apartheid policies.

Youth is at long last being allowed its place in the eisteddfod. Rock and folk, through the medium of Welsh, have helped to revive the language. But as late as the 1979 eisteddfod it was considered unacceptable—so much so that the officials pulled the plug on an impromptu rock concert which drew hundreds away from the conventional pursuits. Now a rock pavilion is officially sanctioned.

A word of warning for the thirsty eisteddfod-goer. Alcohol is banned from the

Gorsedd stones—each marking the place where an eisteddfod has been held. Williams stage-managed the first Gorsedd ceremony at which bardic "degrees" were awarded on 21 June 1792, choosing Primrose Hill in north London as the site for an event which contributes much to the National's colourful pageantry. One of the festival's most moving moments is the welcoming ceremony for Welsh people from abroad visiting the land of their fathers. Dozens of countries are

Left, ancient rites rehearsed at a National Eisteddfod at Barry. Above, dressing up for an International Eisteddfod at Llangollen.

maes and the beer tents so much a part of other Welsh events—miners' galas, agricultural shows and sports meetings—are notable by their absence. This is good news for the public houses and restaurants which stock up in advance, only to be drunk dry in a matter of days; bad news on a hot day when approved-of lemonade tastes tepid. Thirst for spectacle however, overrides all other appetites and the National's rich diversity satisfies most tastes.

The other festival: Quite separate from the National is the Llangollen International Eisteddfod, held every July in that tranquil North Wales town. Staged in a field between the River Dee and the Llangollen Canal, which connects to the waterways of the English Midlands, it is a celebration of nations speaking—rather singing, dancing and making music—to one another.

It was first held soon after the guns fell silent in 1945. Europe was a wreck and the festival sought in a tentative way to heal wounds that were not visible, to bridge gaps opened up by six years of bloody conflict. Forty years on, its success is beyond dispute. Singers, dancers, instrumentalists, orchestras and choirs from all over the world converge on Llangollen for a week of *entente cordiale*. By a miracle of voluntary effort, hundreds of competitors are housed, fed and

generally made a fuss of—and tens of thousands flock to the eisteddfod to listen, look and, maybe, learn that cooperation beats conflict hands down.

The events are competitive, of course, Swedish choirs contest with Canadians and dancers from the Ukraine try to outdo Morris Men from Shropshire, a few steps across the English border. But all is secondary to the spirit of kinship between nations.

Llangollen is a pretty town blessed with one of Wales's most convivial wine bars and some picturesque riverside paths. Quiet it is not during eisteddfod week. Singing, dancing and fraternising go on continuously. For

12 hours a day on the field—and much longer in the town itself—the atmosphere is electric. Fiesta time in rural Wales brings New Orleans and Catalonia to the green hills, Ankara and Argentina to the friendly pubs and cafés. National costumes, brilliant hair styles and complexions of every hue combine with the picture postcard setting to produce a photographer's dream.

The International is given to scoring some noteworthy "firsts": groups from the People's Republic of China and the Soviet Union were first seen in Britain at Llangollen. It precedes the National by a couple of weeks, giving enthusiastic eisteddfod goers just enough time to catch their cultural breath.

Some opinion holds that the two are rivals, competitors in a cultural league where everyone claims the sweetest music, the deftest footwork and the catchiest tunes. A minority of old National supporters regard the International as an upstart which ignores Welsh, "the language of heaven". and threatens to dilute an ancient culture. An equally small group unthinkingly describes the National as an anachronism set in sentimental cement and fixing Welsh in a linguistic ghetto. Neither analysis stands the acid test: a visit.

Complementary rather than competitive, they stand for different values springing from a shared base. The National carries a strong and compelling emotional appeal. Every Welsh woman, every Welsh man defines Welshness in a personal way, but their support for the National is today virtually total. An ancient institution, even allowing for Iolo Morganwg's antics, it continues to stir the blood of Celts and others. It commands respect for people living in a part of the United Kingdom which considers itself different to neighbouring England. Not better, just different.

The International is a coming together of people scattered across the globe, people whose forebears fought each other in the name of who knows what. An affirmation of friendship is always welcome. Every July the Llangollen festival provides just that, cultural *glasnost* ahead of more recent political thaws.

One important role of the modern eisteddfod movement is to help keep traditional Welsh music alive.

WELSH CHOIRS

All Welshmen sing like angels. That's what all Welshmen like to think, anyway. Put any two together and within minutes they'll have a sing-song going. Put 100 of them together and you'll have one of the world's great choirs pounding out one of the world's great melodies, anything from Bach's *Oratorio* to Joseph Parry's *Myfanwy*.

Although there are very good ladies' and mixed choirs, it is the male voice choir that is the best-known part of the Welsh musical tradition. The great choirs—the Morriston Orpheus, the Pendyrus, the Treorchy, the Rhos, the Pontardulais and the Llanelli among them—are carrying on a tradition that goes back a century or more and is inextricably interwoven with Welsh cultural life.

Giraldus Cambrensis, the great Welsh cleric who travelled the country in the Middle Ages, remarked on how the people sang in harmony. For centuries afterwards that love of music was expressed in Welsh harp tunes, in simple unaccompanied singing and in penillion singing, an improvisatory art form unique to Wales.

Choral music came with the arrival of industrialisation and nonconformity. The nonconformist revival in the 18th and 19th centuries was a people's religion. The church was for the toffs,

and ordinary people turned to the chapels with their strong emphasis on preaching and hymn singing. Love of music was also inculcated by the popularity of tonic sol-fa, a method of reading music without the traditional notation.

Keith Griffin, of the Welsh Amateur Music Federation, has another theory about why the Welsh are so musical: it is to do with the language. Welshmen and women open their mouths fully when they speak, he believes, and the voice comes from an open throat, which gives purer vowel sounds reminiscent of Italians. They also seem able to project the voice. He contrasts this with the southern English, who speak between their teeth, hardly opening their mouths.

It was therefore hardly surprising, given this aptitude combined with a cultural association that

placed great importance not just on music but on *Welsh* music expressed in hymns, that choirs were formed.

Scrabbling around in the archives is always fraught with danger since there is the possibility of overlooking someone or something long since lost, but it would appear that the first of the big male voice choirs was formed in Ebenezer chapel, Trecynon, a suburb of Aberdare, in about 1849. Others quickly followed. But the great growth of choral singing occurred in the last quarter of the 19th century, in the heyday of Victorian industrialisation in Wales.

By then, the male voice choirs had become very large indeed, up to 150 strong. They were even going to London to perform before royalty—in Britain, the ultimate accolade.

Few of those Victorian choirs have survived. Recently a population with more money to spend and new ways in which to spend it found choir practice increasingly irksome. As attendances at chapels and Sunday schools declined, so did the choir tradition.

But Welsh people never lost their ability to sing, as anyone who has watched a rugger international at Cardiff Arms Park or attended one of the "festivals of a thousand voices" in London's Albert Hall will testify. And in the late 1960s a new wave of enthusiasm for choral singing broke through. New choirs were formed, the old ones were given a further lease of life. More choirs were created than at any time in the past 100 years.

Wales is not just about male voice choirs, though, and the tradition of musicality has been kept alive throughout the principality by the choral societies, the mixed choirs in which the sopranos and altos find a place alongside those lovely basses, baritones and tenors.

The latter, for some reason, are in short supply. "Where have all the tenors gone?" is a standard cry of choral music directors. Where indeed? Perhaps to Sweden, which in recent years has developed an unexpectedly excellent choral tradition for small, balanced choirs. But, just as all Welshmen believe they sing like angels—after all, Welsh is said to be the language of Heaven—so none of them would dream of conceding that the Swedes are now better.

THE FOOD REVOLUTION

Wales, once regarded as a gastronomic wilderness, is on the up-and-up in the league table of foodies: there are now plenty of good places to eat—both modestly and not so modestly. Nouvelle Cuisine decorates some plates at the top end of the market. The number of pubs serving satisfying bar snacks is growing. Fast food turns up in small villages—even those with long names like Penrhyndeudraeth in Snowdonia, which today has a Chinese take-away.

It was not always so. But the influx of tourists, from Britain as well as overseas, has changed the menu dramatically. Technical colleges and catering establishments are bringing on chefs of high calibre, who are quickly snapped up by discerning restaurateurs—and occasionally poached by the English.

One of Wales's most nourishing and sustaining dishes is a bowl of cawl, a simple soup, well laced with bite-sized chunks of vegetables. Follow that with a few slices of bread made of locally milled flour topped with Caws Aberteifi (a tasty cheese made in Cardigan) and you will feel replete.

Basics, like steak and chips, chicken and chips, fish and chips, sausage and chips are obtainable everywhere from Cardiff to Caernarfon. Note that repetitive addition: chips. Thereby hangs a tale, a cautionary one. Wales is being swamped with healthy eating publicity aimed at cutting down obesity, heart disease and other problems stemming from unsuitable diets. An organisation called Heartbeat Wales, funded by the Government, is doing sterling work. Recently, the steak has become leaner and the chips are cooked in sunflower oil. Lard is out, unsaturated fats in.

The traditional Sunday joint—the equivalent of beef in England—is succulent Welsh lamb. The farmers of Wales have managed to produce a meat which is comparatively fat-free. With a registered sheep population exceeding 10 million, there are enough lamb chops and shoulders

Preceding pages: farmhouse cheese, cellar-matured for six years. Left, traditional butcher. Above, traditional broth.

of mutton in the offing to last for ever.

Traditionalists who demand a good beef steak (with or without chips) will be well served at establishments like the Wellington Hotel in Brecon and the Aleppo Merchant, a pub in the Mid-Wales village of Carno, which has another claim to fame—a gleaming Laura Ashley textiles factory.

Laver bread is not really bread. Made of seaweed, oatmeal and bacon fat, it is not to everyone's taste. Found mainly in South Wales, it can be eaten at any meal, from early

breakfast to post-TV snack. Some prefer it with chips.

Cockles, gathered on the shores of Gower, a peninsula nosing into the Bristol Channel near Swansea, and in the Dee estuary in the north, are another Welsh tradition. The air sung by another Celt—Molly Malone of Dublin, who wheeled her barrow through streets broad and narrow, crying cockles and mussels, alive alive-o—has no Welsh counterpart, but cockle pie (cockles, bacon and spring onions under a pastry roof) strikes a happy chord.

Wales, like Scotland, has its salmon. And sewin, a pink-skinned large trout, is equally popular, and as much sought after as Conwy salmon. Trout taken from Trawsfynydd Lake are the fattest in the land; not everyone cares to eat them because the lake supplies cooling water to the nuclear power station which sits alongside it.

For a land reckoned to be somewhat insular, Wales has a remarkable diversity of eating places. Italians settled in the valleys of the south generations ago, and have established a niche in the catering trade. Cafés run by Rabiottis and Sidolis stand alongside others with "Evans" and "Jones" above the door. Latins and Celts fuse, marry and combine to produce a lively society dishing up interesting food.

buttered, hot, cold. Try one, and the plate will soon be bare.

The Wales Tourist Board is pushing local dishes made with local produce through its "Taste of Wales" campaign. It publishes a recipe book under that title, which is a handy guide to culinary by-ways.

Newer dishes emerging include taste ticklers such as chicken and apricots, grilled fish with prunes. What fails to raise a smile in some parts of rural Wales is the confused licensing law. In the districts of Ceredigion and Dwyfor, pubs are shut on Sundays, and eating opportunities suffer in consequence. So, if you're in Porthmadog or Aberystwyth on the Sabbath, forget that vision of on ice-

The capital city, Cardiff, caters for all tastes. The Riverside and the Happy Gathering are the best of Chinese, which explains why so many of the city's Chinese families eat there. Giacomo Savastano, who comes from Naples, provides excellent cheap pasta dishes at the restaurant on North Street which bears his name. When cash is short, go to Crumbs, a cosy vegetarian eating house in the city centre, and try to spend more than £2 a head.

For a between-meals snack, Welsh cakes are favourite. Flat scone-like cakes the diameter of a tea cup, baked with sultanas and currants, they can be eaten plain,

cold bottle of wine being drunk as the sun shimmers on Cardigan Bay; the National Milk Bars (serviceable providers of non-alcoholic drinks) will have to do.

The vexed question of Sunday drinking is decided once every seven years by means of a referendum. It is likely that the two districts (of the 37 in Wales) holding out will go for "wet" next time round.

Sandwiched between the two "never on Sunday" areas is Merioneth, a district rapidly gaining a reputation for good food. The country house hotel Maes-y-Neuadd at Talsarnau overlooks stunning countryside and serves stunningly good food; it's certainly worth trying the Anglesey Eggs (hard boiled eggs with leeks and potatoes in a cheese sauce) for starters and Monmouth Pudding (breadcrumbs, sugar, butter, egg whites, milk and strawberry jam baked together) to finish.

At Harlech, Ken Goody presides over the Cemlyn (Welsh for frog), a crossed-forks restaurant people drive miles to sample. Booking is essential. The scores of frogs Ken has assembled are, of course, artificial—the bill even comes up in a wicker-work little croaker. A few miles south, at Llanbedr, Augusto Gutto adds a touch of his native Italy at the Salutation. Excellent pasta dishes and great friendliness from Augusto, a

Llandudno has a similar broad sweep of promenade, good gardens, a new sports centre—and a decent spread of eating places. There are chip shops, coffee houses and honest plain restaurants like Summers, which overlooks the main street and provides traditional three-course lunches at modest prices. The cocktail bar, panelled and subdued, is strictly 1930s.

Young enthusiasts—Adam Rattenbury, his wife, Penny, and Tim Kirton—run Chandlers, a brasserie at Trefriw a few miles inland. The Sunday joint is carved in front of you and "seconds" are encouraged. The wine list is almost outshone by the lengthy list of beers from just about every country

former restaurant manager at the famous Portmeirion Hotel across the bay, earn a salute.

It must be said that some resorts do little to bring catering standards up to scratch. Rhyl, on the north coast, has a lot going for it: a beautifully wide promenade, a fine leisure centre and public gardens of great potential. It also boasts (if that's the right word) wall-to-wall chip shops which overpower the senses on a warm day. The reasonable cafés are hard to find. A few miles along the coast,

Left, laver bread. Above, a bed-and-breakfast farmhouse near Rhayader.

from Kenya to Canada.

Pembrokeshire is a good place to be when the early potatoes are harvested; Crickhowell on the banks of the Usk when the tempting afternoon tea at Gliffaes Country Hotel awaits returning anglers; the Ty Newydd in the Rhondda where Saturday night steaks are much in demand.

It has taken Wales some time to come in from the cold in matters gastronomic and the journey has yet to be completed in some parts. But the demand for good food combined with cheerful service is recognised and increasingly met—with or without chips.

RUGGER: A WELSH RELIGION

Twice a year on winter Saturday afternoons, come rain or shine or apocalypse, more than 60,000 people cram themselves into the Arms Park in Cardiff. The occasion is the Big Match: the International. It's the day all Wales has been awaiting for weeks. Wales is facing one of four teams at rugger: England and Ireland one year, France and Scotland the next.

The atmosphere builds up through the morning. By the early afternoon the city is awash with red-bedecked fans who have arrived from Llanwonno, Llandudno and Llancayo by coach, car and other carriage to support "the boys". Red scarves and red hats are worn; giant green leeks, usually cardboard cutouts but often the real thing, are carried; white and green flags with the red dragon superimposed are waved.

Cardiff is unique not just because rugger has reached the status of a quasi-religion in Wales but because the Arms Park is bang in the centre of the city. Where the Murrayfield stadium is a good couple of miles from Princes Street in Edinburgh and Twickenham might just as well be on the south coast for all they know about it in London's Piccadilly, the Cardiff Arms Park in Westgate Street is literally as well as metaphorically a stone's throw from St Mary Street, the city's posh shopping centre.

Fine for masochists: For those without a seat—about half the crowd—the experience can be uncomfortable. It is said in Cardiff that when you can see the Wenallt, the hill behind the city, it is going to rain and when you can't it is raining. Still, those getting wet comfort themselves with the knowledge that as many again would gladly swop places with them.

On international days the Arms Park is the focus of the game; almost everything else comes to a halt. For the remaining 363 days of the year it is the home of Welsh rugger; some would say the home of rugger, even though Twickenham is respectfully known as Headquarters.

Rugger is played everywhere in Wales.

Opposite and above: players line up for a Wales versus Scotland game.

Any piece of land will do to sprout the H-shaped posts. It doesn't have to be rectangular and it won't necessarily in a country like Wales be flat. The most famous club in the country, the mythical Aberflyaff, the product of a Cardiff cartoonist's vivid imagination, plays on a ground whose pavilion end is in all probability several hundred feet higher than the river that is the dead-ball line at the other end.

Water plays an important role in Welsh rugger. The Taff, which before it was

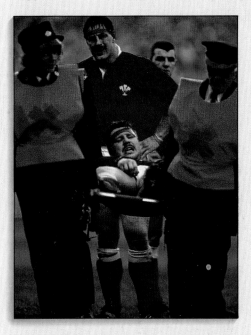

cleaned up made the Danube look like drinking water, runs just outside the west end of the ground. But beer plays an even more important role. Post-match bacchanalia fuelled by the fiery potion puts all the heavenly choirs combined to shame.

The other seminal influence on the game is music. Music is the very soul of Wales; there have been eminent individual singers such as Madame Adelina Patti and Sir Geraint Evans, but music finds its greatest expression in great choirs like the Morriston Orpheus, the Pendyrus and the Treorchy Male Voice. Every Welshman—especially every Welshman with a few beers inside him—

imagines he is the lead tenor in the choir.

The unevenness of tone induced by alcoholic stimulation is, however, negated by mass and the sound of 60,000 voices belting it out louder than Eartha Kitt ever imagined possible has a stimulating effect on the 15 men on the pitch wearing the red jerseys. Englishmen have been known to go faint at the sound, New Zealanders have been known to travel half way across the world to hear it.

The greatest of the songs is *Hen Wlad fy Nhadau*, the Welsh national anthem. But this is only sung once, at the start. *Sospan Fach*, Little Saucepan, the "national anthem" of Llanelli, and two hymns, *Cwm Rhondda*

(known to most English speakers for its opening words Guide Me O Thou Great Jehovah, and its chorus of Bread of Heaven) and *Calon Lan* are sung at the drop of a pin.

One of the three will originate somewhere in the crowd. The refrain will be taken up and the tune will move around the great amphitheatre, urging on "the boys" to even greater effort. Strong men have been known to request *Calon Lan* sung by the Arms Park "choir" as the one tune they would take with them to BBC Radio's mythical land of *Desert Island Discs*.

Strictly speaking, the Arms Park is not the Arms Park at all. It is the Welsh National

Ground. The Arms Park is next door, the place where the Cardiff club plays and on which the players have their picture taken before committing themselves to 80 minutes of heroic action.

This needs some explanation because no-one except a few hidebound members of the Welsh Rugby Union would think of calling the National Ground anything else but the Arms Park. The confusion stems from the change of status of the ground a couple of decades ago. At that time, what is now the National Ground was called the Arms Park and was the home of the Cardiff rugger club, the rugger end of the Cardiff Athletic Club which encompassed cricket, tennis and squash as well.

Then the Welsh Rugby Union—the top end of the trade, as it were—took over the ground, enlarged and rebuilt it into a magnificent stadium, while the Cardiff club built a new ground, technically called the Arms Park, next door on what had until then been the square that was the main home of Glamorgan county cricket.

It is here, on the Arms Park, that the international teams have their picture taken before moving next door to the National Ground for the real thing. Only no-one bothers with such sophistry. It's the Arms Park where it all takes place.

However important, though, the Arms Park/National Ground is only the apex of where it all happens. Rugger is everywhere. Any pantheon dedicated to the game would include names such as Rodney Parade in Newport, St Helens in Swansea, Sardis Road in Pontypridd and Stradey Park in Llanelli. Especially Stradey. Stradey is the home of all that is Welsh in rugger. Down there they don't go in for a lot of English nonsense. The scoreboard gives the names of the teams in Welsh; the crowd speaks Welsh, and its not just to confuse that toffee-nosed lot from Cardiff. It's their first language, which they speak all the time.

At Newport's Rodney Parade the crowd is very anglicised—hardly surprising as the town is almost in England. It's neither as anglicised nor as witty as the new Cardiff ground, where the sheepskin coats and peaked caps could almost reflect the crowd at the Harlequins' ground in London, university men all.

At St Helens there's the whiff of the sea in

Swansea Bay just across the road but it is in Pontypridd, Pontypool, Newbridge and Maesteg that one really feels in the heart of a Welsh crowd. Once they would have been miners. Now the pits have gone and the men are probably employed in Bridgend or Cardiff assembling television sets and video recorders for the Japanese.

Hero worship: The players themselves are much the same as ever, gods in different sizes. The greatest gods are men like Cliff Morgan who in the late 1940s and early 1950s was to rugger what Dennis Compton was to cricket, a buccaneering genius. Or Onllwyn Brace, who brought distinction to the scrum-half job when all he was expected

is so deeply enshrined in Welsh folklore that it has to be mentioned separately.

That autumn a team from New Zealand had been touring Britain and by the time they reached Cardiff for the International against Wales, the last match of their tour, they were unbeaten. They had played 26 times and had won 26 times. Nine days before Christmas, on 16 December, New Zealand met a Welsh team which the previous season had won the Triple Crown, the mythical prize that goes to the national team beating the other three home countries. The match was played to the background of a cacophony of noise and Teddy Morgan scored the only try of the game to send the New Zealanders home with

to do was feed the great men outside him. Billy Cleaver with the fair mop of hair and Merve the Swerve, Mervyn Davies, the back-row forward who led Wales through one of their golden eras in the 1970s when nothing was impossible.

There was not a boy in Wales at the time who would not have wanted to be in these men's boots. Not many men either. There have been others. Perhaps the most famous was a little chap called Teddy Morgan, a doctor, who took part in a match in 1905 that

Opposite, Wales takes on an Irish team. Above, rugger still draws large crowds.

just one defeat on their programme. It was from this match, and a disputed try by the New Zealanders that was disallowed but which might have swung the game for them, that the intense rivalry between Wales and New Zealand has emerged.

If there is one country that Wales always wants to beat, it is England. Welshmen can accept defeat, albeit reluctantly, from anyone except England. But New Zealand matches have an allure over and above even those with England. The Red Devils of Wales against the All Blacks of New Zealand are the sort of matches only fashioned in Heaven.

GREAT LITTLE TRAINS

Lovers of steam who visit Wales are in for a rare treat: nearly a dozen narrow-gauge steam railway lines. These were not designed for the edification of tourists or even the transportation of passengers—they were usually built to transport slate from mountain quarries to seaports. After falling into disuse around the middle of this century, they were resuscitated by enthusiasts who formed railway preservation societies.

What makes a railway narrow-gauge? The term applies to any track between 1ft 6in (450 mm) and 3ft 6in (1,050 mm) wide. Lines more than 3ft 6in are sub-standard gauge; lines less than 1ft 6in are miniature; standard gauge as used by British Rail is 4ft 8.5in (1.4 metres). The attractions of the "little trains", other than the steam, are their intimate size and their leisurely progress which gives passengers a grand opportunity to enjoy the scenery.

Rescue bid: Britain's very first railway preservation society was formed in Wales in 1950 to save the Talyllyn railway. This, the world's oldest functioning steam-hauled, narrow-gauge railway, was on the verge of extinction. The Talyllyn has its headquarters at Tywyn in the heart of Cardigan Bay. From here, a slightly more than seven-mile (12-km), 2ft 3in (675 mm) track runs inland following the river valley through spectacular scenery, much of which is in the Snowdonia National Park. At Dogloch station the line crosses an impressive viaduct and walks from the station will take you to Dogloch Waterfalls.

The Talyllyn's rolling stock includes the *Talyllyn*, a steam engine built in 1864. Visit the society's Narrow-gauge Railway Museum at Tywyn Wharf station and see the best collection of narrow-gauge relics in Britain. These include engines from Britain, Ireland and France.

North of Tywyn, and still on Cardigan Bay, stands Porthmadog, the home of two preserved narrow-gauge railways. The Ffestiniog line originally opened in 1836 with horse-drawn rolling stock which brought

Preceding pages: Vale of Rheidol Railway. Right, a "great little train" at Morfa Harlech.

slate from the mines at Blaenau Ffestiniog to the port of Porthmadog. It had a maximum gradient of one in 70 which permitted laden wagons to freewheel from quarry to port.

In 1860, the Ffestiniog became the first steam-powered narrow-gauge railway in the world: visitors came from far and wide to view this engineering marvel. It was then that the line began to carry passengers as well as slate. In 1951 a preservation society was formed to save the Ffestiniong which had stopped operating. Volunteers rushed forward and by 1955 the railway had started up again. Today it's a great success.

The Ffestiniog two-ft (600-mm) track runs for almost 14 miles (22 km) through oak

The Welsh Highland Railway, Porthmadog's second narrow-gauge line, was formerly the longest narrow-gauge railway in Wales. Its two-ft (600 mm) track opened in 1923 but was, from its inception, doomed to failure, having started too late to enjoy any real chance of industrial survival. However, after the success of the Ffestiniog, the future looks bright for the Welsh Highland whose current one-mile track runs through some of the most scenic parts of the country.

On the coast, between Porthmadog and Tywyn and running for about two miles (three km) above a magnificent sandy beach and so close to the waves of Cardigan Bay that you fear it will get its feet wet, is the

forests and past luxuriant rhododendrons through what is claimed to be the most scenic narrow-gauge route in Wales. As the train proceeds, the valley unfolds and reveals superb views of Snowdonia National Park.

The Ffestiniog's oldest engines are from 1863, but the line is even better known for its double-ended articulated engines which were built in the society's workshop. Yet there is a disappointment for purists: the Ffestiniog has converted all its engines from coal to oil firing because of the risk of forest fires. Drown your sorrow in draught beer in the buffet car—a drink which no other British railway serves.

Fairbourne railway. The line, originally horse-drawn, was built to carry materials for the building of Fairbourne village.

The Fairbourne is actually a miniature rather than a narrow-gauge railway, with a track which is 15in (375 mm) wide. It operates with replicas of famous narrow-gauge locomotives hauling period-style wooden coaches. Yet the Fairbourne is possibly the most functional of all "little railways", carrying housewives and businessmen rather than tourists from Fairbourne to the ferry which crosses the Mawddah Estuary to Barmouth.

Until recently the Vale of Rheidol narrow-gauge railway, which has its headquarters at

Aberystwyth, was unique: it was the only narrow-gauge line owned by British Rail rather than by a preservation society and the only line on which British Rail regularly operated steam locomotives. However, in 1988 British Rail divested itself of this operation. The track—almost 12 miles (19 km) long—was opened in 1902 for the purpose of transporting lead and timber and passengers, and has a two-ft (600-mm) gauge. Yet, in spite of this narrow-gauge the tiny locomotives are more than eight ft (two metres) wide and each weighs just over 25 tons.

The one-hour journey is spectacular, especially the final third where, as the veteran steam engines snort their way up steep gradi-

Close to the border with England is the Welshpool and Llanfair Light railway. This line, often called the "Farmers' Line", was built early this century to carry passengers and their products to the market towns of Welshpool and Llanfair. The route winds its way through a rich mosaic of pastoral and wooded hill country, climbing steep gradients over a switchback eight-mile (13 km) route between the Severn and Banwy valleys. At one stage the train puffs and puffs and puffs its way up a one in 30 gradient.

The line, which has a gauge of 2ft 6in (750 mm), was re-opened by enthusiasts in 1963 after having been closed down in 1956. The society prides itself on the international fla-

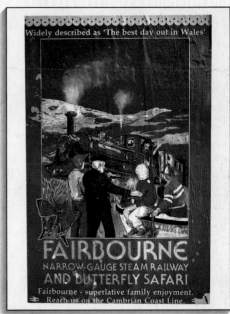

ents, around tight bends and on ledges overhanging precipitous drops, you look back to where you were 10 minutes before. Finally, the track passes through a deep rock-cutting to end at the "Devil's Bridge" terminus, at an altitude of 679 ft (204 metres).

Actually, there are three bridges, one above the other. According to legend, the lowest was built by the devil who claimed as payment the first soul to cross. The village dog was sent over.

Left, train at Blaenau Ffestiniog. Above, Porthmadog station on the Ffestiniog line (left) and a vintage poster.

vour of its coaches and locomotives and you will have the opportunity to travel in vintage coaches from Austria or comfortable modern ones from Sierra Leone while being pulled by a locomotive from Germany or from a sugar plantation in the West Indies.

Back in the Snowdonia National Park is the somewhat different Snowdon Mountain railway which departs from Llanberis. This is Britain's only rack-and-pinion railway—which means, in brief, that the drive of the engine is through rack pinions on the rails and that the wheels of the engine merely serve to carry its weight.

Since its inception, nearly 100 years ago,

the Snowdon Mountain railway has been strictly a passenger operation and has never needed to be rescued by preservation societies and their like. (The line is so popular that advanced booking is advisable in July, August and September. Trains do not run in severe weather or when the wind is high.) It takes almost one hour to ride the five miles (eight km) of 2ft 7½ in (800 mm) track which runs to within 66 ft (19 metres) of the summit of Mount Snowdon. Gradients are as steep as one in five-and-a-half.

On a clear day the unfolding views are unsurpassed those rivalled only by those enjoyed by walkers who decide to make it to the 3,560-ft (1,069-metre) summit under

two companies which, for nearly a century, served the Dinoric slate quarries. The track bed is from one and the rolling stock is from another. The two-mile (three-km) track, dwarfed by mountains which are reflected in the lake, runs along the edge of Llyn (*lake*) Padarn. It has a two-ft (600-mm) gauge. On a good day you will enjoy superb views of Snowdon.

The Bala Lake railway is another lakeside railway in the Snowdonia National Park. It runs for nearly five miles (eight km) between Bala and Llanuwchllyn along lovely Llyn Tegid, the largest natural lake in Wales.

Other newer societies which have only short lengths of track are the Brecon Moun-

their own steam. The trip is exciting and not for those of a nervous disposition.

Timid passengers were aboard when the railway opened on Easter Monday, 1896. Engine No. 1, the *Ladas*, fell into a ravine. Two passengers who wrongly anticipated that the coaches would also fall leapt for safety: one of them was killed. The company has operated without a No. 1 engine ever since and has never had another accident.

Narrow-gauge enthusiasts should not dash off when they return to Llanberis but should make their way across town to Gilfach Ddu station and the Llanberis Lake railway. This line has been scavenged from

tain, the Teifi Valley and the Gwili. The last named has a standard rather than a narrow-gauge track. All are in the southern half of the country.

A word of warning: preserved railways do not run during the winter and, for the remainder of the year, schedules are varied and irregular. Check before starting on your trip. Some lines, on occasion, substitute diesel for steam locomotives.

Railway enthusiasts visiting Wales need not confine themselves to travelling on preserved lines. Some of the most glorious country is traversed by tracks of British Rail which can also whisk the steam enthusiast from one preserved line to another.

Breath-taking is British Rail's 58-mile (93-km) line between Machynlleth and Pwllheli. The sea is rarely out of sight on this Cambrian Coast odyssey, with the train speeding alongside golden beaches, through windswept dune-land and, on one dramatic stretch, clinging to steep cliffs.

En route, the track crosses three river estuaries, the highlight being the half-mile-long Barmouth timber trestle bridge spanning the Mawddach estuary. Look out also for Harlech and Criccieth castles and the Italianate village of Portmeirion. Those with steam withdrawal symptoms will break their journey at Tywyn, Fairbourne and/or Porthma-

the Vale of Rheidol at Aberystwyth and the Festiniog at Blaenau Ffestiniog.

Travelling on British Rail rather than on preserved lines provides the visitor with the chance to meet locals rather than other tourists. Although the stiff upper-lipped Brit, commuting for the umpteenth year on the Basingstoke to London line, may never yield more than a courteous nod of the head and a curt "Good morning", the Welsh housewife travelling between Llanwrtyd and Llandrindod Wells for her weekly shopping will be delighted to chat with you, especially if you are a foreigner—although preferably not from England.

Your cup—not to mention your glass—

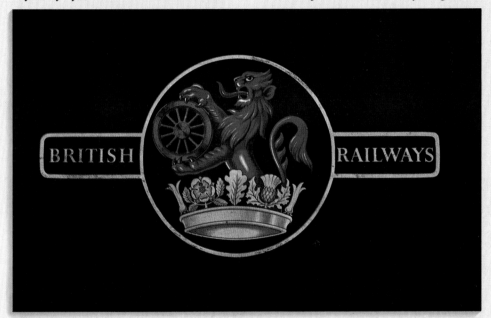

dog from which narrow-gauge steam trains depart.

Other scenic British Rail routes are the 83-mile (133-km) trip from Chester to Holyhead; the 121-mile (195-km) journey from Shrewsbury via Llanelli to Swansea; the 81-mile (130-km) journey from Shrewsbury to Aberystwyth and the 28-mile (45-km) run from Llandudno Junction to Blaenau Ffestiniog. The last two provide the opportunity to join narrow-gauge steam railways:

Left, the Cambrian coast line. Above, train at Aberystwyth. Next pages, coracle fishermen; the Roman steps, near Harlech; Monmouth pub.

may well run over if you travel on the Chester-Holyhead line, for here you will be entertained not only by the Welsh and possibly the English but also the Irish. (Holyhead is the terminal for the ferry to the Irish Republic.)

Finally, those in search of luxury and with a desire to be thoroughly spoilt might consider joining the "Black Prince" on its infrequent seven-day safaris around the principality during the summer. The train, composed of rolling stock from the Orient Express, is accompanied by luxurious buses which transport passengers from stations and sidings to outstanding sights. Nights are spent in hotels rather than on board the train.

THE NOBLE TIME

JUVENIA
——— 1860 ———

Golden Age ®
COLLECTION

STEEL - STEEL/GOLD - 18KT GOLD AND WITH PRECIOUS STONES

Worldwide list of JUVENIA Agents available on request

JUVENIA MONTRES SA - 2304 LA CHAUX-DE-FONDS - SWITZERLAND
Tel. 41/39 26 04 65 Fax 41/39 26 68 00

So, you're getting away from it all.

Just make sure you can get back.

AT&T Access Numbers
Dial the number of the country you're in to reach AT&T.

ANGUILLA	1-800-872-2881	**COLOMBIA**	**980-11-0010**	JAMAICA††	0-800-872-2881
ANTIGUA (Public Card Phones)	#1	*COSTA RICA	114	MEXICO◊◊◊	95-800-462-4240
ARGENTINA♦	001-800-200-1111	**CURACAO**	**001-800-872-2881**	MONTSERRAT†	1-800-872-2881
BAHAMAS	**1-800-872-2881**	DOMINICA	1-800-872-2881	**NICARAGUA**	**174**
BELIZE♦	555	DOMINICAN REP.††	1-800-872-2881	PANAMA♦	109
BERMUDA†	1-800-872-2881	ECUADOR†	119	PARAGUAY†	0081-800
*BOLIVIA	0-800-1111	*EL SALVADOR	190	PERU†	191
BONAIRE	**001-800-872-2881**	GRENADA†	872	ST. KITTS/NEVIS	1-800-872-2881
BRAZIL	**000-8010**	*GUATEMALA	190	**ST. MAARTEN**	**001-800-872-2881**
BRITISH VIRGIN IS.	1-800-872-2881	*GUYANA††	165	**SURINAME**	**156**
CAYMAN ISLANDS	1-800-872-2881	HAITI†	001-800-972-2883	URUGUAY	00-0410
CHILE	**00◊-0312**	HONDURAS†	123	*VENEZUELA†	80-011-120

Countries in bold face permit country-to-country calling in addition to calls to the U.S. *Public phones require deposit of coin or phone card. †May not be available from every phone. ††Collect calling only. ♦ Not available from public phones. ◊ Await second dial tone. ◊◊◊ When calling from public phones, use phones marked "Ladatel." © 1993 AT&T.

Here's a travel tip that will make it easy to call back to the States. Dial the access number for the country you're visiting and connect right to AT&T **USADirect**® Service. It's the quick way to get English-speaking operators and can minimize hotel surcharges.

If all the countries you're visiting aren't listed above, call 1 800 241-5555 before you leave for a free wallet card with all AT&T access numbers. International calling made easy—it's all part of **The *i* Plan.**℠

THE *i* PLAN™

AT&T

TRAVEL TIPS

GETTING THERE

BY AIR

You can fly straight into Wales via Cardiff Airport, 12 miles (19 km) from Wales's capital. It is linked by three direct summer services from North America, from Toronto, and New York. There are also connecting scheduled services into Cardiff via Amsterdam and Dublin from a wide range of North American airports. In addition to Amsterdam and Dublin, scheduled flights also operate between Cardiff and Belfast, Leeds and Glasgow.

For those wishing to visit North Wales first, Manchester Airport is less than an hour's drive from the Welsh border. It is the focal point of over 100 European and intercontinental routes.

BY SEA

The only direct sea routes into Wales are from Ireland. Five services operate: Dublin to Holyhead (B & I); Dun Laoghaire to Holyhead (Sealink British Ferries); Rosslare to Fishguard and Rosslare to Pembroke Dock (B & I); and Cork to Swansea (Swansea/Cork Ferries).

BY RAIL

British Rail's 125 InterCity Service is a real distance-shrinker – less than two hours, capital to capital, from London (Paddington Station) to Cardiff, for example. Speedy 125 trains also link Birmingham, Sheffield, York and Newcastle with Cardiff, and there's a fast, regular service from London (Euston Station) to Holyhead in North Wales, calling in at the north coast resorts. This coast is also served by direct services from Manchester, Liverpool and Hull.

BY ROAD

Continual motorway connects Wales with London, Heathrow and Gatwick Airports. And the motorway extends deep into southwest Wales; the scenic Pembrokeshire coast in the far west, for example, is now an easy, straightforward drive of no more than a handful of hours.

Along the North Wales coast, there's the excellent A55 expressway. This new road, which avoids all the old bottlenecks and links with Manchester Airport and Britain's motorway network, has resulted in dramatic improvements in communications between North Wales and the rest of the country. Similar improvements to roads into Mid Wales from the M5/M6 via the M54 make for quick and easy access, especially from Birmingham Airport and central England.

BY COACH

Good road links also mean quick journey times – at surprisingly low prices. Convenient express services to Wales operate from almost all major towns and cities in England and Scotland. London services usually start at Victoria Station. Tel: 071-730-0202.

TRAVEL ESSENTIALS

VISAS & PASSPORTS

The same regulations apply to Wales as to the rest of Britain. Overseas citizens must have a valid passport, but in the majority of cases do not need a visa. US and Canadian citizens generally receive a stamp on their passports, entitling them to stay for up to six months.

MONEY MATTERS

The pound sterling is a decimal currency, divided into 100 pence. Coins come in the following denominations – £1 (100p), 50p, 20p, 10p, 5p, 2p, and 1p; and notes in four denominations, £50, £20, £10 and £5. Some of the pre-decimal silver coins are still in circulation, but these are the same size as their decimal equivalents. No £1 notes remain in circulation.

You can bring any amount of money into the UK in any form, but the bulk should be in travellers cheques. Many people find it helpful to buy these in pounds sterling so that they can be exchanged easily in most places. Banks are the best places to convert foreign currency, not hotels or privately owned *bureaux de change*.

Major international credit cards are acceptable in an increasing number of British hotels, shops and restaurants but not necessarily away from major towns and cities or in small privately owned hotels and guest houses. The most popular cards are Access, American Express, Mastercard and Visa. It is advisable to purchase a small amount of currency before you arrive for immediate necessities and tips at the airport, rail station or ferry terminal. But as this currency would be in notes with the smallest denomination being £5, buy a bar of chocolate or a newspaper on arrival so that you have a selection of coins readily available.

HEALTH

Should you have any medical problems, consult your doctor before you travel and ask for a card with your medical profile. This, if kept with your other identification, could prove very useful in the case of an emergency.

Make sure that your health insurance coverage is adequate. Should you have to be hospitalised or be in need of what would be classified as non-emergency treatment, you will have to pay the full fees but would be able to recoup these from your insurance company on your return home.

The National Health Service in Britain charges no fees for the treatment of accidents, emergencies and infectious diseases. For more information on Medical Services, see section on *Emergencies*.

WHAT TO WEAR

The visitor to Wales should bring comfortable, practical clothing and have a good pair of walking shoes. Casual clothes are perfectly acceptable, even for medieval banquets, but a few of the upmarket country hotels will expect men to wear a collar, tie and jacket for evening dinner.

A light raincoat (a "mac") is highly recommended as Welsh weather is so unpredictable. In recent years Wales has experienced a heatwave in April, snow in May and a drought in November! So be prepared and bring a small selection of clothes for all seasons.

Many visitors to Wales enjoy walking in the countryside and some also attempt to walk to the summit of Mount Snowdon and other peaks. The mountains are to be respected; as the weather can change in a matter of minutes on higher ground, adequate clothing, footwear, a map and a compass are essential. If one's visit coincides with a period of heavy rainfall an inexpensive pair of "wellies" (Wellington boots) obtainable for a few pounds from most shoe shops is a very good investment, even though you may decide to leave them at your favourite hotel or guest house rather than take them home with you.

WHAT TO BRING

Apart from your own special personal requirements, there is no need to bring with you any equipment other than possibly a travel plug adaptor. (The standard voltage throughout Britain is 240v AC, 50 HZ). Medications are available at chemists (drug stores) and photographic supplies are readily available everywhere. Any Tourist Information Centre should be able to advise you as to where you should go to buy your special requirements.

ANIMAL QUARANTINE

Due to quarantine requirements (six months for animals, 35 days for birds, or if the stay is shorter, until taken out of the country again), bringing your pets necessitates a licence, which can be obtained from The Ministry of Agriculture, Fisheries & Food, Hook Rise South, Tolworth, Surbiton, Surrey, KT6 7NF. Tel: (01)337 6611.

The penalties for landing an animal or bird without a licence are severe – at present the maximum penalty is an unlimited fine and/or one year's imprisonment. There are no exceptions to this rule, which is enforced to keep out rabies.

CUSTOMS

Items which may not be brought into Britain include plants, vegetables, fresh meats, controlled drugs, animals or pets, firearms and ammunition.

A red and green "Clearway System" is in operation at most ports and airports in Britain. Go through the Red Channel if you have goods to declare (or if you are unsure of importation restrictions), or the Green Channel (which is subject to spot checks by a Customs Officer) if you have nothing to declare (i.e. are not exceeding your permitted allowance of tobacco, perfume, spirits and wine).

Visitors arriving in cars from Ireland can obtain red or green windscreen stickers on the boat. Where the "Clearway System" is not in operation, report to the Customs Officer in the Baggage Hall. You must declare anything you intend to leave or sell in Britain.

TIPPING

This is very much left to the individual. The following is intended only as a guide to customary practice:
Hotels: Most hotel bills include a service charge, usually 10–12.5 percent, but in some larger hotels 15 percent. Where a service charge is not included, it is customary to divide 10 to 15 percent of the bill among the staff who have given good service.
Restaurants: Some restaurant bills include a service charge. Where a service charge is not included it is customary to leave a tip of 10 to 15 percent of the bill.
Taxis: 10 to 15 percent of the fare.
Hairdressers: £1 plus about 50p to the assistant who washes your hair.
Petrol (Gas) Stations: Tips are not expected.

PORTER SERVICES

Porters are a rare sight at railway stations these days. Most of the larger hotels, however, employ porters, whereas in smaller hotels the waiter or barman, or even the owner himself will help you with your baggage. About 30p per suitcase would be considered a reasonable tip.

EXTENSION OF STAY

When moving on, it is always advisable to make an advance reservation. If staying at a hotel which belongs to a chain or consortium such as "Welsh Rarebits" the hotel will make the reservation on your behalf and at no cost to you. But if your requirements are not perfectly straightforward your best advice is to call at your nearest TIC (Tourist Information Centre) and ask about their "Book a Bed a Head" scheme.

GETTING ACQUAINTED

HOW WALES IS GOVERNED

Wales returns 38 members to the (British) House of Commons in Westminster. Unlike England, there are more Labour than Conservative members in Wales. Plaid Cymru, the Welsh National Party, has three members represented.

Matters of Welsh concern are discussed in the Welsh Grand Committee and time in each parliamentary session is put aside in the Commons to debate Government policy and action over the entire area of Welsh administration. Considerable administrative autonomy exists in Wales in the person of the Secretary of State, who has a seat in the British Cabinet. He carries out ministerial functions in Wales relating to housing, health, road services, local government, primary, secondary and further education (but not the University), agriculture, town and country planning, new towns, forestry, tourism, etc. He has direct responsibility for Welsh economic development.

In short, it is his function to ensure that the Government as a whole is aware of the needs and conditions of the principality. He is advised by his civil servants and by various statutory bodies. His central office is in Cardiff – the Welsh Office – in Cathays Park; there is also an office in London, a few yards away from the Houses of Parliament.

On 7 June 1979 there was a new representation when Wales elected its four members to sit in the European Parliament. The country, for this purpose, was divided into South Wales, Southeast Wales, Mid & West Wales and North Wales.

Local Government is organised basically in two tiers, comprising eight large counties (Clwyd, Dyfed, Gwent, Gwynedd, Mid Glamorgan, Powys, South Glamorgan and West Glamorgan), within which there are 37 districts; the counties are responsible for strategic planning, transportation planning, education, the police and fire services and the personal social services. The districts provide more local services.

THE ECONOMY

Well over half of the land area of Wales is in agricultural use, although conditions vary considerably from the high moorland and mountainous regions of North Wales to such arable areas as part of Gwent, Dyfed and the Vale of Glamorgan. Farmers have not been too happy of late. The European Economic) has at various times introduced stringent milk production quotas and weakened the support system for beef.

As the cereal surplus problem is being faced, Welsh sheep farmers too are concerned about their future. Many farmers are therefore diversifying – some with considerable success as cheese producers and fish farmers but primarily as tourism entrepreneurs. Tourism is second to agriculture in the Welsh economy and is Wales's major growth industry. Tourism now employs about 100,000 – more than three times the combined total of those who work in coal and steel.

The "How Green Was My Valley" image of Wales, of miners trudging their way home is no more. Wales is now in the forefront of a range of new technologies. More than one in five of Welsh manufacturing workers are employed by foreign-owned companies – North American, European and Japanese.

Wales now boasts disc production, optics, electro-acoustics, office furniture, petrochemicals, instrument and automotive engineering, oil refining, electricity generating – and even Welsh whisky and wine industries. Despite this new vibrancy and the exciting regeneration of dock areas in Newport, Cardiff and Swansea, parts of Wales still experience a remarkably high level of unemployment.

GEOGRAPHY & POPULATION

The land area of Wales is 8,000 sq miles (20,720 sq km), about the size of Massachusetts or half the size of Switzerland. It is approximately 170 miles long by 60 miles wide (270 by 100 km) and has 750 miles (1,200 km) of coastline. Wales is mainly an upland country with the greater part being over 600 feet above sea level. One quarter of it is above 1,000 ft (305 metres).

The population numbers 2.73 million, slightly less than that of New Zealand. The capital city is Cardiff – population 275,000. Over 75,000 of the total population of Wales live within half an hour of here – a population that grew with the explosion of the Industrial Revolution.

Each part of Wales possesses physical features that have given it qualities of their own. The South has its beautiful sandy beaches, Mid Wales has its gently

KPM

KÖNIGLICHE
PORZELLAN
MANUFAKTUR
Berlin

BERLIN MASTERPIECES

ROCAILLE,
Breslauer Stadtschloß
The unusual reliefs and
opulent embellishments
of this rococo design
places extremely high
demands on the artistic
abilities of the craftsmen.

SCHINKEL Basket
Design: app. 1820
by Karl Friedrich Schinkel.

KURLAND, *pattern 73*
The first classicistic service
made by KPM was created
around 1790 by order of
the Duke of Kurland.

KPM BERLIN · Wegelystraße 1 · Kurfürstendamm 26a · Postal address: Postfach 12 21 07, D-10591 Berlin · Phone
(030) 390 09 - 226 · Fax (030) 390 09 - 279 · U.K. AGENCY · Exclusif Presentations, Ltd. · 20 Vancouver Road
Edgware, Middx. HA8 5DA · Phone (081) 952 46 79 · Fax (081) 951 09 39 · JAPAN AGENCY · Hayashitok Co., Ltd.
Nakano-Cho. Ogawa. Marutamachi · Nakagyo-Ku. Kyoto 604 · Phone (075) 222 02 31 / 231 22 22 · Fax (075) 256 45 54

rolling hills and the North craggy mountains and Yr Wyddfs – Mount Snowdon, at 3,560 ft (1,085 metres) the highest point in England and Wales.

TIME ZONES

Wales, like the rest of Britain, lies in the Greenwich Mean Time Zone. In spring, the clock is moved forward one hour for British Summer Time and in the autumn moved back again to G.M.T. In the early summer months, it is light until 10p.m., especially on the west coast of Wales. Zones west of Greenwich have earlier times (e.g. New York, five hours), whereas zones to the east have later times (e.g. Tokyo, nine hours).

CLIMATE

Welsh weather is always unpredictable. Because of the mountainous nature of the country, it can be raining on one side of the mountain and dry and sunny all day on the other. Always be prepared and carry a lightweight raincoat or a collapsible umbrella.

May/June and September/October are usually the most pleasant and comfortable times to travel in Wales and although July and August were once considered to be the warmest months, they are now often the wettest. The month of April a few years ago was the warmest and driest since records have been kept and December 1988 was the mildest in living memory. Heavy snow is something of a rarity and generally only remains on the higher ground for no more than a few days at a time.

CULTURE & CUSTOMS

Dewi Sant, or Saint David, a saint of the Celtic Church, was son of Sandde, Prince of Powys, and Non. He became the Abbot of Ty Ddewi/Saint David's and died on 1 March A.D. 588. He was buried in what is today Ty Ddewi (Saint David's Cathedral) in the former county of Pembrokeshire, now part of Dyfed. So respected was he that medieval pilgrims believed that two pilgrimages to Ty Ddewi were worth one pilgrimage to Rome. Fifty churches in South Wales alone bear his name.

St David's Day (1 March) is now the traditional day of the Welsh, celebrated by Welsh people all over the world, wearing either of the national emblems: a leek or daffodil. Usually the day's celebrations would include either a Noson Llawen, an Eisteddfod or a dinner with guest speaker.

THE NATIONAL FLAG

This depicts a red dragon passant on a green and white field. No-one really knows how the red dragon became the emblem of Wales. However, it seems that the early Britons probably used it as a battle standard after the Roman occupation and that it may derive from a Roman standard. One

clue to this theory is that the English word "dragon" and the Welsh *draig* both come from the same Latin root, *draco*.

Draig was used in Welsh poetry to symbolise a warrior or a leader, while British leader was sometimes called Pendragon, or chief dragon, as was King Arthur's father.

In the 7th century, Cadwaladr, Prince of Gwynedd, carried a battle standard bearing a Red Dragon. Legend gathered around the Prince asserting that he would return to deliver his people.

The same idea appears in a legend recorded by an 8th-century historian about a fight between a Red Dragon (Wales) and a White Dragon (England) which foretold the eventual triumph of the Red Dragon. These deeply rooted convictions that a Welsh Prince would reign again were preserved by the bards.

Centuries later they helped Henry Tudor to gain support as he marched through Wales, bearing the Red Dragon as his standard. After winning the English Crown at Bosworth Field, he placed the standard in St Paul's Cathedral. Henry also introduced the Red Dragon into the Royal Arms. This was later displaced by James VI of Scotland with the Scottish Unicorn.

In 1801 the Red Dragon again won heraldic recognition – this time as a Royal Badge representing Wales. An addition was made to it in 1953 by placing it on a shield, surrounded by a ribbon bearing the quotation *Y Ddraig Goch ddyry Cychwyn* (The Red Dragon lends impetus). The whole of this was surmounted by a Crown.

For a time, this badge was used on the Welsh flag, but did not find universal favour in Wales and, in 1959, the Queen commanded that the original Red Dragon on a green and white field be flown as the official Welsh flag.

Welsh flags of varying sizes may be purchased from: **Mott & Jones (Flagmakers Ltd.)**, 14 Cambrian Place, South Dock, Swansea. Tel: (0792) 473139

ELECTRICITY

The standard voltage throughout Wales is 220 volts. Most hotels and guest houses have dual 220/110 volt sockets for razors.

BUSINESS HOURS

Business hours are generally 9a.m.–5.30p.m. from Monday to Saturday. In cities such as Cardiff, Newport and Swansea many "corner shops" are open seven days a week until 10p.m. In country areas, many small villages and towns still have an "early closing day". This is often on a Wednesday afternoon.

HOLIDAYS

Public holidays in Wales are identical to those in England and usually amount to eight days a year. These are:

New Year's Day Bank Holiday, 1 January
Good Friday
Easter Monday
May Day Holiday (1st Monday after 1 May)
Spring Bank Holiday (a Monday in late May)
Christmas Day, 25 December
Boxing Day, 26 December

RELIGIOUS SERVICES

Wales can boast a long and continuous history of Christian conviction, although church attendances have declined in recent years. Wales is largely non-conformist – with a great number of chapels, churches and a few spectacular cathedrals. The Archbishop of Wales is head of the disestablished church of the Anglican communion.

Most church services are held on a Sunday morning and evening. Details of these and other services are usually available at hotel reception desks and Tourist Information Centres.

COMMUNICATIONS

MEDIA

Newspapers: The *Western Mail,* printed in Cardiff and owned by Thomson Regional Newspapers, claims to be "The National Newspaper of Wales". It is the only daily paper with a good coverage of Welsh news as well as British and foreign news. Its "News of Wales" has tended to be biased towards South Wales but a North Wales edition was introduced in 1988. In North Wales, the *Daily Post,* printed in Liverpool, has a smattering of Welsh news in its Welsh edition.

The three main cities – Cardiff (*South Wales Echo*), Swansea (*Swansea Evening Post*) and Newport (*The Argus*) have evening papers which concentrate on local news, sport and entertainment. There is a high degree of advertising in each of these papers. There are many local weekly papers throughout Wales and one weekly "national" newspaper, *Y Cymro* (The Welshman) which is printed in the Welsh language.

All major daily papers printed in London or Manchester are readily available at newsagents throughout Wales. Wales's first Sunday paper, *Wales on Sunday*, appeared in the spring of 1989 and was created by Thomson Regional Newspapers as a national newspaper with a Welsh focus.

Television & Radio: Cardiff has major television studios for both the BBC and commercial television (HTV). Both companies provide programmes in English and in Welsh. Their Welsh language output for television is transmitted via the local counterpart of the national Channel 4: S4C (*Sianel 4 Cymru*).

BBC Wales (located at Broadcasting House, Llandaff) is the biggest and most productive broadcasting centre outside London. It is the home of two separate BBC radio services: Radio Wales (English language) and Radio Cymru (Welsh language). Both services provide on average 65 hours a week of programmes.

In television BBC Wales originates nearly eight hours a week of English television programmes as an opt-out service for BBC 1 or BBC 2. Welsh news and events are featured in *Wales Today* each evening

BBC Wales is one of the major contributors to the S4C Welsh language service, supplying most of the news and sporting programmes as well as a nightly "soap" about the inhabitants of Cwm Deri.

The commercial station in Wales, HTV, has invested about £20 million to create the most modern television production centre in Europe on a 60-acre site on the outskirts of Cardiff. Welsh news and events are featured in an early evening programme. The company maintains close links with major national events in Wales and produces programmes of high quality, including current affairs, music and entertainment and agriculture.

Although BBC Wales has studios in Swansea and Bangor and HTV Wales have a presence in Mold, more broadcast television is produced in Cardiff than anywhere else in the UK other than London. Many of Wales's new independent companies are based in the regenerated dockland area of Cardiff whilst Caernarfon is undoubtedly the thriving media centre of North Wales.

Three commercial radion stations have a presence in Wales – Marcher Sound in northeast Wales, Red Dragon Radio in Cardiff and Gwent and the most successful Swansea Sound covering southwest Wales.

POSTAL SERVICES

Post offices in cities and major towns throughout Wales are open from 9a.m.–5.30p.m. Monday to Friday and from 9a.m.–12.30p.m. on Saturdays. Most villages also have post offices, but these are referred to as sub-post offices and are usually part of a grocery or general store. Opening hours are the same as main post offices but in some villages shops often close for a half-day (usually a Wednesday) during the week.

The postage rate within the UK for letters or cards is 24p (1st class) and 18p (2nd class). Airmail cards or letters to Europe cost 28p or 39p to anywhere else in the world.

For the fastest weekend refunds anywhere in the world.

Ensure your holiday is worry free even if your travellers cheques are lost or stolen by buying American Express Travellers Cheques from;

Lloyds Bank

Royal Bank of Scotland

Abbey National[*]

Bank of Ireland

Halifax Building Society[*]

Leeds Permanent Building Society[*]

Woolwich Building Society[*]

National & Provincial Building Society

Britannia Building Society[*]

American Express Travel Offices.

As well as many regional building societies and travel agents.

[*]Investors only.

Not all travellers cheques are the same.

 Travellers Cheques

The Post Office will receive mail for you providing you instruct the sender to label the envelope "Poste Restante". It should be sent to a main post office nominated by you from where it may be collected.

TELEPHONE & TELEX

There is a minimum charge of 10p to use a public telephone. Most telephone booths accept 2p, 5p, 10p, 20p, 50p and £1 coins. You can direct dial any number in Britain for the minimum charge of 10p, although the time you buy for your money is dictated by the distance involved. A local call will give you three minutes for 10p.

When you dial, using either the almost extinct rotary dial or the modern press-button telephone, don't pause too long between digits. After dialling there may be a pause before you hear a tone; hold on for up to 15 seconds on calls within the UK and up to 60 seconds on international calls to allow the equipment time to connect your call. To access the international network, dial 010 followed by your country code (e.g. 1 for the United States).

To contact the operator for assistance or if you experience difficulty in obtaining a dialled call, dial 100. Dial 100 also for all International enquiries. For directory enquiries within the UK dial 192. No money is required to call the operator but a charge is made when calling directory enquiries from a private phone.

Most of the larger hotels in Wales have telex facilities, available to guests at a small charge. The number of hotels with a fax facility is growing at an extremely rapid pace.

EMERGENCIES

SECURITY & CRIME

PRINCIPAL POLICE STATIONS

SOUTHEAST WALES

CWMBRAN
Gwent Constabulary, Croesyceiliog, Cwmbran. Tel: (0633) 838111
CHEPSTOW,. Tel: (0291) 623993
MONMOUTH,. Tel: (0600) 712321

SOUTHWEST WALES

CARMARTHEN
Dyfed Powys Constabulary, Carmarthen. Tel: (0267) 236444

NORTH WALES

COLWYN BAY
North Wales Police, Colwyn Bay. Tel: (0492) 517171
DOLGELLAU. Tel: (0341) 422222
LLANDUDNO,. Tel: (0492) 860260
WREXHAM,. Tel: (0978) 290222

SOUTH WALES

BRIDGEND
South Wales Constabulary, Bridgend. Tel: (0656) 655555
CARDIFF,. Tel: (0222) 222111

MID WALES

ABERYSTWYTH,. Tel: (0970) 612791
NEWTOWN,. Tel: (0686) 625704

EMERGENCY SERVICES

Dial 999 on your nearest telephone (no coins required) and ask for the emergency service you want – FIRE, POLICE, AMBULANCE or COASTGUARD.

LOSS

Lost credit cards should be reported immediately to:
Access/Master Card, Southend on Sea.
Tel: (0702) 352255
American Express, Brighton. Tel: (0273) 696933
Diners Club, Farnborough. Tel: (0252) 516261
Visa, Northampton. Tel: (0604) 230230
Valuables: Most hotels have a safe or a safe box where your valuables may be deposited. When travelling, it is always advisable to conceal such valuables as cameras when left unattended in a car or coach. Always lock your car.

MEDICAL SERVICES

Although advisable to have your own medical insurance, citizens of EEC countries and some other countries are entitled to medical treatment under reciprocal arrangements.

Emergency treatment is given free at hospital casualty departments. Major hospitals are listed here:

SOUTH WALES

NEWPORT
Royal Gwent Hospital, Newport. Tel: (0633) 252244
ABERGAVENNY
Nevill Hall Hospital, Abergavenny. Tel: (0873) 852091
CARDIFF
Cardiff Royal Infirmary, Cardiff. Tel: (0222) 492233
St David's Hospital, Cardiff. Tel: (0222) 344141
BRIDGEND
Bridgend General Hospital, Quarella Road, Bridgend. Tel: (0656) 6662166
SWANSEA
Morriston Hospital, Heol Maes Eglwys, Cwn-rhydyceirw, Swansea. Tel: (0792) 702222

SOUTHWEST WALES

CARMARTHEN
West Wales General Hospital, Glan Gwili, Carmarthen. Tel: (0267) 235151
HAVERFORDWEST
Withybush General Hospital, Fishguard Road, Haverfordwest. Tel: (0437) 4545

MIDWALES

ABERYSTWYTH
Bron Glais Hospital, Aberystwyth. Tel: (0970) 623131
SHREWSBURY
Royal Shrewsbury Hospital, Mytton Oak Road, Shrewsbury. Tel: (0743) 231122

NORTH WALES

BANGOR
Ysbyty Gwynedd, Penrhos Road, Bangor. Tel: (0248) 370007
LLANDUDNO
Llandudno General Hospital, Llandudno. Tel: (0492) 860066
ST ASAPH (for Rhyl & Prestatyn)
Glan Clwyd Hospital, Bodelwyddan, St Asaph. Tel: (0745) 583910
WREXHAM
Ysbyty Maelor Wrecsam, Croesnewydd Road, Wrexham. Tel: (0978) 291100

GETTING AROUND

ORIENTATION

Wales is much more accessible than most people think. British Rail's proud boast is that it can take you from one capital city (London) to another (Cardiff) in 100 minutes by its high-speed train. These trains run during most of the day at hourly intervals and depart London from Paddington Station.

But, having arrived in Wales, how does one get around? There are only two answers: with difficulty or by car. To see the best of Wales and to explore its quieter areas, a car is essential. With four people sharing, it may well be worthwhile having the services of a knowledgeable chauffeur-guide (see Things To Do section) but if you are happy to rent a car and do the driving yourself, don't pick up your car in London or another large city – travel by train or bus to Wales first and rent your car in a smaller city or town where the traffic is much lighter and quieter country roads

are virtually on your doorstep. This will give you a confidence booster, especially if you aren't used to driving on the left-hand side of the road.

Car hire in Britain is not cheap, although many excellent deals are available if you can pick up and return your car to the same destination. Some of these smaller companies, however, have very few automatic cars available, so it's advisable to book this type in advance.

There is no air link between South and North Wales, nor is it possible to travel by train from South to North without going through England. The "Britrail Pass" holder needs to work hard to get value for his money in Wales. The two main lines run east to west along the north coast (Chester to Holyhead) and the south coast (Newport to Fishguard). Both services link up with ferry services to and from Ireland.

In Mid-Wales it is possible to travel by rail, again from east to west (Shrewsbury to Aberystwyth), but the two railway journeys that are the most scenic and memorable are the Central Wales line through the heart of Wales (Swansea-Llandrindod Wells-Shrewsbury) and the Cambrian Coastline (Aberystwth-Aberdovey-Harlech-Criccieth-Pwllheli).

There is only one way of travelling between north and south Wales by public transportation in one day, and that is by bus or coach. This is a daily service year-round operated by National Welsh and Crosville Wales. The service, Traws Cambria, operates between Bangor (north Wales) and Cardiff via Aberystwyth, Swansea and a number of small towns on the west coast. Journey time is eight hours and sample fares are around £14 single for entire journey or around £22 period return (three months). There is a 25 percent discount on adult fares for men and women over 60.

Travellers arriving in Wales through Cardiff (Wales) Airport (10 miles west of city centre) can take a taxi (cost to General Railway Station £8 to £10) or a bus. Service X51 operates hourly between the airport and Cardiff's main bus station for less than £2.

The best general map of Wales is published by the Wales Tourist Board. This map not only list all major tourist sites but is packed with useful information and telephone numbers, town maps, a gazetteer and suggested road tours (cost approx. £1.20). Another useful map is called AutoWales. This is free and is obtainable at most offices of the British Tourist Authority worldwide.

DOMESTIC TRAVEL

CAR HIRE

ABERDARE, Mid Glamorgan
Abedare Ford, New Cardiff Road, Aberdare. Tel: (0685) 877700
ABERYSTWYTH, Dyfed
Ford Rent A Car, Meirion Motors, Glenyrafon Industrial Estate, Aberystwyth. Tel: (0970) 611545

ANGLESEY, Gwynedd
Swan National Rental, Kingslands Road, Holyhead.
Tel: (0407) 764614
Hertz, Swift Service Centre, London Road, Holyhead.
Tel: (0407) 763818
BLACKWOOD, Gwent
Ford Rent A Car, Arrow Ford, Belmont Garage,
Newbridge Road, Pontllanfraith. Tel: (0495) 225423
BRECON, Powys
Ford Rent A Car, Elston of Brecon, The Modern
Garage, Brecon. Tel: (0874) 622401
CAERPHILLY, Mid Glamorgan
Ford Rent A Car, R. J. Brown Rent A Car, The
Truck Centre, Pontygwindy Estate, Caerphilly. Tel:
(0222) 852222
CARDIFF, South Glamorgan
Avis Rent A Car Ltd., 14-22 Tudor Street, Cardiff.
Tel: (0222) 342111
Budget Rent A Car, c/o Driveside, Collingdon
Road, Cardiff. Tel: (0222)465060
Europcar,1-11,Byron Street,Cardiff.Tel:(0222) 498978
Hertz, 9, Central Square, Cardiff. Tel: (0222) 224548
All Travellers Rent A Car, Cardiff International
Hotel, Mary Ann Street, Cardiff. Tel: (0222) 222098
Swan National Rentals, 10, Dominions Way,
Industrial Estate, Newport Road, Cardiff. Tel:
(0222) 496256
CARMARTHEN, Dyfed
Ford Rent A Car, Towy Garage Ltd., The Bridge,
Carmarthen. Tel: (0267) 236482
CHEPSTOW, Gwent
Ford Rent A Car, Larkfied of Chepstow Ltd.,
Newport Road, Chepstow. Tel: (0291)628155
COLWYN BAY, Clwyd
Ford Rent A Car, Gordon Ford (Colwyn Bay) Ltd.,
130, Conway Road, West End, Colwyn Bay. Tel:
(0492) 532201
HAVERFORDWEST, Dyfed
Ford Rent A Car, W. H. Baker Ltd., Salutation
Square, Haverfordwest. Tel: (0437) 3772
LLANDOVERY, Dyfed
Castle Garage Ltd., Broad Street, Llandovery. Tel:
(0550) 20335
LLANDUDNO, Gwynedd
Europcar, L.S.P. Motors Ltd., Mostyn Broadway,
Llandudno. Tel: (0492) 878608
LLANGEFNI, Gwynedd
Ford Rent A Car, Ivor Jones Motors, Chapel Street,
Llangefni. Tel: (0248) 750142
MERTHYR TYDFIL, Mid Glamorgan
Ford Rent A Car, W. H. Baker (Merthyr Tydfil) Ltd.,
Pentrebach Road, Merthyr Tydfil. Tel: (0685) 74121
NEATH, West Glamorgan
Ford Rent A Car, C. E. M. Day, Ltd., Neath Abbey
roundabou Neath. Tel: (0639) 641234
NEWPORT, Gwent
Avis Rent A Car Ltd., Gwent Service Station, 158,
Cardiff Road, Newport. Tel: (0633) 259023
Budget Rent A Car, Motorwell Service Station,
Granville Square, George Street Bridge, Newport.
Tel: (0623)214326

PONTYPRIDD, Mid Glamorgan
Ford Rent A Car, R. J. Brown Ltd., Station Square
Garage, Pontypridd. Tel: (0443) 409211
PORT TALBOT, West Glamorgan
Ford Rent A Car, C. E. M. Day Ltd., Acacia Avenue,
Sandfields, Port Talbot. Tel: (0639) 887661
RHOOSE, South Glamorgan
Europcar, (Advanced Reservations only), Cardiff
(Wales) Airport, Rhoose. Tel: (0446) 711705
SWANSEA, West Glamorgan
Avis Rent A Car Ltd., NCP Car Park, Orchard
Street, Swansea. Tel: (0792) 460939
Europcar, 187-189 Lower Oxford Street, Swansea.
Tel: (0792) 650526
Ford Rent A Car, C. E. M. Day Ltd., Beaufort Road,
Plas Marl Industrial Estate Swansea. Tel: (0792)
310410
Hertz, Ael-Y-Bryn, Carmathen Road, Swansea. Tel:
(0792) 586117
Practical Used Car Rental, Clare Street, Manselton,
Swansea. Tel: (0792) 641037
Swan National Rentals, Lower Oxford Street,
Swansea. Tel: (0792) 643336
TENBY, Dyfed
Silcox Self Drive Ltd., Frog Street Arcade, Tenby.
Tel: (0834) 2459
WREXHAM, Clwyd
Kirbys (Wrexham) Ltd., Holt Road, Wrexham. Tel:
(0978) 365720

WHERE TO STAY

HOTELS

Wales offers a wide range of accommodation from
small cottages and farmhouses offering Bed and
Breakfast to hotels of international standard. There
are very few hotels with more than 100 bedrooms
outside the capital, Cardiff. Prices vary from about
£15 a night to over £100 at the most expensive hotel.

Hotels and guest houses as well as self-catering
properties and caravan parks are inspected and
graded by the Wales Tourist Board. The Board
publishes *Where to Stay in Wales* annually; it
contains the most comprehensive list of accommodation available.

In North America, it is possible to book independently owned hotels that are members of Inter-
Hotels or the "Welsh Rarebits" consortia through
the Wales Reservation Centre which has a toll-free
number. USA 1-800-444-9988 and Canada 212-

688-9563. Information on where to stay in Wales is also available at all British Tourist Authority offices worldwide.

In London, one can obtain this information and make the necessary reservations at the Wales Centre in the heart of London's West End: Wales Centre, British Travel Centre, 4, Lower Regent Street, London W1. Tel: (071) 409 0969. Once you arrive in Wales, call in at a Tourist Information Centre. Most operate a free Bed Booking Service.

WELSH RAREBIT HOTELS, INNS & FARMHOUSES

This section includes a complete cross-section of accommodation. All are highly individualistic, are privately owned and personally run, offer genuine Welsh hospitality – and exceptional value for money. Prices are as guidelines only. They are for double rooms (two people) and include full Welsh breakfast.

SOUTH WALES

MONMOUTH
King's Head Hotel, Monmouth. Tel: (0600) 2177. A 17th-century coaching inn. £45–£55.

USK
Cwrt Bleddyn Hotel, Usk. Tel: (063349) 521. A country hotel with modern leisure complex. £97.

NEAR CARDIFF
Egerton Grey Country House, Porthkerry. Tel: (0446) 711666. A small manor house of great character. £60–£120.

BRIDGEND
Coed y Mwstwr Hotel, Coychurch. Tel: (0656) 860621. An elegant Victorian country house. £80.

NEAR SWANSEA
Fairyhill Country Hotel, Reynoldston. Tel: (0792) 390139. An historic house on the beautiful Gower peninsula. Over £60.

SOUTHWEST WALES

TENBY
Penally Abbey Hotel, Penally. Tel: (0834) 3033. A character hotel with many four poster beds. £70–£80.

ST DAVID'S
St Non's Hotel, St David's. Tel: (0437) 720239. A friendly hotel close to the magnificent cathedral. £70.

FISHGUARD
Wolfscastle Country Hotel, Wolfscastle. Tel: (043787) 225. Small and friendly with a superb restaurant. £38–£55.

MIDWALES

CARDIGAN
Penbontbren Farm Hotel, Cardigan. Tel: (0239) 810248. A taste of traditional Wales at its best. £52–£58.

CRICKHOWELL
The Bear Hotel, Crickhowell. Tel: (0873) 810408. An historic coaching inn of great character. £65.

LLANGAMMARCH WELLS
The Lake Hotel, Llangammarch Wells. Tel: (05912) 202. A superb country house set in 50 acres. £85–£130.

ABERYSTWYTH
Conrah Country Hotel, Chancery, Aberystwyth. Tel: (0970) 617941. An elegantly restored 19th-century mansion. £75–£95.

ABERDOVEY
Hotel Plas Penhelig, Aberdovey. Tel: (0654) 767676. A country house set in beautiful gardens. £81.

LLANWDDYN
Lake Vyrnwy Hotel, Llanwddyn. Tel: (069173) 692. An uniquely located sporting hotel. £44–£74.

WELSHPOOL
Heart of Wales Farmhouses.
(1) **Tynllwyn Farm** Tel: (0938) 553175.
(2) **Gungrog Farm** Tel: (0938) 553381.
(3) **Moat Farm** Tel: (0938) 553179.
(4) **Highgate Farm** Tel: (0686) 625981.
(5) **Cyfie Farm** Tel: (069184) 451.
Experience a genuine Welsh farmhouse welcome. £26–£32.

NORTH WALES

HARLECH
Hotel Maes-y-Neuadd. Tel: (0766) 780200. A beautiful country house in a superb setting. £97.

PWLLHELI
Plas Bodegroes, Pwllheli. Tel: (0758) 612363. A small Georgian house with elegant restaurant. £80–£120.

CAERNARFON
Seiont Manor. Tel: (0286) 673366. A luxury property with the highest standards. £99.

BEAUMARIS
Ye Olde Bull's Head. Tel: (0248) 810329. A 500-year-old inn of great character. £68.

LLANDUDNO
Bodysgallen Hall. Tel: (0492) 584466. One of Britain's most popular country house hotels. From £128–£185.

LLANRWST
Meadowsweet Hotel. Tel: (0492) 640732. A small Victorian hotel with fine restaurant. £38.

DENBIGH
Llanrhaeadr Hall. Tel: (074578) 313. An historic mansion nicely set in the verdant Vale of Clwyd. £56–£75.

MOLD
Soughton Hall. Tel: (0352)86811. An outstandingly well-preserved example of a Georgian country mansion.£50–£65.

WREXHAM
Llwyn Onn Hall. Tel: (0978) 261225. A handsome country house set in open parkland. £64–£75.

CORWEN
Tyddyn Llan Country House. Tel: (049084) 264. A small Georgian house of great charm. £48–£52.

LLANARMON DYFFRYN CEIRIOG
The Hand Hotel. Tel: (069176) 264/666. A charming hotel located not far from the interesting Chirk Castle. £70.

BED & BREAKFAST

In Wales, this term usually refers to accommodation in private homes. Prices usually range from £12 to £20 a person. During the main summer season, Bed & Breakfast signs appear everywhere and although it is rarely essential to book in advance, it is advisable to call at the nearest Tourist Information Centre for guidance on accommodation that has been thoroughly checked out by the Wales Tourist Board.

Most country inns in Wales offer food of some description. Relatively few inns, however, offer good quality accommodation as well as good food. Here is a selection of 28 inns of character noted for their welcome, atmosphere and food. All have fewer than 14 letting bedrooms and prices for bed and a full Welsh breakfast start from approximately £15 a person.

BEAUMARIS, Isle of Anglesey
Ye Olde Bull's Head. **Tel**: (0248) 810329. 11 bedrooms.

CARDIGAN, Dyfed
Black Lion Hotel. Tel: (0239) 612532. 11 bedrooms.

HAY-ON-WYE, Powys
Old Black Lion. **Tel**: (0497) 820841. 10 bedrooms.

LLANDOGO, Gwent (Wye Valley)
Sloop Inn. **Tel**: (0594) 530291. 4 bedrooms.

LLANDOVERY, Dyfed
King's Head Inn. **Tel**: (0550) 20393. 4 bedrooms.

LLANGOLLEN, Clwyd
Britannia Inn (Horseshoe Pass). **Tel:** (0978) 860144. 5 bedrooms.

LLANGORSE, Brecon, Powys
Red Lion. **Tel:** (087 484) 238. 10 bedrooms.

LLANGURIG, Powys
Blue Bell Inn. **Tel:** (055 15) 254. 10 bedrooms.

LLANEFYDD, near Denbigh, Clwyd
Hawk & Buckle Inn. **Tel:** (074 579) 249. 10 bedrooms.

MONMOUTH, Gwent
Queen's Head Inn. **Tel:** (0600) 2767. 4 bedrooms.

MONTGOMERY, Powys
Dragon Hotel. **Tel:** (0686) 668359/668287. 15 bedrooms.

NOTTAGE, Porthcawl, Mid Glamorgan
Rose & Crown. **Tel:** (0656) 784850. 8 bedrooms.

PANTMAWR, near Llangurig, Powys
Glansevern Arms. **Tel:** (055 15) 240. 8 bedrooms.

PENMAENPOOL, near Dolgellau, Gwynedd
George III Hotel. **Tel:** (0341) 422525. 14 bedrooms

PENYBONT, near Llandrindod Wells, Powys
Severn Arms Hotel. **Tel:** (0597) 851224. 10 bedrooms.

RAGLAN, Gwent
Beaufort Arms Hotel. **Tel:** (0291) 690412. 15 bedrooms.

TRECASTLE, Powys
Castle Hotel. **Tel:** (087 482) 636354. 10 bedrooms.

YOUTH HOSTELS

NORTH WALES

BALA, Gwynedd
Youth Hostel, Plas Rhiwaedog, Rhos-Y-Gwaliau, Bala, Gwynedd LL23 7EU. Tel: (0678) 520215

BANGOR, Gwynedd
Youth Hostel, Tan-Y-Bryn, Bangor, Gwynedd LL57 1PZ. Tel: (0248) 353516

BRYN GWYNANT, Gwynedd
Youth Hostel, Bryn Gwynant, Caernarfon, Gwynedd LL55 4NP. Tel: (076686) 251

CAPEL CURIG, Gwynedd
Youth Hostel, Plas Curig, Betws-y-Coed, Gwynedd LL24 0EL. Tel: (06904) 225

CHESTER
Youth Hostel, Hough Green House, 40, Hough Green, Chester CH4 8JD. Tel: (0244) 680056

COLWYN BAY, Clwyd
Youth Hostel, Foxhill, Nant-Y-Glyn, Colwyn Bay, Clwyd LL29 6AB. Tel: (0492) 530627

CYNWYD, Clwyd
Youth Hostel, The Old Mill, Cynwyd, Corwen, Clwyd LL21 0LW. Tel: (0490) 2797

FFESTINIOG, Gwynedd
Youth Hostel, Caerblaidd, Llan Ffestiniog, Blaenau Ffestiniog, Gwynedd LL41 4PH. Tel: (076676) 265

IDWAL COTTAGE, Gwynedd
Youth Hostel, Idwal Cottage, Nant Ffrancon, Bethesda, Bangor, Gwynedd LL57 3LZ . Tel: (0248) 600225

LLANBEDR, Gwynedd
Youth Hostel, Plas Newydd, Llanbedr, Gwynedd LL45 2LE. Tel: (034123) 287

LLANBERIS, Gwynedd
Youth Hostel, Llwyn Celyn, Llanberis, Caernarfon, Gwynedd LL55 4SR. Tel: (0286) 870280

LLANGOLLEN, Clwyd
Youth Hostel, Tyndwr Hall, Tyndwr Road, Llangollen, Clwyd LL20 8AR. Tel: (0978) 860330

LLEDR VALLEY, Gwynedd
Youth Hostel, Lledr House, Pont-Y-Pant, Dolwyddelan, Gwynedd LL25 0DQ. Tel: (06906) 202

MAESHAFN, Clwyd
Youth Hostel, Holt Hostel, Maeshafn, Mold, Clwyd CH7 5LR. Tel: Regional Office (0222) 396766

PENMAENMAWR, Gwynedd
Youth Hostel, Penmaenbach, Penmaenmawr, Gwynedd LL34 6UL. Tel: (0492) 623476

PEN-Y-PASS, Gwynedd
Youth Hostel, Pen-Y-Pass, Nant Gwynant, Caernarfon, Gwynedd LL55 4NY. Tel: (0286) 870428

ROWEN, Gwynedd
Youth Hostel, Rhiw Farm, Rowen, Conwy, Gwynedd LL32 8YW. Tel: Regional Office (0222) 396766

SNOWDON RANGER, Gwynedd
Youth Hostel, Snowdon Ranger, Rhyd Ddu, Caernarfon, Gwynedd LL54 7YS. Tel: (028685) 391

MID WALES

BLAENCARON, Dyfed
Youth Hostel, Blaencaron, Tregaron, Dyfed SY25 6HL. Tel: (0974) 298441

BORTH, Dyfed
Youth Hostel, Morlais, Borth, Dyfed SY24 5JS. Tel: (0970) 871498

BRYN POETH UCHAF, Dyfed
Youth Hostel, Hafod-Y-Pant, Cynghordy, Llandovery, Dyfed SA20 0NB. Tel: (05505) 235

CORRIS, Powys
Youth Hostel, Old School, Old Road, Corris, Machynlleth, Powys SY20 9TS. Tel: (0654) 761686

DOLGOCH, Dyfed
Youth Hostel, Dolgoch, Tregaron, Dyfed SY25 6NR. Tel: (0974) 298680

GLASCWM, Powys
Youth Hostel, The School, Glascwm, Llandrindod Wells, Powys LD1 5SE. Tel: (0982) 570415

KINGS, Gwynedd
Youth Hostel, Kings, Dolgellau, Gwynedd LL40 1TB. Tel: (0341) 422392

KNIGHTON, Powys
Youth Hostel, Old Primary School, West Street, Knighton, Powys LD7 1EN. Tel: (0547) 528807

NANT-Y-DERNOL, Powys
Youth Hostel, Tan-Yr-Allt, Llangurig, Llanidloes, Powys SY18 6RZ. Tel: (05515) 246

TYNCORNEL, Dyfed
Youth Hostel, Tyncornel, Llanddewi-Brefi, Tregaron, Dyfed SY25 6PH. Tel: Regional Office (0222) 396766

YSTUMTUEN, Dyfed
Youth Hostel, Glantuen, Ystumtuen, Aberystwyth, Dyfed SY23 3AE. Tel: (097085) 693

WEST WALES

BROAD HAVEN, Dyfed
Youth Hostel, Broad Haven, Haverfordwest, Dyfed SA62 3JH. Tel: (0437) 781688

MARLOES SANDS, Dyfed
Youth Hostel, Runwayskiln, Marloes, Haverfordwest, Dyfed SA62 3BH. Tel: (0646) 636667

PENTLEPOIR, Dyfed
Youth Hostel, The Old School, Pentlepoir, Saundersfoot, Dyfed SA69 9BJ. Tel: (0834) 812333

POPPIT SANDS, Dyfed
Youth Hostel, Sea View, Poppit, Cardigan, Dyfed SA43 3LP. Tel: (0239) 612936

PWLL DERI, Dyfed
Youth Hostel, Castell Mawr, Tref Asser, Goodwick, Dyfed SA64 0LR. Tel: (03485) 223

ST DAVID'S, Dyfed
Youth Hostel, Llaethdy, St David's, Haverfordwest, Dyfed SA62 6PR. Tel: (0437) 720345

TREVINE, Dyfed
Youth Hostel, 11, Ffordd-Yr-Afon, Trevine, Haverfordwest, Dyfed SA62 5AU. Tel: (0348) 831414

BRECON BEACONS & SOUTH WALES

CAPEL-Y-FFIN, Gwent
Youth Hostel, Capel-Y-Ffin, Abergavenny, Gwent NP7 7NP. Tel: (0873) 890650

CARDIFF, South Glamorgan
Youth Hostel, 2, Wedal Road , Roath Park, Cardiff, South Glamorgan CF2 5PG. Tel: (0222) 462303

LLANDDEUSANT, Dyfed
Youth Hostel, The Old Red Lion, Llanddeusant, Llangadog, Dyfed SA19 6UL. Tel: (05504) 634/619

LLWYN-y-CELYN, Powys
Youth Hostel, Llwyn-Y-Celyn, Libanus, Brecon, Powys LD3 8NN. Tel: (0874) 624261

LLWYNYPIA, Mid Glamorgan
Youth Hostel, Glyncornel, Llwynypia, Mid Glamorgan CF40 2JF. Tel: (0443) 430859

PORT EYNON, West Glamorgan
Youth Hostel, The Old Lifeboat House, Port Eynon, Swansea, West Glamorgan SA3 1NN. Tel: (0792) 390706

TY'N-Y-CAEAU, Powys
Youth Hostel, Ty'n-y-Caeau, Groesffordd, Brecon, Powys LD3 7SW. Tel: (087486) 270

YSTRADFELLTE, Mid Glamorgan
Youth Hostel, Tai'r Heol, Ystradfellte, Aberdare, Mid Glamorgan CF44 9JF. Tel: (0639) 720301

FOOD DIGEST

WHAT TO EAT

In many Welsh seaside resorts it is regrettably still chips with everything, and the increase in fast-food, hamburger and pizza restaurants in cities such as Cardiff are sadly a sign of the times. Wales, however, is no longer a gastronomic desert. Standards have improved dramatically in recent years.

Cardiff can boast an amazing selection of international cuisines with some of its Chinese and Indian restaurants comparing favourably with the best in Britain. The most comprehensive selection of tradi-tional Welsh dishes is served at a Cardiff restaurant, *Blas ar Cymru* (Taste of Wales). Lamb and *sewin* (sea trout) are Welsh specialities and laver bread is as distinctive to Wales as is haggis to Scotland.

On your travels throughout Wales, look out for the *Blas ar Cymru*/Taste of Wales symbol. You'll find it at hotels, restaurants, farmhouses, guest houses and country inns which serve tempting Welsh foods prepared at their very best.

The Taste of Wales scheme embraces many styles of cooking. For the traditionalists, there are dishes such as succulent Welsh lamb. The more modern, lightly prepared style of cuisine is also very much a part of Taste of Wales – try some lightly poached sewin (sea-trout), for example.

Taste of Wales puts emphasis on fresh, high quality produce cooked with flair and imagination. The Welsh larder is a bountiful one, catering for all tastes. The county of Dyfed is known as the cheese store of Wales. The green heartlands of Powys and Gwynedd give us the star of Welsh cuisine, lamb. And since Wales is surrounded by the sea on three of its four sides, sea-food figures strongly. Try Gower oysters, Cardigan Bay lobsters, Menai mussels and Conwy salmon.

Don't miss out on Taste of Wales. You'll enjoy imaginative new dishes and old favourites, all using fresh, local ingredients.

WHERE TO EAT

RESTAURANTS

The following is a selection of the best restaurants in Wales with an approximate idea of the price per head for a meal, without wine.

ABERAERON, Dyfed
Hive on the Quay, Cadwgan Place, Aberaeron. Tel: (0545) 570445. £15–£20.

ABERDOVEY, Gwynedd
Old Coffee Shop, 13, New Street, Aberdovey. Tel: (065472) 767652. £10–£19.

ABERGAVENNY, Gwent
Walnut Tree Inn, Llandewi Skirrid, Abergavenny. Tel: (0873) 2797. £20+.

ABERYSTWYTH, Dyfed
Gannets, 7, St James' Square, Aberystwyth. Tel: (0970) 617164 £10+.

BRECHFA, Dyfed
Ty Mawr, Brechfa. Tel: (026789) 332. £10–£15.

CAERNARFON, Gwynedd
Bakestone, 26, Hole in the Wall Street, Caernarfon. Tel: (0286) 5846. £10–£15.

CARDIFF, South Glamorgan
Blas ar Gymru (A Taste of Wales), 48, Crwys, Road, Cardiff. Tel: (0222) 382132 £10-£15
Armless Dragon, 97, Wyvern Road, Cathays, Cardiff. Tel: (0222) 382357. £20.
La Brasserie, 60, St Mary's Street, Cardiff. Tel: (0222) 372164. £15-£20.
Le Cassoulet, 5, Romilly Crescent, Canton, Cardiff. Tel: (0222) 221905. £20-£30.
Champers, 61, St Mary's Street, Llandaff, Cardiff. Tel: (0222) 373363. £15-£20.
Everest, 43-45, Salisbury Road, Cathays, Cardiff. Tel: (0222) 374881. £10-£15.
Happy Gathering, 233, Cowbridge Road East, Canton, Cardiff. Tel: (0222) 621152. £10-£15.
Noble House, 9-10, St David's House, Wood Street, Cardiff. Tel: (0222) 388430. £15-£29.
Riverside, 44, Tudor Street, Cardiff. Tel: (0222) 372163. £13-£20.
Salvatore's, 14, Romilly Crescent, Canton, Cardiff. Tel: (0222) 372768. £16-£20.
Thai House, 23, High Street, Cardiff. Tel: (0222) 387404. £12-£25.
Trillium, 40, City Road, Cardiff. Tel: (0222) 463665. £20+.

CHEPSTOW, Gwent
Beckfords, 15/16 Upper Church Street, Chepstow. Tel: (0291)626665. £22.

CILGERRAN, Dyfed
Castle Kitchen, Cilgerran. Tel: (0239) 615055. £12+.

DINAS MAWDDWY, Gwynedd
Old Station Coffee Shop, Dinas Mawddwy. Tel: (06504) 338. Under £12.

ERBISTOCK, Clwyd
Boat Inn, Erbistock. Tel: (0978) 780143. £12-£20.

GLANWYDDEN, Gwynedd
Queen's Head, Glanwydden. Tel: (0492) 46570. £10-£15.

HARLECH, Gwynedd
Castle Cottage, Pen Llech, Harlech. Tel: (0766) 546570. £15-£20.

HARLECH, Gwynedd
The Cemlyn, High Street, Harlech. Tel: (0766) 780425. £20-£30.

HAVERFORDWEST, Dyfed
Jemima's, Nash Grove, Freystrop, Haverfordwest. Tel: (0437) 891109. £12-£31.

LLANBERIS, Gwynedd
Y Bistro, 43-45, High Street, Llanberis. Tel: (0286) 871278. £25-£34.

LLANDUDNO, Gwynedd
Craigside Manor, Colwyn Road, Little Orme, Llandudno. Tel: (0492) 45943. Under £10.
Lanterns Restaurant, 7, Church Walks, Llandudno. Tel: (0492) 77924. £22-£28.

LLANGOLLEN, Clwyd
Caesar's, Deeside Lane, Llangollen. Tel: (0978) 860133. £10-£15.
Gales, 18, Bridge Street, Llangollen. Tel: (0978),860089. Under £15.

MATHRY, Dyfed
Ann Fitzgerald's Farmhouse Kitchen, Mawbs Fawr, Mathry. Tel: (03483) 831347. £17-£34.

NEWPORT, Dyfed
Cnapan, East Street, Newport. Tel: (0239) 820575. £16-£26.

PONTYPRIDD, Mid Glamorgan
John & Maria's, 1-3, Broadway, Pontypridd. Tel: (0443) 402977. £10-£15.

SWANBRIDGE, South Glamorgan
Sully House, Nr Penarth. Tel: (0222) 530448. £20+.

SWANSEA, West Glamorgan
Annie's, 56, St Helen's Road, Swansea. Tel: (0792) 55603. £18-£26.
La Braseria, 28, Wind Street, Swansea. Tel: (0792) 469683. £15-£25.

TREFRIW, Gwynedd
Chandler's, Trefriw. Tel: (0492) 640991. £20+.

TRELLECH, Gwent
Village Green, Trellech. Tel: (0600) 860119. £15-£20.

WELSH HOOK, Dyfed
Stone Hall, Welsh Hook, Wolf's Castle. Tel: (0348) 840212. £15+.

HOTELS

All "Welsh Rarebits" hotels (*see* "Where to Stay" section) are noted for the quality of their food. Many boast outstanding restaurants and all feature local fresh produce.

Other hotels noted for their restaurants in Wales include the following:

ABERGWESYN
Llanwrtyd Wells, Powys
Llwynderw Hotel. Tel: (05913) 238

ABERSOCH, Gwynedd
Porth Tocyn Hotel. Tel: (075881) 3303

BROAD HAVEN, Dyfed.
Druidstone Hotel. Tel: (0437) 781221

CONWY, Gwynedd
Old Rectory, Llan Sanffraid Glan Conwy. Tel: (0492) 580611

DOLGELLAU, Gwynedd
George III Hotel. Tel: (0341) 422525

LLANDUDNO, Gwynedd
St Tudno Hotel. Tel: (0492) 874411

MACHYNLLETH, Powys
Ynyshir Hall, Eglwysfach. Tel: (0654) 781209

MUMBLES, West Glamorgan
Norton House Hotel. Tel: (0792) 404891

PORTMEIRION, Gwynedd
Hotel Portmeirion. Tel: (0766) 770228

ROSSETT, Clwyd
Llyndir Hall. Tel: (0244) 571648

TALYLLYN, Gwynedd
Minffordd Hotel. Tel: (0654) 761665

THREE COCKS, Powys
Three Cocks Hotel. Tel: (04974) 215

DRINKING NOTES

Pubs in Wales, as elsewhere in Britain, are evolving in many cases into wine bars or restaurants. Brewers are spending millions of pounds on refurbishment. Nowhere is this more apparent than in Cardiff, where the old established brewery company S.A. Brain turned many of the real pubs in the city centre into trendy bars.

New relaxed licensing laws now mean that many pubs in towns and cities are open on weekdays from 11a.m.–11p.m. and usually from noon–3p.m. and 7–11p.m. on Sundays. But do not rely on these hours. The choice is left to the landlord, and in country areas most pubs will be closed between 3p.m. and 6p.m. in the afternoons.

There are only two areas of Wales where pubs are not permitted to open on Sundays – Ceredigion (the county of Cardigan which includes the University town and seaside resort of Aberystwyth) and Dwyfor (the Lleyn Peninsula in North Wales which includes such resorts as Pwllheli, Criccieth and Abersoch). If you are residents in a hotel in these areas, however, you may drink on Sundays.

Pubs in Wales are usually either brewery owned (or financed) or free houses. Free houses do not give their drinks away free – in these areas the pub owners are free to choose the type of beer and drinks they sell. They may buy from several breweries thus giving their clients greater freedom of choice. Free houses generally have greater character than brewery owned pubs.

Most pubs in Wales now serve at least one type of "real ale" – that is, beer brewed in the traditional method and cask-conditioned. The three largest Welsh breweries are all in the South: Brains (Cardiff) and Felinfoel and Buckleys (Llanelli). Brains has approximately 200 of its own pubs in Cardiff and the surrounding area whilst Felinfoel, brewers of Double Dragon ale in West Wales is justifiably proud of the fact that it is the oldest canner of beer in the world.

Swn y Mor (Sound of the Sea) Welsh Chwisgi was launched by Brecon Brewery in the early 1980s and is now a big success story, with export orders increasing dramatically each year.

Wine bars and café-bars have become fashionable in recent years; but as with pubs and inns the food element is now in many cases as important as the drink.

For good Welsh company as well as good Welsh cheer, find out where the local Male Voice Choir quench their thirst after their twice-weekly rehearsal, or visit a cattle or sheep market when the farmers are in town.

THINGS TO DO

COUNTRY

First and foremost, Wales is renowned for its castles. More than 100 are open to the public – everything from the powerful "showpiece" castles of Caernarfon, Harlech and Caerphilly to lesser known, but no less spectacular, fortresses hidden deep in the country.

It is also renowned for its narrow gauge railways – the Ffestiniog, Talyllyn, Vale of Rheidol, Llanfair and Welshpool, Llanberis Lake and the Brecon Mountains Railway. And it's the only place where you can catch a train to the top of the highest mountain in England and Wales; then, within a few miles, go deep underground and explore old slate caverns.

Apart from its outstanding castles, narrow gauge railways and museum, Wales offers a great variety of attractions. Comprehensive information, including details of current opening times and admission prices, is available from the Wales Tourist Board but here are 10 very different experiences that you shouldn't miss on your visit to Wales:

Portmeirion, near Porthmadog: an unique Italianate village and architectural work of art.
Caerleon Roman Fortress, near Newport: the only excavated Roman barracks building in Britain.
Big Pit, Blaenafon: an unique underground tour of a coalmine.
Welsh Mountain Zoo, Colwyn Bay: in a beautiful setting and with a wide collection of animals.

Dylan Thomas' Boathouse, Laugharne: the home and inspirational setting of Wales's most famous 20th-century Anglo-Welsh poet.

Llanfairpwllgwyngyllgogerychwyrndrobwllllanty-siliogogogoch, Isle of Anglesey: the railway station with the world's most photographed placename.

Dolaucothi Gold Mines, near Llandovery: first exploited by the Romans and last worked in the 1930s.

Rhyl Sun Centre, Rhyl: a must for families with children. A tropical island setting in North Wales.

Waverley Paddle Steamer, Penarth near Cardiff: cruises along the South Wales coast each June and is the only steam-powered paddle steamer left in Britain.

Bodnant Gardens, Conwy Valley: undoubtedly one of the best in Britain. 100 acres of trees, shrubs and flowers.

CASTLES

NORTH WALES

Most castles also house exhibitions on their own heritage and history.

Beaumaris Castle, Isle of Anglesey, Gwynedd. Tel: (0248) 810361 Open all year. Begun in 1295 and on the World Heritage List as a site of outstanding universal value, it has the best example of concentric walls within walls in Britain.

Bodelwyddan Castle, 2 miles west of St Asaph, off A55, Clwyd. Tel: (0745) 583539. Following an earlier building, this is another example of Victorian neo-Classicism on a heroic scale. Beautifully restored and used as a girls' school, it now houses some of the National Portrait Gallery's Victorian paintings.

Caernarfon Castle, Caernarfon, Gwynedd. Tel: (0286) 77617). Open all year. A medieval stronghold of immense significance, this majestic fortress with lofty towers was built by Edward I in 1301.

Chirk Castle, 1 mile West of Chirk, off A55, Clwyd. Tel: (0691) 777701. Magnificent medieval castle built in 13th century and occupied ever since as rich stately home.Also has a deep circular dungeon and acres of 18th-century parkland.

Conwy Castle, Conwy, Gwynedd. Tel: (0492) 592358. Open all year. An outstanding feat of medieval military construction; one of the great fortresses of Europe with wonderful views from its turrrets.

Criccieth Castle, Criccieth, Gwynedd. Tel: (0766) 522227. Open all year. Commanding superb views over Tremadog Bay, this castle was captured and burnt in 1404 and never rebuilt.

Denbigh Castle, Denbigh Castle, Clwyd. Tel: (0745) 713979. Most noted for its triple-towered gatehouse, this 14th-century castle has had a turbulent history and crowns a rocky outcrop in the delightful Vale of Clwyd.

Harlech Castle, Harlech, Gwynedd. Tel: (0766) 780552. Open all year. Built on a rocky crag high above the coastal flats, this is another site of outstanding universal value with great defensive strength; it has great majesty and commands superb views.

Penrhyn Castle, 1 mile east of Bangor, on A5122, Gwynedd. Tel: (0248) 353084. Grand 19th-century castle built on a massive scale and elaborately decorated.

Powis Castle, 1 mile south of Welshpool, on A483, Powys. Tel: (0938) 554336. Original medieval construction transformed into grand stately home but most noted for its beautiful and brilliantly designed gardens.

SOUTH WALES

Caerleon Roman fortress, Caerleon, 4 miles northeast of Newport, Gwent. Tel: (0633) 422518. Open all year. Remains of important fortress with modern exhibition and life-size figures.

Cardiff Castle, Cardiff Castle, South Glamorgan. Tel: (0222) 372737. Unique combination of Roman fort, Norman and medieval stronghold, and Victorian Gothic fantasy; perhaps the most bizarre building of the Victorian era.

Caerphilly Castle, Caerphilly, Mid Glamorgan. Tel: (0222) 883143. Open all year. One of the greatest surviving medieval fortresses, deriving its stunning impact from its vast size and distinctive water defences, it is an extraordinary sight with a great variety of things to see.

Carreg Cennen Castle, off A483, southeast of Llandeilo, Dyfed. Tel: (0588) 822291. Open all year. Commanding magnificent views of Brecon Beacons National Park, 13th-century building stands on a great crag almost 300 feet above the River Cennen.

Castel Coch, 5 miles northwest of Cardiff, off A470, South Glamorgan. Tel: (0222) 810101. Open all year. An astonishingly different construction, this 13th-century ruin was transformed in the 19th-century by an opium-inspired architect, resulting in one of the most romantic buildings in Wales with pointed turrets adorning the steep hillside.

Chepstow Castle, Chepstow, Gwent. Tel: (02912) 4065. Guarding a major crossing from England to Wales high up on its cliff above the River Wye, this strategic construction the history of fortification from medieval times also houses life-size models of the medieval lords.

Kidwelly Castle, Kidwelly, Dyfed. Tel: (0554) 890104. Open all year. Remarkably complete, grand medieval castle with with distinctive gatehouse.

Raglan Castle, Raglan, off A40, Gwent. Tel: (0291) 690228. Open all year. Situated in beautiful countryside, this 15th-century castle has distinctive French influences and a prominent Great Tower with water defences.

Tretower Castle & Court, Tretower, 3 miles northwest of Crickhowell, off A40, Powys. Tel: (0874) 730279. Open all year. The glorious late medieval house replacing the earlier castle stronghold with its solid 13th-century keep creates vivid impressions of the life of the 15th and 16th-century gentry.

TRAVEL PACKAGES

Wales is often not included in package tours of Britain or otherwise forms a very minor part of an all-Britain coach tour. This is why it remains Britain's best-kept secret. Nevertheless, Wales is an ideal destination for people seeking the unusual and the tour operators listed in this section, although mainly small organisations, do cater for a wide range of special interests.

MARKET DAYS

An important entry in the farmer's diary, when everyone comes to town looking for a bargain or a chat. The small market towns come to life – streets are filled with stalls whilst the serious business of hard bargaining circulates amongst the pens. It's worth noting down these days for a colourful insight into the Welsh country way of life.

LIVESTOCK MARKETS

MONDAYS

Abergele: weekly
Cardigan: weekly
Carmarthen: weekly – sheep only
Dolgellau: weekly & seasonal
Hay-on-Wye: weekly
Lampeter: fortnightly
Llanybydder: fortnightly
Llandeilo Bridge: alternate weeks
Llanfyllin: seasonal
Mold: weekly
Monmouth: weekly
Nelson: weekly
Valley: monthly
Welshpool: weekly
Wrexham: weekly

TUESDAYS

Abergavenny: weekly
Brecon: weekly
Bryncir: weekly
Corwen: weekly
Cowbridge: weekly
Denbigh: weekly
Gowerton: weekly
Haverfordwest: weekly
Llandovery: alternate weeks
Llandysul: weekly
Llanfair Caereinion: weekly – seasonal
Llangadog: alternate weeks
St Clears: alternate weeks
Tregaron: alternate weeks
Whitland: alternate weeks

WEDNESDAYS

Carmarthen: weekly – dairy, cows, heifers, store lambs, pigs

Llangefni: weekly – store stock
Llanrwst: weekly
Machynlleth: weekly
Mold: weekly
Neath: weekly
Oswestry: weekly
Pembroke: fortnightly
Sennybridge: weekly

THURSDAYS

Bala: weekly
Carmarthen: weekly – cattle only
Cenmaes Road: weekly
Knighton: weekly
Llangefni: weekly
Llanwrtyd Wells: fortnightly & seasonal
Newtown: fortnightly
St Asaph: weekly
Talybont on Usk: weekly

FRIDAYS

Caerwen: weekly
Denbigh: weekly
Dolgellau: monthly
Knighton: weekly
Monmouth: weekly
Mold: weekly
Llanrwst: weekly
Newcastle Emlyn: weekly
Rhayader: weekly
Ruthin: weekly
Sarn: seasonal

SATURDAYS

Caersws: alternate weeks & seasonal
Llanidloes: alternate weeks & seasonal

GENERAL MARKETS

Many weekly markets are held in which stallholders set up shop either under cover or in the streets. Some coincide with livestock markets.
Aberdare: Sundays
Abergavenny: Tuesdays, Fridays
Aberystwyth: Mondays
Ammanford: Fridays
Bangor: Fridays, Saturdays
Barmouth: Thursdays
Blackwood: Fridays, Saturdays
Blaenafon: Fridays
Brecon: Tuesdays, Fridays
Bridgend: Fridays, Saturdays
Brynmawr: Saturdays
Builth Wells: Mondays, Fridays
Caernarfon: Saturdays
Cardiff: Monday–Saturday
Cardigan: Saturdays, Mondays
Carmarthen: Wednesdays, Saturdays
Chepstow: Sundays
Clydach: Sundays
Colwyn Bay: Tuesdays, Saturdays

Crickhowell: Thursdays
Cwmbran: Wednesdays, Saturdays
Cwmcarn: Wednesdays, Saturdays
Denbigh: Wednesdays
Ebbw Vale: Thursdays
Fishguard: Thursdays
Flint: Thursdays
Haverfordwest: Monday–Saturday
Holyhead: Fridays, Saturdays
Holywell: Thursdays, Saturdays
Lampeter: alternate Tuesdays
Llandovery: Saturdays
Llangollen: Tuesdays
Llanidloes: Saturdays
Llanleli: Thursdays, Saturdays
Llanwrst: Tuesdays
Machynlleth: Wednesdays
Maesteg: Fridays
Merthyr Tydfil: Tuesdays, Saturdays
Milford Haven: Fridays
Mold: Wednesdays, Saturdays
Monmouth: Fridays, Saturdays
Neath: Wednesdays, Saturdays
Newcastle Emlyn: Fridays
Newcastle Emlyn: Fridays
Newport, Gwent: Saturdays
Newtown: Tuesdays, Saturdays
Pontypool: Thursdays
Pontypridd: Wednesdays, Saturdays
Port Talbot: Tuesdays, Saturdays
Porthcawl: Sundays (*summer*)
Prestatyn: Tuesdays, Fridays
Pwllheli: Wednesdays
Rhayader: Wednesdays
Rhyl: Mondays, Thursdays, Saturdays
Swansea: Monday–Saturday

TOUR OPERATORS

CLASSIC COACH TOURS & FISHING TRIPS

PEMBROKE DOCK, Dyfed
Tudor Line Cruises, Hobbs Point, Pembroke Dock.
Tel: (0646) 685627

BEAUMARIS, Gwynedd
Starida, Little Bryn, Bryn lane, Beaumaris. Tel:
(0248) 810251

COACH TOURS

LLANDUDNO, Gwynedd
Alpine Coaches Garage, Builders Street West,
Llandudno. Tel: (0492) 879133

LLANDUDNO, Gwynedd
Crosville Wales, Imperial Buildings, Llandudno
Junction. Tel: (0492) 596969

SEA CRUISES

TENBY, Dyfed
Coastal & Island Cruises, Sheerwater, The Harbour,
Tenby. Tel: (0834) 3179

ST DAVID'S, Dyfed
Thousand Island Expeditions, Cross Square, St
David's. Tel: (0437) 721686

CHAUFFEUR GUIDE TOURS IN WALES

Waverley/Balmoral Excursions Ltd., Anderstone
Quay, Glasgow. Tel: (041) 221 8152

WALKING TOURS

Welsh Wanderer, 13, Millington Court, Spencers
Wood, Reading. Tel: (0734) 882515

SPECIAL INTEREST GROUP TOURS

Margaret Butler, City Walks, 210, Cyncoed Road,
Cardiff. Tel: (0222) 752679

TOUR GUIDES

The Wales Official Tourist Guide Association can be
contacted at Cae'r Felin, Chwilog, Pwllheli, Gwynedd LL53 6SW. Tel: (0766) 810889. Guides can be
booked through Tourist Information Centres.

Members are the only qualified tourist guides in
Wales registered by the Wales Tourist Board.
Association Members will undertake any kind of
guided tour, ranging from hourly tours by car and
coach from a designated centre, to extended tours
throughout Wales of any duration.

KEY
D/G Driver/Guide
D Dutch
Da Danish
F French
G German
I Italian
S Spanish
Sw Swedish
GB Round Britain Tours
* Welsh Speakers

WREXHAM, Clwyd
Derek Jones, Y Stabl, 30, Acton Gardens, Box
Lane, Wrexham. Tel: (0978) 351212 **D/G**

LLANDYSUL, Dyfed
Susanna Van Eeghen, Typoeth, Llandysul SA44
4RS. Tel: (055934) 483 **F D**

ABERGAVENNY, Gwent
Olwen Jones, 73, North Street, Abergavenny NP7
7EB. Tel: (0873) 77866

NEWPORT, Gwent
Alun Booth, 54, Allt-yr-Yn Road, Newport NP9 5EJ. Tel: (0633) 251524 **D/G GB**

USK, Gwent
Rosemary Phillips, Willowdene, Llantrisant, Near Usk NP5 1LR. Tel: (063349) 397 **D/G**

CAERFILI, Mid Glamorgan
The Cottage, Pwll-y-Pant, Caerfili. Tel:(0222) 869160/886117

CAERNARFON, Gwynedd
June Hartshorn, Maesteg, High Street, Llanberis Caernarfon. Tel: (0286) 871187

CARDIFF, South Glamorgan
Audrey Griffiths, 3, Church Street, Taffs Well, Cardiff CF4 7PG. Tel: (0222) 811970 **D/G GB**
Jennet Abram, 8, Thornbury close, Rhiwbuna, Cardiff CF4 1UT. Tel: (0222) 627133
Margaret Butler, 210, Cyncoed Road, Cardiff CF2 6RS. Tel: (0222) 752679
Philip Boots, 4 Wynnstay close, Carlton Mews, Grangetown, Cardiff.CF1 7NB. Tel: (0222) 229436. **D/G**

DINAS POWYS, South Glamorgan
Lesley Jeffrey, Playhill, 2, The Common, Dinas Powys CF6 4DL. Tel: (0222) 512404

LLANTWIT MAJOR, South Glamorgan
Michael Gill, 7, Tewdrig Close, Llantwit Major. Tel: (04465) 3740

SWANSEA, West Glamorgan
Len Ley, 2, Alder Avenue, Ystradgynlais, Near Swansea. Tel: (0639) 844102. **D/G I**

CRICKHOWELL, Powys
Miriam Ward, 35, Everest Drive, Crickhowell NP8 1DH. Tel: (0873) 811484

LONDON
Katrine Prince, Greencroft Gardens, London NW6 3LN. Tel: (081) 624 5138. **F G I**
Liza Spencer, 7, Baronsmede Court, Baronsmede, London W5 4LN. Tel: (071) 567 9409. **F I**
Mike Wale , 7, Baronsmede Court, Baronsmede, London W5 4LN. Tel: (071) 567 9409. **F**

BRADFORD
Nick Baggio, Ivy House, 16 Russell Street, Bradford.BD5 0JB. Tel: (0274) 727060. **I**

WARMINSTER
Joan Robertson, Glebe House, Chitterne, Warminster. Tel: (0985) 50382

WORCESTER PARK, Surrey
Inge Garstang, Solbakken, Grafton Road, Worcester Park KT4 7JN. Tel: (01) 337 7659. **D**

CULTURE PLUS

MUSEUMS

No visit to Wales is complete without a visit to one of its many museums. The National Museum of Wales has three oustanding museums in Cardiff alone, as well as the Museum of the Welsh Woollen Industry in the Teifi Valley in West Wales and the Welsh Slate Museum in Llanberis at the foot of Snowdon in North Wales. Although many of the museums listed are small, the variety is considerable.

NORTH WALES

HOLYWELL, Clwyd
Grange Cavern Military Museum.
Tel: (0352) 713455

LLANGOLLEN, Clwyd
Chwarel Wynne Slate Mine & Museum.
Tel: (069172) 343

LLANGOLLEN, Clwyd
Llangollen Motor Museum. Tel: (0978) 860324

WREXHAM, Clwyd
Maelor Heritage Centre. Tel: (0978) 290048

BANGOR, Gwynedd
Doll Museum at Penrhyn Castle. Tel: (0248) 353084

BEAUMARIS, Gwynedd
Museum of Childhood. Tel: (0248) 810448

BETWS-Y-COED, Gwynedd
Conwy Valley Railway Museum. Tel: (0690) 710568

CAERNARFON, Gwynedd
Segontium Roman Fort Museum. Tel: (0286) 5625

HOLYHEAD, Gwynedd
Holyhead Maritime Museum. Tel: (0407) 762816

LLANBERIS, Gwynedd
Oriel Eryri (Museum of the North). Tel: (0286) 870636

LLANBERIS, Gwynedd
Welsh Slate Museum. Tel: (0286) 870630

LLANDUDNO, Gwynedd
Llandudno Doll Museum & Model Railway.
Tel: (0492) 870424

MID WALES

ABERYSTWYTH, Dyfed
Ceredigion Museum. Tel: (0970) 617911

LLANDYSUL, Dyfed
Museum of the Welsh Woollen Industry.
Tel: (0559) 370929

NEWTOWN, Powys
Robert Owen Museum. Tel: (0686) 626345

WELSHPOOL, Powys
Powys Land Museum & Canal Centre.
Tel: (0938) 554656

SOUTH WALES

LAUGHARNE, Dyfed
Dylan Thomas' Boathouse. Tel: (0994) 427420

KIDWELLY, Dyfed
Kidwelly Industrial Museum. Tel: (0554) 891078

PEMBROKE, Dyfed
National Museum of Gypsy Caravans, Romany Crafts & Lore. Tel: (0646) 681308

CALDICOT, Gwent
Caldicot Castle, Museum & Country Park.
Tel: (0291) 420241

CHEPSTOW, Gwent
Model Farm Folk Museum & Craft Centre.
Tel: (02915) 231

USK, Gwent
Gwent Rural Life Museum. Tel: (02913) 3777

BLAENAVON, Mid Glamorgan
Big Pit Mining Museum. Tel: (0495) 790311

CARDIFF, South Glamorgan
Techniquest ("Hands On" Science Museum).
Tel: (0222) 460211
National Museum of Wales. Tel: (0222) 397951
Welsh Regiment Military Museum at Cardiff Castle. Tel: (0222) 822083
Welsh Industrial & Maritime Museum.
Tel: (0222) 481919

ST. FAGANS, South Glamorgan
Welsh Folk Museum. Tel: (0222) 569441

GOWER, West Glamorgan
Gower Farm Museum. Tel: (0792) 391195

PORT TALBOT, West Glamorgan
Afan Argoed Country Park & Welsh Miners Museum. Tel: (0639) 850564

NEATH, West Glamorgan
Cefn Coed Museum. Tel: (0639) 750556

SWANSEA, West Glamorgan
Maritime & Industrial Museum. Tel: (0792) 650351

ARTS CENTRES & THEATRES

A number of modern purpose-built art centres throughout Wales attract leading companies and first class productions throughout the year. In addition to their stage facilities, many of these centres have attractive exhibition areas, art galleries, cinemas, bars, coffee shops and restaurants.

Drop in at any time for a relaxing couple of hours. There's a theatre within easy driving distance of most holiday centres.

NORTH WALES

Theatr Clwyd
Mold, Clwyd CH7 1YA. Tel: (0352) 755114

Theatr Gwynedd
Ffordd Deiniol, Bangor, Gwynedd.
Tel: (0248) 351707/8

Theatr Seilo, Bangor Street, Caernarfon, Gwynedd.
Tel: (0286) 4073

MID WALES

Aberystwyth Arts Centre, Penglais, Aberystwyth, Dyfed SY23 3DE. Tel: (0970) 622882

Theatr Ardudwy, Coleg Harlech, Harlech, Gwynedd LL46 2PU. Tel: (0766) 780667

Theatr Felinfach, Felinfach, Llanbedr Pont Steffan, Lampeter, Dyfed SA48 8AF. Tel: (0570) 470697

Theatr Hafren, Llanidloes Road, Newtown, Powys SY16 1BE. Tel: (0686) 625007

Theatr Mwldan, Caridgan, Dyfed SA43 1JY.
Tel: (0239) 621200

Theatr y Castell/Castle Theatre, St Michael's Place, Aberystwyth, Dyfed SY23 2AU.
Tel: (0970) 614606

Wyeside Arts Centre, Castle Street, Builth Wells, Powys LD2 3BN. Tel: (0982) 552555

SOUTH WALES

Berwyn Centre, Nantymoel, Bridgend, Mid Glamorgan. Tel: (0656) 840439

Brangwyn Hall, Swansea, West Glamorgan. Tel: (0792) 470002

Chapter Arts Centre, Market Road, Canton, Cardiff. Tel: (0222) 396061

Congress Theatre, 51, Gwent Square, Cwmbran, Gwent NP44 1PL. Tel: (0633) 868239

Dolman Theatre, 5, Kingsway, Newport, Gwent. Tel: (0633) 63670

Dylan Thomas Theatre, 7, Gloucester Place, Swansea, West Glamorgan. Tel: (0792) 473238

Grand Theatre, Singleton Street, Swansea, West Glamorgan SA1 3QJ. Tel: (0792) 475715

Llandovery Theatre, Stone Street, Llandovery, Dyfed. Tel: (0550) 20113

New Theatre, Park Place, Cardiff CF1 3LN. Tel: (0222) 394844

St David's Hall, The Hayes, Cardiff CF1 2SH. Tel: (0222) 371236

St Donat's Art Centre, St Donat's Castle, Llantwit Major, CF6 9WF. Tel: (0446) 792151

Tailiesin Arts Centre, University College, Singleton Park, Swansea SA2 8PZ. Tel: (0792) 295438

Torch Theatre, St Peter's Road, Milford Haven, Dyfed SA73 1SR. Tel: (0646) 95267

ART GALLERIES

Few people realise that one of the best collections of French Impressionist paintings in the world with works by such artists as Renoir, Cézanne, Monet and Manet is to be found in the National Museum of Wales in Cathays Park, Cardiff. The Museum also has numerous sculptures by Rodin and Degas including Rodin's *The Earth* and *The Moon* and *The Kiss*.

Other art galleries in Wales include Turner House, Penarth, South Glamorgan (a small attractive gallery holding temporary exhibitions of pictures and objêts d'art from the National Museum of Wales and other sources); Glyn Vivian Art Gallery and Swansea Art Gallery both in Swansea, West Glamorgan; Graham Sutherland Gallery, Picton Castle, Near Haverfordwest, Dyfed; Oriel Plas Glyn y Weddw, Llanbedrog, near Pwllheli, Gwynedd; Tegfryn Art Gallery, Cadnant Road, Menai Bridge, Isle of Anglesey; Tunnicliffe Gallery, Llangefni, Isle

of Anglesey (an outstanding collection of interest to ornithologists to be opened in 1990); Mostyn Art Gallery, Vaughan Street, Llandudno, Gwynedd; National Portrait Gallery, Bodelwyddan Castle, near Bodelwyddan, St Asaph.

CONCERTS

The spectacular ultra-modern 2,000-seater St David's Hall in Cardiff is undoubtedly Wales's premier concert venue. World-class symphony orchestras, massed Welsh choirs, jazz bands, rock groups and international superstars perform here regularly. St David's Hall ofers a tremendous variety of events, is open all year and offers an exciting programme on most nights of the week.

BALLET

Britain's best touring ballet companies perform at the New Theatre in Cardiff, in the Grand Theatre in Swansea and occasionally in the smaller purpose-built theatres in West, Mid and North Wales.

OPERA

The Welsh National Opera is now regarded as one of the world's leading opera companies. The company is based in Cardiff and does three or four "seasons" a year in the city (usually May and June, September and October).

These performances are held in the impressive New Theatre in the city centre. With over 80 years of entertainment behind it, the New Theatre has recently been refurbished but still retains its traditional design, ornate decor and red velvet. It seats 1,100.

The WNO also has at least one "season" at the Grand Theatre in Swansea (usually July). In February 1989, the orchestra performed for the first time in New York at the Brooklyn Academy before the Princess of Wales (Princess Di) and a host of other VIPs and ardent opera followers.

MOVIES

Many conventional cinemas have closed in Wales, leaving probably no more than 20 throughout the country, and those mainly in the larger towns and cities. Cardiff once again offers the most exciting cinema viewing at its Chapter Arts Theatre, one of Britain's largest arts centres which includes among its studios and workshops, two cinemas, two galleries, a theatre, a restaurant and two bars. The Chapter offers a year-round programme for movie fans.

JAZZ

Players of international repute are frequent visitors to Cardiff, and the *Four Bars* (a Brains pub, immediately opposite Cardiff Castle) can usually guarantee a live session on most nights of the week all year round.

Apart from the annual Welsh Jazz Festival, the success story of the 1980s and now acknowledged as one of the foremost in Europe is the annual Brecon Jazz Festival (held in August). Another small town in North Wales, Llangollen, better known perhaps for its International Musical Eisteddfod, has also launched its very own annual Jazz Festival (May).

WELSH CHOIRS

Most towns and rural areas boast a choir of one kind or another, with male choirs by far the most numerous. Obtain a copy of *Events in Wales* from the Wales Tourist Board or call at your nearest Tourist Information Centre to find out details of concerts. If the dates do not correspond with your visit, then all is not lost.

The majority of choirs have no objection to visitors sitting quietly at the back of the hall during their weekly or twice weekly rehearsals. (August is usually a blank month). This is for many an experience of a lifetime. Some the the more thirsty choristers retire to a nearby pub after rehearsal. Try to join them and savour the best of Welsh fun and friendship. There are more than 100 male voice choirs in Wales. Here are details of some of the best.

ABERYSTWYTH MALE CHOIR
Rehearsals: Full choir: Thursdays, 7.45p.m.
Part practice: Sundays, 7.30p.m. (August excepted)
Further details: Mr. Richie Hughes. Tel: (0970) 624494

BRYTHONIAID MALE CHOIR (Blaenau Ffestiniog).
Rehearsals: Mondays and Thursdays, 7.30p.m.
Further details: Mr. A.L. Davies. Tel: (0766) 830381

CALDICOT MALE VOICE CHOIR (near Newport)
Rehearsals: Mondays and Thursdays, 7p.m.
Further details: Mr. I. Watkins. Tel: (0291) 422894

COR MEIBON CAERFYRDDIN (Carmarthen)
Rehearsals: Tuesdays and Fridays, 7.30p.m.
Further details: Mr. T.J. Lewis. Tel: (0267) 234470

DOWLAIS MALE CHOIR (near Merthyr Tydfil)
Rehearsals: Wednesdays and Sundays, 7.30p.m.
Further details: Mr. M. Price. Tel: (0685) 73721

DUNVANT MALE CHOIR (near Swansea)
Rehearsals: Tuesdays and Fridays, 7.30p.m.
Further details: Mr. A. M. Rees. Tel: (0792) 201115

COR MEIBION LLANELLI
Rehearsals: Mondays and Thursdays, 6.45p.m.
Further details: Mr. M. Mason. Tel: (0554) 758101 extn. 206 (daytime); (0544) 755985

COR MEIBION MAELGWYN (near Llandudno)
Rehearsals: Sundays, 8.30p.m.; Wednesdays, 7.30p.m.
Further details: Mr. H. G. Jones. Tel: (0492) 44507

COR MEIBION MORLAIS (Rhondda)
Rehearsals: Wednesdays and Fridays, 7.30p.m.
Further details: Mr. B. Young. Tel: (0443) 685095

THE MORRISTON ORPHEUS CHOIR (near Swansea)
Rehearsals: Sundays and Wednesdays, 7.30p.m.
Further details: Mr. G. Bailey. Tel: (0792) 73278

PENDYRUS MALE CHOIR (Rhondda)
Rehearsals: Sundays, 7p.m.; Wednesdays, 7.30p.m.
Further details: Mr. J. H. Lewis. Tel: (0443) 730383

PONTARDDULAIS MALE CHOIR (near Swansea)
Rehearsals: Wednesdays and Sundays, 7p.m.
Further details: Mr. J. Davies. Tel: (0792) 586330

RHYMNEY SILURIAN MALE CHOIR (near Caerphilly)
Rehearsals: Tuesdays and Fridays, 7.30p.m.
Further details: Mr. G. M. Morris. Tel: (0685) 841431

COR MEIBION Y TRAETH (Isle of Anglesey)
Rehearsals: Tuesdays, 7.45p.m.
Further details: Mr. R. W. Williams. Tel: (0248) 724300

TREDEGAR ORPHEUS MALE CHOIR
Rehearsals: Wednesdays and Fridays, 7p.m.
Further details: Mr. H. Hatton. Tel: (049525) 3852

COR MEIBION TRELAWNYD (near Rhyll)
Rehearsals: Sundays and Tuesdays, 8p.m. Not in August.
Further details: Mr. E. T. Williams. Tel: (0745) 591119

TREORCHY MALE CHOIR
Rehearsals: Sundays, 3.30p.m.; Tuesdays and Thursdays, 7.30p.m.
Further details: Mr. I. Morgan. Tel: (0443) 435852

YSTRADGYNLAIS MALE CHOIR (Swansea Valley)
Rehearsals: Wednesdays, 7p.m.; Fridays, 6.45p.m.
Further details: Mr. G. R. Griffiths, Tel: (0639) 843371

DIARY OF EVENTS

There are the cultural festivals of song and dance known as *eisteddfodau*, country fairs and agricultural shows, sheepdog trials and market days, medieval pageants and Victorian weeks, theatre and music festivals, jazz in the streets and guided walks in the country. And in the cities and towns, you can enjoy everything from word-famous opera to performances by international artistes.

The Wales Tourist Board publishes an annual Events booklet, usually available at the beginning of each year. Here is a small selection of important events held:

March: St David's Day Gala Concert at St David's Hall, Cardiff.

April: Antiques Fair, Brecon; Newport Drama Festival, Newport, Gwent; Folk Festival, Ammanford; Welsh International Car Rally, Cardiff.

May: Old May Day Fair, Welsh Folk Museum, Cardiff; Victorian Extravaganza, Llandudno; Colwyn Drama Festival, Colwyn Bay; Festival of Music & Drama, Llantilio Crosseny, near Abergavenny; Media Festival, Cardiff; South Wales Male Voice Choirs Concert, Cardiff or Swansea; Choral Festival, Llandudno; Bach Festival, St David's Cathedral, St David's; Montgomery Agricultural Show, Welshpool; Steam and Vintage Rally, Abergavenny; Llangollen International Jazz Festival, Llangollen;

June: Eisteddfod Genedlaethol Urdd Gobaith Cymry (Welsh League of Youth National Eisteddfod) – alternate venue North/South each year; Rhyl Community Festival Week, Rhyl; Beaumaris Festival, Isle of Anglesey; Welsh National Steam and Agricultural Show, Builth Wells; Eisteddfod Mon (Isle of Anglesey Eisteddfod); Agricultural Show, Aberystwyth; Deeside Community Festival, Clwyd; Gwyl Ifan – Welsh Folk Dancing Festival, Cardiff; Aberdare Summer Festival, Aberdare; Antiques Fair at Tredegar House, Newport; Three Peaks Yacht Race, Barmouth/Caernarfon; Ceiriog Valley Country Fair, near Chirk; Flower & Music Festival, Pontypridd.

July: Margam Festival at The Orangery, near Port Talbot; Festival of Music & the Arts, Criccieth; Llangollen International Musical Eisteddfod, Llangollen; Community & Arts Festival, Chepstow; Summer Festival, Abergavenny; Festival of Arts & Music, Llanfyllin; Welsh Proms, St David's Hall, Cardiff; The Snowdon Race (Fell Running), Llanberis; Royal Welsh Agricultural Show, Builth Wells; Gower Festival at Gower's Parish Churches; Fishguard Music Festival, Fishguard; Summer Festival, Aberystwyth; Carnival Week, Barry; Conwy Festival of the Performing Arts, Conwy; Sioe Eifionnydd (Agricultural Show), Porthmadog; Swansea Sky-Diving Boogie, Swansea Airport.

August: National Eisteddfod of Wales – alternate venue North/South each year, e.g. 1989 Llanrwst, 1990 Rhymney Valley; Menai Strait Regatta, Beaumaris and Caernarfon; Welsh National Sheepdog Trials (1989 Bala); Medieval Fayres at Beaumaris Castle, Isle of Anglesey; Agricultural & Horticultural Show, Nevern, Dyfed; Agricultural Show & Sheep Dog Trials, Gower; North Wales Agricultural Show, Port Dinorwic; Agricultural & Horticultural Show, Fishguard; Brecon County Agricultural Show, Brecon; Game Fair, Haverfordwest; Anglesey County Agricultural Show, Llangefni; United Counties Agricultural Show, Carmarthen; Vale of Glamorgan Festival of Music, St Donat's Arts Festival, Machynlleth; Merioneth Country Agricultural Show; Monmouthshire Agricultural Show, Monmouth; International Folk Music Festival, Pontardawe; Beddgelert Dog Show, Beddgelert; Denbigh Flower Show, Denbigh; Llantwit Major Flower Festival, South Glamorgan; Victorian Festival, Llandrindod Wells.

September: Welsh International Four Days Walk, Llanwrtyd Wells; North Wales Music Festival, St Asaph; Swansea Festival of Music & the Arts, Swansea; Cardiff International Festival of Theatre, Cardiff.

October: Swansea Festival of Music & the Arts, Swansea; Cardiff International Festival of Theatre, Cardiff; Cardiff Literature Festival, Cardiff; Holyhead Arts Festival, Isle of Anglesey; The National Trust Snowdonia Marathon, Llanberis.

November: Lamb Show and Sale at Royal Welsh Showground, Builth Wells; Ten Mile Road Race, Llandudno; Railway Modelling Club Show, Pontypridd; Mid Wales Beer Festival, Llanwrtyd Wells; Cardiff Festival of Music, Cardiff; Llanelli Arts Festival, Llanelli.

NIGHTLIFE

BANQUETS

Three Welsh castles stage medieval banquets – usually on as many as five or six evenings a week during the main summer months. Those with a taste for such fantasies can "join the Baron and Baroness in the romantic candlelit splendour" of Caldicot, Cardiff or Ruthin, being "welcomed and attended by the gracious and talented ladies of the Court in their colourful medieval gowns, and served with mead, wine and succulent dishes".

The banquets usually start at 7.30 or 8p.m. and last approximately two and half hours. The all-inclusive cost (meal, wine, entertainment) is in the region of £25 a person. Advance booking is advisable; dress is informal.

Caldicot Castle, Caldicot, Nr. Newport, Gwent. Tel: Caldicot (0291) 421425
Cardiff Castle, Cardiff, South Glamorgan. Tel: Cardiff (0222) 372737
Ruthin Castle, Ruthin, Clwyd (North Wales).

In Swansea, you can experience an even more authentic Welsh evening. The "Hwyrnos" or "Welsh Night" in Green Dragon Lane, Swansea (opposite Barclays Bank in Wind Street; tel: Swansea 0792-641437) offers exceptional food and outstanding entertainment for around £20-plus per head which includes wine. Here you will savour Welsh lamb at its best and be invited to join in the singing. Dress is informal, doors open at 7.30p.m. and the programme starts at around 8p.m. The bar is licensed until 1a.m. This is one venue where they will guarantee to teach you a few words of Welsh! Similar "experience" is being offered in Cardiff during 1989; for details contact the Swansea Hwyrnos.

NIGHTSPOTS

SOUTH WALES

USK
Savvas Country Club, Usk. Tel: (02913) 2223

CARDIFF
Cha Chas Night Club, 5, St Mary Street, Cardiff. Tel: (0222) 398072
Coco Savanna, Greyfriars Road, Cardiff. Tel: (0222) 377014
Jacksons, Westgate Street, Cardiff. Tel: (0222) 390851
Philharmonic & Lloyds, 76, St Mary Street, Cardiff. Tel: (0222) 222595

SWANSEA
Aviary Nightclub, Northampton Lane, Swansea. Tel: (0792) 651775
Barons Nightspot, College Street, Swansea. Tel: (0792) 650123
Bentleys, Castleton Walk, Mumbles, Swansea. Tel: (0792) 361043

SOUTHWEST WALES

CARMARTHEN
Harveys Club, Queen Street, Carmarthen. Tel: (0267) 234378

CARMARTHEN
The Riviera Club, The Quay, Carmarthen. Tel: (0267) 237348

SAUNDERSFOOT
Sands Disco, Milford Street, Saundersfoot. Tel: (0834) 813728

MID WALES

BARMOUTH
Sandancer Nightclub, Pavillion Buildings, Marine Parade, Barmouth. Tel: (0341) 280198

NEWTOWN
Crystles Night Club, Broad Street, Newtown. Tel: (0686) 624275

NORTH WALES

CAERNARFON
Majestic, Bangor Street, Caernarfon. Tel: (0286) 76069

BANGOR
Octagon, Dean Street, Bangor. Tel: (0248) 354977

LLANDUDNO
Broadway Boulevard, Mostyn Broadway, Llandudno. Tel: (0492) 879614

COLWYN BAY
Nik-Als Club, Eirias Park, Colwyn Bay. Tel: (0492) 531123

TOWYN
Bentley Jasmins, Towyn Road, Towyn. Tel: (0745) 336422

WREXHAM
The Cotton Club, Mold Road, Wrexham. Tel: (0978) 357186

GAMBLING

CARDIFF
Les Croupiers, St Mary Street, Cardiff. Tel: (0222) 382810

CARDIFF
Tiberius Sporting Club Casino, Greyfriars Road, Cardiff. Tel: (0222) 342991

RHYL
Downtown Club, Rhyl. Tel: (0745) 351861

SHOPPING

WHAT TO BUY

You are almost spoilt for choice in Wales, whether you find yourself in the cities of Cardiff or Swansea or in the coastal towns and mountain villages.

In recent years there has been a dramatic improvement in the quality of Welsh goods sold in craft shops throughout Wales but look around, don't necessarily buy in the obvious shop. Much of the cheaper range of Welsh souvenirs are still imported. Insist on buying a Welsh product. Check it out in the shop and don't wait until you get home before discovering that the little Welsh doll you bought was made in Hong Kong.

Hand-carved love spoons, authentic maps and prints, cassettes of Welsh choirs, woolly sweaters, gloves, hats and scarves are good value and are easy

Our history could fill this book, but we prefer to fill glasses.

When you make a great beer, you don't have to make a great fuss.

BREAK THE LANGUAGE BARRIER!

If you travel internationally, for business or pleasure - or if you are learning a foreign language - TI's electronic language -products can make communication a lot easier.

The **PS-5800** is a versatile 3-language dictionary with 30,000 entry words in each language. Available in English/German/French or English/Italian/French, it includes, travel sentences, business words, memory space to build and store your own vocabulary, currency and metric conversions, and more.

The **PS-5400** is a powerful 5-language translator fea-

turing up to 5,000 words and 1,000 structured sentences in English, German, French, Italian, and Spanish. Travel-related sentences, conveniently grouped by category, facilitate conversation in the language of your choice. To keep you on time and on top, there's also world time, alarm reminders, calculator, and metric conversions.

The **PS-5800** and **PS-5400**. Two pocket-sized ways to break the language barrier!

For more information, fax your request to:
Texas Instruments France, (33) 39 22 21 01

TEXAS INSTRUMENTS

to pack. Wales also has a wide range of excellent craft workshops where you can see the skills and buy the products of professional craft, gift and textile producers. The best of these are registered with the Wales Craft Council (for a free attractive/informative guide contact them at 20 Severn Street, Welshpool, Powys, tel: 0938-55313).

SHOPPING AREAS

Cardiff's shopping centre is acknowledged as one of Britain's finest and most compact. One of its great attractions is that to go from any point of the centre to another is never more than a reasonable walking distance – a walk made simple and pleasant by the pedestrianised shopping streets and extensive system of charming Edwardian arcades.

All major departmental stores in Cardiff are part of or are close to an ultra-modern shopping precinct called the St David's Centre. The smaller shops in the arcades boast a wide range of speciality shops, boutiques, book and craft shops, soft furnishings, buttons, etc. Not to be missed is the covered market in Cardiff.

The market is also a highlight of any shopping visit to Swansea, Wales's second city. Here, as in Cardiff, most of Britain's many departmental stores rub shoulders with long-established family stores. In the old covered market here, you should still be able to buy cockles and laver bread (a Welsh delicacy prepared from seaweed) from the ladies of Penclawdd or some farmhouse cheese and home-grown vegetables from farmers' wives from Gower or Carmarthenshire. The market at nearby Carmarthen is also bustling with local produce.

The largest shopping town in Mid Wales is Aberystwyth, although small market towns such as Machynlleth have an amazing choice of "speciality" shops. In North Wales, the elegant seaside resort of Llandudno boasts an excellent variety of shopping, whereas Bangor and Wrexham are also considered to be good centres. In the mountain resort of Betws-y-Coed, every shop seems to sell Welsh crafts, while almost every shop in the border town of Hay-on-Wye sells second hand books.

SHOPPING HOURS

Most shops are open between 9a.m. and 5.30p.m. six days a week (Mondays to Saturdays). Some of the larger deparment stores in towns and cities stay open late on Thursday evenings. In country areas, smaller shops close for one afternoon a week (usually a Wednesday). Cardiff, Newport, Swansea and most of the larger towns have a good number of "corner" shops that seem to remain open until late at night on seven days of the week. And in tourist areas during the season many of the shops remain open until mid-evening.

EXPORT PROCEDURES

Many visitors will find it worthwhile to take advantage of the Retail Export Scheme whereby they can reclaim VAT (value added tax) on goods purchased for export. Note that not all shops operate this scheme, and there is often a minimum purchase price (there are also minimum values which apply to travellers from European Community countries). Shops operating the scheme may ask to see your passport before completing the VAT form. This form must be presented with the goods to the Customs Office at the point of departure from Britain) or to customs at the point of importation into an EC country) within three months of purchase. After the Customs Officer has certified the form it should be returned to the shopkeeper, who will then send you the VAT refund, from which a small administration fee may be deducted.

CLOTHING SIZES

Dresses/Knitwear/Lingerie

Britain:	10	12	14	16		
USA:	8	10	12	14		

Shoes

Britain:	5	6	7	8	9	10	11
USA:	6.5	7.5	8.5	9.5	10/10.5	11	12

SPORTS

PARTICIPANT

Walking is by far the most popular activity with visitors to Wales, although to the majority a two or three-mile stroll would be the ultimate. Much of the best walking or hiking is to be found in one of the three National Parks – Brecon Beacons, Pembrokeshire Coast and Snowdonia – or in one of the areas of Wales especially designated for their outstanding natural beauty e.g. the Wye Valley and Gower Peninsula in South Wales and the Lleyn Peninsula and the coastline of the Isle of Anglesey in the North.

The serious walker will no doubt wish to tackle one of Wales's long-distance footpaths – the Offa's Dyke Walk from Chepstow to Prestatyn (200 miles/320 km) or the 168-mile (270-km) Pembrokeshire Coastal Footpath. Both offer the walker spectacular scenery and everchanging light and landscapes.

Wales boasts more than a 100 golf courses and all welcome visiting golfers. Only one club, the Royal

Porthcawl, insists on a letter of introduction or a valid membership card from one's home club. The best courses are the links courses to be found around the Welsh coastline. These include Porthcawl, Ashburnham, Tenby, Aberdovey, Harlech and Conwy.

Golf green fees in Wales must be as cheap as in almost any part of Britain. The average daily fee during the week ranges between £5 and £10; although this may be doubled on weekends or Bank Holidays.

SPECTATOR

Wales's national sport is Rugby Football, played between September and May. The major first-class clubs are all located in South Wales, between Newport in the east and Llanelli in the west. Fixtures are usually on a Saturday, although many clubs play mid-week games – usually on a Tuesday or Wednesday evening. Almost every small village and town has a rugby team and the sport is fast gaining ground in North Wales.

International matches are all held in Cardiff at the spectacular new National Stadium, still referred to as Cardiff Arms Park. Tickets for these matches are always extremely difficult to obtain as tickets are all allocated through member clubs.

Association Football (soccer) is the other main winter sport played throughout Wales. The three best teams who play in the English league are Cardiff, Swansea and Wrexham. As with rugby, most games take place on a Saturday and practically every village and town throughout the country boasts at least one soccer team.

The third major sport, this time played in summer (but as strange and foreign to most overseas visitors as are rugby and soccer), is cricket. Wales has one "championship" team (Glamorgan) which competes with the best counties in England. Most "home" matches are played in Cardiff or Swansea, although occasionally, the team will play in other towns e.g. Neath, Ebbw Vale, Abergavenny and Colwyn Bay in North Wales.

Athletics meetings are held regularly in the summer months. The two best stadia are in Cwmbran (Gwent) and Swansea.

Wales's newest spectator sport, ice hockey, attracts capacity crowds for all "home" fixtures in support of the "Cardiff Devils" at the recently opened National Ice Rink in Cardiff.

Details of major spectator sporting events taking place in Wales – from the Round Britain Cycle Race to the RAC Car Rally through the forests of Mid Wales – are included in *Events in Wales*, published annually by the Wales Tourist Board.

LEISURE CENTRES

In the 1970s most local authorities (councils) in Wales built swimming pools, but since the mid-1980s leisure centres have been developed throughout the country. These centres are open to all and provide a wide range of leisure and health facilities. In almost all cases there are squash courts and a swimming pool, a health suite and a gymnasium. In Cardiff alone, five new leisure centres have recently opened with another three within 10 miles of the city centre at Penarth, Barry and Cowbridge. Wales's only 50-metre international swimming pool, Wales Empire Pool, is located near to Cardiff's main railway station.

SPECIAL INFORMATION

DOING BUSINESS

Welsh Development Agency, Pearl House, Greyfriars Road, Cardiff. Tel: (0222) 222666

Welsh Office, Cathays Park, Cardiff. Tel: (0222) 825111

Confederation of British Industry, Pearl Assurance House, Greyfriars Road, Cardiff. Tel: (0222) 232536

Dept. of Trade and Industry, Companies House, Crown Way, Maindy, Cardiff. Tel: (0222) 388588

Chamber of Commerce & Industry, 101, Exchange Buildings, Mount Stuart Square, Cardiff. Tel: (0222) 481648

DISABLED

For specific information contact:
Wales Council for the Disabled, Llysifor, Crescent Road, Caerphilly. Tel: (0222) 887325/6/7/8

A joint publication with the Wales Tourist Board listing attractions etc. accessible to disabled guests and titled *Accessible Wales* is available from the above address and at Tourist information centres costing £2.50. An all-Britain holiday information service for disabled visitors is available from:

Holiday Care Service, 2, Old Bank Chambers, Station Road, Horley, Surrey. Tel: (0293) 774535

LANGUAGE

English is spoken throughout Wales by practically all the population. There are various regional dialects, but most visitors to Wales find it easier to understand the Welsh when they speak English than to get to grips with most Scots or English regional dialects.

The most distinctive feature of Wales is its own Welsh language which has its origin in the cradle of European civilisation. It is still very much a living language for about 20 percent of the population and is spoken at home, studied at schools, colleges and universities and used on radio and television.

Welsh is a Celtic branch of the Indo-European family of languages and is related more closely to Breton than to Irish and Scots Gaelic. It has been used as a written language since A.D. 600 (300 years before French and German were first written) and has changed in few major respects since. The 400th anniversary of the first translation of the Bible into Welsh by Bishop William Morgan was celebrated in 1988.

Written Welsh is standard but spoken Welsh varies greatly in accent, particularly between North and South Wales. Interest in the language has gained ground especially in the more anglicised parts of South Wales, where there has been a remarkable growth in nursery groups, bilingual schools and adult language classes.

Channel 4 Wales (S4C) has its own showing of Welsh television programmes (22 hours per week) and Radio Cymru transmits for an average 12 hours per day. Some 400 books are published in Welsh each year.

PRONUNCIATION OF WELSH

Welsh has 28 letters in its alphabet (English 26 letters) but has no j, k, q, v, x or z. Welsh is a phonetic language in all but one instance – the letter "y" has two sounds which the English ear can detect:
1. As the "u" sound in understand.
2. As the "ea" sound in the word lea.

There are some sounds in Welsh which are very different from their English equivalents. The following is a basic guide, with Welsh in Italics, followed by English.

c *cath* = *cat*
cat (never as in receive)
ch *chwaer* = *sister*
loch
dd *yn* dd*a* = *good*

them
f y fam = *the mother*
of
ff ff*enstr* = *window*
off
g *gardd* = *garden*
garden (never as in George)
h h*et* = *hat*
hat (never silent as in honest)
ll ll*aw* = *hand*

There is no equivalent sound. Place the tongue on the upper roof of the mouth near the upper teeth, ready to pronounce l; then blow rather than voice the l.
th *byth* = *ever*
three (never as in English the)

The vowels in Welsh are a e i o u w y; all except "y" can be long or short:
long a *tad* = *father*
similar to English hard
short a *mam* = *mother*
similar to English ham
long e *hen* = *old*
similar to English sane
short e *pen* = *head*
similar to English ten
long i *mis* = *month*
similar to English geese
short i *prin* = *scarce*
similar to English tin
long o *mor* = *sea*
similar to English more
short o *ffon* = *walking stick*
similar to English fond
long w *swn* = *sound*
similar to English moon
short w *gwn* = *gun*
similar to English look
y has two sounds:

1. CLEAR
dyn = *man*, a long "ee" sound almost like English geese
cyn = *before*, a short "I" sound almost like English tin
2. OBSCURE
Sometimes like the sound in English run
Examples: y = *the*; yn = *in*; *dynion* = *men*.

It is well to remember that in Welsh the accent usually falls on the last-syllable-but-one of a word: e.g. cadair = chair

A FEW GREETINGS

Bore da
Good morning
Dydd da
Good day
Prynhawn da
Good afternoon
Noswaith dda
Good evening
Nos da
Good night

Sut mae?
How are you?
Hwyl
Cheers
Diolch
Thanks
Diolch yn fawr iawn
Thanks very much
Croeso
Welcome
Croeso i Cymru
Welcome to Wales
Da
Good
Da lawn
Very good
Iechyd da!
Good health!
Nadolig Llawen!
Merry Christmas!
Blwyddyn Newydd Dda!
Good New Year!
Dymuniadau
Best wishes
Cyfarchion
Greetings
Penblwydd hapus
Happy birthday

FURTHER READING

HISTORY

David Williams: *A History of Modern Wales*, John Murray
Gwyn A. Williams: *When Was Wales?* Pelican

POETRY & LITERATURE

Walford Davies & Ralph Maud (Editors): *Dylan Thomas – Collected Poems 1934-1953*, Dent
Islwyn Jenkins (Editor): *The Collected Poems of Idris Davies*, Gomer
Meic Stephens: *The Oxford Companion to the Literature of Wales*, Oxford
Gwyn Thomas: *Selected Short Stories*, Seren
J. P. Ward: *The Poetry of R. S. Thomas*, Poetry Wales Press

MISCELLANEOUS

David Greenslade: *Welsh Fever (Welsh Activities in the U.S. and Canada Today)*, D. Brown & Sons
Gwyn Jones & Thomas Jones (Translators): *The Mabinogion* (11 stories regarded as a masterpiece of medieval European literature), Everyman Classics
Lewis Lloyd: *Australians From Wales*, Gwynedd Archives & Museums
Jan Morris: *The Matter of Wales*, Penguin
Trefor M. Owen: *Welsh Folk Customs*, Gomer
W. A. Poucher: *Wales* (a photographic review of Welsh mountains), Constable
Ann Sutton: *The Textiles of Wales*, Bellew
Roger Thomas (Editor): *Castles in Wales*, AA/Wales Tourist Board
Wynford Vaughan Thomas: *Wales*, Mermaid Books

BIOGRAPHIES

W. H. Davies: *The Autobiography of a Super-Tramp*, Oxford
Melvyn Bragg: *Rich* (The Life of Richard Burton), Hodder & Stoughton
Paul Ferris: *Dylan Thomas*, Penguin Library Biographies
Graham Jenkins: *Richard Burton – My Brother*, M. Joseph
Michael Parnell: *Laughter from the Dark* (A Life of Gwyn Thomas), John Murray
Emlyn Williams: *George – An Early Autobiography*, Hamish Hamilton
Emlyn Williams: *Emlyn – A Sequel to George*, Penguin

LEARNING WELSH

Catchphrase – A course in spoken Welsh, Sain (Two cassettes and/or book)
Heini Gruffydd: *Welcome to Welsh*, Y Lolfa (book & cassette)
Heini Gruffydd: *Welsh is Fun & Welsh is Fun-tastic*, Y Lolfa
T. J. Rhys Jones: *Teach Yourself Living Welsh*, Hodder & Stoughton
These books are just a selection of what is available. *Taflen* at 12 Duke Street Arcade, Cardiff, CF1 7AZ Tel: (0222) 227530, can supply further information and offer a full postal service worldwide.

THE COLOUR OF LIFE.

A holiday may last just a week or so, but the memories of those happy, colourful days will last forever, because together you and Kodak Ektachrome films will capture, as large as life, the wondrous sights, the breathtaking scenery and the magical moments. For you to relive over and over again.

The Kodak Ektachrome range of slide films offers a choice of light source, speed and colour rendition and features extremely fine grain, very high sharpness and high resolving power.

Take home the real colour of life with Kodak Ektachrome films.

LIKE THIS?

OR LIKE THIS?

A KODAK FUN PANORAMIC CAMERA BROADENS YOUR VIEW

The holiday you and your camera have been looking forward to all year; and a stunning panoramic view appears. "Fabulous", you think to yourself, "must take that one".

Unfortunately, your lens is just not wide enough. And three-in-a-row is a poor substitute.

That's when you take out your pocket-size, 'single use' Kodak Fun Panoramic Camera. A film and a camera, all in one, and it works miracles. You won't need to focus, you don't need special lenses. Just aim, click and... it's all yours. The total picture

You take twelve panoramic pictures with one Kodak Fun Pano ramic Camera. Then put the camera in for developing and printing.

Each print is 25 by 9 centimetres. Excellent depth of field. True Kodak Gold colours.

The Kodak Fun Panoramic Camera itself goes back to the factory, to be recycled. So that others too can capture one of those spectacular phoooooooooootooooooooooooos.

USEFUL ADDRESSES

Wales Tourist Board, Brunel House, 2, Fitzalan Road, Cardiff CF2 1UY. Tel: (0222) 499909

Wales Information Bureau, British Travel Centre, 4, Lower Regent Street, London W1V 9PB. Tel: (01) 409 0969

British Travel Centre, 4, Lower Regent Street, London SW1. Tel: (01) 730 3400

Welsh Arts Council, 9. Museum Place, Cardiff CF1 2NY. Tel: (0222) 394711

Welsh Office, Information Division, Crown Buildings, Cathays Park, Cardiff. Tel: (0222) 825111

Welsh Development Agency, Pearl House, Greyfriars Road, Cardiff. Tel: (0222) 222666

Urdd Gobaith Cymru, Welsh League of Youth, Swyddfa'r Urdd, Aberystwyth, Dyfed. Tel: (0970) 623744

National Eisteddfod Office, Unit 40, Cardiff Business Park, Llanishen, Cardiff. Tel: (0222) 76377

Mid Wales Development, Ladywell House, Newtown, Powys. Tel: (0686) 26965

The National Trust, North Wales, Trinity Square, Llandudno, Gwynedd. Tel: (0492) 860123

Snowdonia National Park, Penrhyndeudraeth, Gwynedd LL48 6LS. Tel: (0766) 770274

Brecon Beacons National Park, Glamorgan Street, Brecon, Powys. Tel: (0874) 4437

Pembrokeshire Coast National Park, Information Services, County Offices, Haverfordwest, Dyfed. Tel: (0437) 764591

Wales Craft Council, 20, Severn Street, Welshpool, Powys. Tel: (0938) 555313

National Museum of Wales, Cathays Park, Cardiff. Tel: (0222) 397951

Royal Welsh Agricultural Society, Llanelwedd, Builth Wells, Powys. Tel: (0982) 553683

Wales Official Tourist Guides Association, Gwennie Johnson, Cae'r Felin, Chwilog, Pwllheli, Gwynedd LL53 6SW. Tel: (0766) 810889

European Centre for Traditional & Regional Cultures, Parade Street, Llangollen, Clwyd. Tel: (0978) 861292

National Language Centre, Nant Gwrtheyrn, Llithfaen, Gwynedd. Tel: (075885) 334

Prince of Wales Award Scheme, Shire Hall, Mold, Clwyd. Tel: (0352) 75 2121

CADW – Welsh Historic Monuments, Brunel House, 2, Fitzalan Road, Cardiff.CF1 2UY. Tel: (0222) 465511

Welsh National Opera, John Street, Cardiff. Tel: (0222) 464666

Youth Hostel Association, Regional Office, 1, Cathedral Road, Cardiff.CF1 9HA. Tel: (0222) 396766

Welsh Folk Museum, St Fagans, Cardiff. Tel: (0222) 569441

National Library for Wales, Aberystwyth, Dyfed. Tel: (0970) 623816

National Sports Council for Wales, Sophia Gardens, Cardiff. Tel: (0222) 397571

TOURIST INFORMATION CENTRES

NORTH WALES

* Indicates seasonal opening only.

BANGOR, Gwynedd
Theatr Gwynedd, Deiniol Road, Bangor, Gwynedd LL57 2RE. Tel: (0248) 352786 *

BETWS-Y-COED, Gwynedd
Royal Oak Stables, Betws-y-Coed, Gwynedd LL24 0AH. Tel: (0690) 710426 *

BLAENAU FFESTINIOG, Gwynedd
High Street, Blaenau Ffestiniog, Gwynedd LL41 3HD. Tel: (0766) 830360

CAERNARFON, Gwynedd
Oriel Pendeitsh, Caernarfon, Gwynedd LL55 2PB. Tel: (0286) 672232

COLWYN BAY, Clwyd
Station Road, Colwyn Bay, Clwyd LL29 8BU. Tel: (0492) 530478

CONWY, Gwynedd
Castle Street, Conwy, Gwynedd LL32 8AY. Tel: (0492) 592248

HALKYN, Clwyd
Little Chef Services A55, Halkyn, Holywell, Clwyd
CH8 8DF. Tel: (0352) 780144 *

HOLYHEAD, Gwynedd
Marine Square, Salt Island Approach, Holyhead,
Gwynedd LL65 1DR. Tel: (0407) 762622

LLANBERIS, Gwynedd
Oriel Eryri (Museum of the North), Llanberis,
Gwynedd LL55 4UR. Tel: (0286) 870765 *

LLANDUDNO, Gwynedd
1/2 Chapel Street, Llandudno, Gwynedd LL30
2YU. Tel: (0492) 876413

LLANFAIR P.G., Gwynedd
Station Site, Llanfair P.G., Gwynedd LL61 5UJ.
Tel: (0248) 713177

LLANGOLLEN, Clwyd
Town Hall, Llangollen, Clwyd LL20 5PD. Tel:
(0978) 860828

MOLD, Clwyd
Town Hall, Mold, Clwyd CH7 1AB. Tel: (0352)
75933

PORTHMADOG, Gwynedd
High Street, Porthmadog, Gwynedd LL49 9LP.
Tel: (0766) 512981

PRESTATYN, Clwyd
Scala Cinema, Prestatyn, Clwyd LL19 9LH. Tel:
(0745) 8544365 *

PWLLHELI, Gwynedd
Y Maes, Pwllheli, Gwynedd LL53 6HE. Tel:
(075861) 3000

RHYL, Clwyd
Town Hall, Central Promenade, Rhyl, Clwyd LL18
5NL. Tel: (0745) 355068

RUTHIN, Clwyd
Craft Centre, Ruthin, Clwyd LL15 1BB. Tel:
(08242) 3992

WREXHAM, Clwyd
Guild Hall, Wrexham, Clwyd LL11 1AY. Tel:
(0978) 357845

MID WALES

ABERAERON, Dyfed
Cerdigion District Council, Tourist Information
Centre, The Harbour, Aberaeron, Dyfed SA46 0BT.
Tel: (0545) 570602 *

ABERDOVEY, Gwynedd
Snowdonia National Park/Wales Tourist Board
Visitor Centre, The Wharf, Aberdovey, Gwynedd
LL35 0ED. Tel: (0654) 767321 *

ABERYSTWYTH, Dyfed
Ceredigion District Council, Tourist Information Centre,
Aberystwyth, Dyfed SY23 7AG. Tel: (0970) 612125

BALA, Gwynedd
Snowdonia National Park/Wales Tourist Board
Visitor Centre, High Street, Bala, Gwynedd LL23
7NH. Tel: (0678) 520367 *

BARMOUTH, Gwynedd
Wales Tourist Board, Tourist Information Centre,
The Old Library, Barmouth, Gwynedd LL42 1LU.
Tel: (0341) 280787 *

BLAENAU FFESTINIOG, Gwynedd
Snowdonia National Park/Wales Tourist Board
Visitor Centre, High Street, Blaenau Ffestiniog,
Gwynedd LL41 3HD. Tel: (0766) 830360 *

BUILTH WELLS, Powys
Wales Tourist Board, Tourist Information Centre,
Groe Car Park, Builth Wells, Powys LD2 3BT .
Tel: (0982) 553307 *

CARDIGAN, Dyfed
Theatr Mwldan, Tourist Information Centre, Bath
house Road, Cardigan, Dyfed SA43 1HY.
Tel: (0239) 613230

CORRIS, Gwynedd
Wales Tourist Board, Tourist Information Centre,
Corris Craft Centre, Corris, Gwynedd SY20 9SP.
Tel: (0654) 761244 *

DOLGELLAU, Gwynedd
Snowdonia National Park/Wales Tourist Board
Visitor Centre, Eldon Square, Dolgellau, Gwynedd
LL40 1PU. Tel: (0341) 422888 *

ELAN VALLEY, Powys
Wales Tourist Board, Tourist Information Centre,
Elan Valley Visitor Centre, Elan Valley, Rhayader,
Powys LD6 5HP. Tel: (0597) 810898 *

HARLECH, Gwynedd
Snowdonia National Park/Wales Tourist Board
Visitor Centre, High Street, Harlech, Gwynedd
LL46 2YA. Tel: (0766) 780658 *

KNIGHTON, Powys
Offa's Dyke Association, The Old School, West
Street, Knighton, Powys LD7 1EW.
Tel: (0547) 528753

LLANDRINDOD WELLS, Powys
Radnor District Council, Tourist Information Centre, Old Town Hall, Memorial Gardens, Llandrindod Wells, Powys LD1 5DL. Tel: (0597) 822600 *

LLANFYLLIN, Powys
Wales Tourist Board, Tourist Information Centre, Montgomeryshire District Council Offices, Llanfyllin, Powys SY22 5DB. Tel: (069184) 8868

LLANWRTYD WELLS, Powys
Tourist Information Point, The Bookshop, Llanwrtyd Wells, Powys LD5 4SS. Tel: (0591) 3391

MACHYNLLETH, Powys
Wales Tourist Board, Tourist Information Centre, Canolfan Owain Glyndwr, Machynlleth, Powys SY20 8EE. Tel: (0654) 702401

NEWQUAY, Dyfed
Ceredigion District Council, Tourist Information Centre, Church Street, Newquay, Dyfed SA45 OBT. Tel: (0545) 560865

NEWTOWN, Powys
Wales Tourist Board, Tourist Information Centre, Central Car Park, Newtown, Powys SY16 2PW. Tel: (0686) 625580 *

PRESTEIGNE, Powys
Wales Tourist Board, Tourist Information Centre, The Old Market Hall, Presteigne, Powys.LD8 2AW. Tel: (0544) 260193 *

RHAYADER, Powys
Wales Tourist Board, Tourist Information Centre, The Old Swan, West Street, Rhayader, Powys LD6 5AB. Tel: (0597) 810591 *

TYWYN, Gwynedd
Wales Tourist Board, Tourist Information Centre, High Street, Tywyn, Gwynedd LL35 9AD. Tel: (0654) 710070

WELSHPOOL, Powys
Wales Tourist Board, Tourist Information Centre, Vicarage Gardens Car Park, Welshpool, Powys SY21 7DD. Tel: (0938) 552043 *

SOUTH WALES

ABERDULAIS, West Glamorgan
Wales Tourist Board, Tourist Information Centre, Aberdulais Basin, West Glamorgan SA10 8ED. Tel: (0639) 633531 *

ABERGAVENNY, Gwent
Wales Tourist Board & Brecon Beacon National Park Tourist Centre, Swan Meadow, Cross Street, Abergavenny, Gwent NP7 5HE. Tel: (0873) 857588

BAGLE BROOK, West Glamorgan
Wales Tourist Board, Tourist Information Centre, Beefeater Restaurant, Sunnycroft Road, Baglan, West Glamorgan SA12 8DS. Tel: (0639) 823049

BARRY, South Glamorgan
Wales Tourist Board, Tourist Information Centre, The Promenade, Barry Island, South Glamorgan CF6 8TJ. Tel: (0446) 747171

BLAENAVON, Gwent
Wales Tourist Board, Tourist Information Centre, Big Pit Mining Museum, Blaenavon, Gwent NP4 9XP. Tel: (0495) 790122

BRECON, Powys
Brecon Beacons National Park Centre, Watton Mount, Brecon, Powys LD3 7DF. Tel: (0874) 624437

BRECON, Powys
Brecon Beacons National Park Centre, The Mountain Centre, Libanus, Brecon, Powys LD3 8ER. Tel: (0874) 623366

BRECON, Powys
Wales Tourist Board, Tourist Information Centre, Cattle Market Car Park, Brecon, Powys LD3 9DA. Tel: (0874) 622485

BROAD HAVEN, Dyfed
Pembrokeshire Coast National Park Centre, Car Park, Broad Haven, Dyfed SA62 3JH. Tel: (043783) 412

CAERPHILLY, Mid Glamorgan
Tourist Information Centre, Old Police Station, Park Lane, Caerphilly, Mid Glamorgan CF8 1AA. Tel: (0222) 851378 *

CARDIFF, South Glamorgan
Wales Tourist Board, Tourist Information Centre, 8-14 Bridge Street, Cardiff. South Glamorgan CF5 2EJ. Tel: (0222) 227281

CARMARTHEN, Dyfed
Wales Tourist Board, Tourist Information Centre, Lammas Street, Carmarthen, Dyfed SA31 3AQ. Tel: (0267) 231557

CHEPSTOW, Gwent
Wales Tourist Board, Tourist Information Centre, The Gatehouse, High Street, Chepstow, Gwent NP6 5LH. Tel: (02912) 3772

MERTHYR TYDFIL, Mid Glamorgan
Wales Tourist Board, Tourist Information Centre, 14a, Glebeland Street, Merthyr Tydfil, Mid Glamorgan CF47 8AU. Tel: (0685) 79884

CWMCARN, Gwent
Wales Tourist Board, Tourist Information Centre, Cwmcarn Forest Drive Visitor Centre, Near Cross Keys, Gwent NP1 5AL. Tel: (0495) 272001

FISHGUARD, Dyfed
Wales Tourist Board, Tourist Information Centre, 4, Hamilton Street, Fishguard, Dyfed SA65 9HL. Tel: (0348) 873484

NEWPORT, Dyfed
Pembrokeshire Coast National Park Centre, East Street, Newport, Dyfed SA42 0SY. Tel: (0239) 820912

HAVERFORDWEST, Dyfed
Wales Tourist Board & Pembrokeshire Coast National Park Tourist Information Centre, 40, High Street, Haverfordwest, Dyfed SA62 6SD. Tel: (0437) 820144

NEWPORT, Gwent
Wales Tourist Information Centre, Newport Museum & Art Gallery, John Frost Square, Newport, Gwent NP9 1HZ. Tel: (0633) 842962

HAY-ON-WYE, Powys
Tourist Information Centre, Craft Centre , Oxford Road, Hay-On-Wye, Powys HR3 5AE. Tel: (0497) 820144

PEMBROKE, Dyfed
Pembrokeshire Coast National Park Centre, Drill Hall, Pembroke, Dyfed. Tel: (0646) 682148

PEN-Y-CAE, West Glamorgan
Craig-Y-Nos Country Park, Pen-Y-Cae, Swansea Valley, West Glamorgan SA9 1GL. Tel: (0639) 730395

LLANDOVERY, Dyfed
Pembrokeshire Coast National Park Tourist Information Centre, Broad Street, Llandovery, Dyfed SA20 0AR. Tel: (0550) 20693 *

KILGETTY, Dyfed
Kingsmoor Common, Kilgettty, Dyfed SA68 0YA. Tel: (0834) 813672 *

MONMOUTH, Gwent
Wales Tourist Information Centre, National Trust Shop, Church Street, Monmouth, Gwent NP6 3BX. Tel: (0600) 3899

PONT ABRAHAM, Dyfed
Wales Tourist Board, Tourist Information Centre, Pont Abraham Services, Junction 49, M4, Near Cross Hands, Dyfed SA4 1FP. Tel: (0792) 883838

PONT NEDD FECHAN, West Glamorgan
Wales Tourist Board, Tourist Information Centre, Pont Nedd Fechan, Near Glynneath, West Glamorgan SA11 5NR. Tel: (0639) 721795

PONTYPRIDD, Mid Glamorgan
Pontypridd Historical & Cultural Centre, The Old Bridge, Pontypridd, Mid Glamorgan CF37 3PE. Tel: (0443) 402077

PORTHCAWL, Mid Glamorgan
Wales Tourist Board, Tourist Information Centre, The Old Police Station, John Street, Porthcawl, Mid-Glamorgan CF36 3DT. Tel: (0656) 786639/782211

ST DAVIDS, Dyfed
Pembrokeshire Coast National Park Centre, City Hall, St Davids, Dyfed SA62 6SB. Tel: (0437) 720392

SARN, Mid Glamorgan
Wales Tourist Board, Tourist Information Centre, Sarn Park Services, Junction 36, M4, Near Bridgend, Mid Glamorgan CF32 9SY. Tel: (0656) 654906

SAUNDERSFOOT, Dyfed
Tourist Information Centre, The Harbour, Saundersfoot, Dyfed SA69 9HE. Tel: (0834) 811411

SWANSEA, West Glamorgan
Tourist Information Centre, Oystermouth Square, Mumbles, West Glamorgan SA3 4DQ. Tel: (0792) 361302

MONMOUTH, Gwent
Wales Tourist Information Centre, National Trust Shop, Church Street, Monmouth, Gwent NP6 3BX. Tel: (0600) 3899

SWANSEA, West Glamorgan
Tourist Information Centre, Singleton Street, Swansea, West Glamorgan SA1 3QN. Tel: (0792) 468321

TENBY, Dyfed
Tourist Information Centre, The Norton, Tenby, Dyfed SA70 8AP. Tel: (0834) 2402

TINTERN, Gwent
Wales Tourist Board, Tourist Information Centre, Abbey Entrance, Tintern Abbey, Tintern, Gwent NP6 6TE. Tel: (0291) 689431

TREDEGAR, Gwent
Wales Tourist Information Centre, Bryn Bach Country Park, Tredegar, Gwent NP2 3AY. Tel: (0495) 711816

OTHER TICs OFFERING INFORMATION ON WALES

SANDBACH, Cheshire
Sandbach Service Area, M6 Northbound, Sandbach, Cheshire CW11 0TD. Tel: (0270) 760460

CHESTER, Cheshire
Town Hall, Northgate Street, Chester, Cheshire CH1 2HF. Tel: (0244) 313126

OSWESTRY, Salop
Mile End Services, Oswestry, Salop FY11 4SE. Tel: (0691) 662488

MANCHESTER
Manchester International Airport, International Airways Hall, Greater Manchester, M22 5NY. Tel: (061) 436 3344

CONSULATES

BELGIUM
Belgian Consul, Empire House, Docks, Cardiff. Tel: (0222) 488111

COSTA RICA
Costa Rica, Consul, 62, St Mary Street, Cardiff. Tel: (0222) 226554

DENMARK
Danish Consul, 70, James Street, Cardiff. Tel: (0222) 480003

FINLAND
Finnish Consul, Mount Stuart House, Mount Stuart Square, Cardiff. Tel: (0222) 480704

LIBERIA
Liberian Consul, Cory Buildings, Cardiff. Tel: (0222) 481141

NETHERLANDS
Netherlands Consul, 4th Floor, 113-116, Bute Street, Cardiff. Tel: (0222) 488636

NORWAY
Norwegian Consul, Empire House, Mount Stuart Square, Cardiff. Tel: (0222) 489711

SWEDEN
Swedish Consul, 4, Dunraven Crescent, Talbot Green, Llantrisant. Tel: (0443) 222538

TURKEY
Turkish Consul, Empire House, Docks, Cardiff. Tel: (0222) 461144

ART/PHOTO CREDITS

INDEX

THE KODAK GOLD GUIDE TO BETTER PICTURES.

Good photography is not difficult. Use these practical hints and Kodak Gold II Film: then notice the improvement.

Move in close. Get close enough to capture only the important elements.

Frame your Pictures. Look out for natural frames such as archways or tree branches to add an interesting foreground. Frames help create a sensation of depth and direct attention into the picture.

One centre of interest. Ensure you have one focus of interest and avoid distracting features that can confuse the viewer.

Use leading lines. Leading lines direct attention to your subject i.e. – a stream, a fence, a pathway; or the less obvious such as light beams or shadows.

Maintain activity. Pictures are more appealing if the subject is involved in some natural action.

Keep within the flash range. Ensure subject is within flash range for your camera (generally 4 metres). With groups make sure everyone is the same distance from the camera to receive the same amount of light.

Check the light direction. People tend to squint in bright direct light. Light from the side creates highlights and shadows that reveal texture and help to show the shapes of the subject. If shooting into direct sunlight fill-in flash can be effective to light the subject from the front.

CHOOSING YOUR KODAK GOLD II FILM.

Choosing the correct speed of colour print film for the type of photographs you will be taking is essential to achieve the best colourful results.

Basically the more intricate your needs in terms of capturing speed or low-light situations the higher speed film you require.

Kodak Gold II 100. Use in bright outdoor light or indoors with electronic flash. Fine grain, ideal for enlargements and close-ups. Ideal for beaches, snow scenes and posed shots.

Kodak Gold II 200. A multipurpose film for general lighting conditions and slow to moderate action. Recommended for automatic 35mm cameras. Ideal for walks, bike rides and parties.

Kodak Gold II 400. Provides the best colour accuracy as well as the richest, most saturated colours of any 400 speed film. Outstanding flash-taking capabilities for low-light and fast-action situations; excellent exposure latitude. Ideal for outdoor or well-lit indoor sports, stage shows or sunsets.

INSIGHT GUIDES

COLORSET NUMBERS

You'll find the colorset number on the spine of each Insight Guide.